MICRO MASTERY:

KEYBOARDING AND WORD PROCESSING APPLICATIONS

Grace L. Marshall
Business Educator
Canton, Connecticut

Berle Haggblade
Professor, Information Management
California State University, Fresno

Library of Congress Cataloging-in-Publication Data

Marshall, Grace L.
Micro mastery: keyboarding and word processing applications/
Grace L. Marshall, Berle Haggblade.
p. cm.
Includes indexes.
Summary: Provides drills, timed writings, and formatting
exercises to teach basic keyboarding, using AppleWorks,
Word Perfect, or MicroSoft Works.
ISBN: 0-538-61877-9
1. Word processing—Juvenile literature. [1. Word processing.
2. Typewriting.] I. Haggblade, Berle. II. Title.
Z52.4.M33 1994
652.5—dc20 92-35186
CIP
AC

3 4 5 6 7 8 H 00 99 98 97 96

Printed in the United States of America

Executive Editor: *Karen Schmohe*
Developmental Editor: *Richard E. Adams*
Product Manager: *Al Roane*
Senior Marketing Manager: *Dick Walker*
Production Editor: *A. Yvonne Stearns*
Senior Designer: *Elaine St. John-Lagenaur*
Production Artists: *Steven McMahon, Sophie Renieris*
Associate Photo Editor/Stylist: *Linda Ellis*
Associate Director/Photography: *Diana Fleming*
Assistant Photographer: *Mimi Ostendorf-Smith*

SOUTH-WESTERN PUBLISHING CO.

PREFACE

MICRO MASTERY: KEYBOARDING AND WORD PROCESSING APPLICATIONS is designed to be used with any word processing hardware and software. As word processing concepts are introduced, they are discussed in general and the student is referred to the User's Manual for the particular software being used for specific function keys and sequences needed to complete the actions for the concepts.

Problems that incorporate student interests at the upper middle school and lower high school levels are used after basic word processing skills are learned. All problems are formatted for full sheets of paper and call for the development of problem-solving skills for students of varying abilities. Of the 121 problems presented in the text, 63 problems (more that 52%) use retrieved files from previous lessons.

A Teacher's Edition of **MICRO MASTERY: KEYBOARDING AND WORD PROCESSING APPLICATIONS** contains information on textbook organization, teaching philosophy of the text, guidelines for grading in **MICRO MASTERY**, specific suggestions for teaching the lessons, supplementary drill dictation lists, and a technique check sheet. In addition, reminders for technique, formatting, and special instructions appear in most sections of each lesson. Problems that will be retrieved for later use are indicated in the Teacher's Edition. Solutions to problems are included in the Teacher's Edition.

OBJECTIVES

Students who complete the text should accomplish several major objectives.

- Achieve sufficient keyboarding skill to be able to operate the keyboard by touch.
- Master correct techniques of position, fingering, and stroking, and develop appropriate response patterns.
- Attain optimum speed and accuracy according to their individual capabilities.
- Review and improve basic English skills of punctuation, spelling, and proofreading.
- Acquire the habit of using their keyboard as a basic communication tool in the preparation of personal and school papers.

ORGANIZATION

MICRO MASTERY: KEYBOARDING AND WORD PROCESSING APPLICATIONS, with 90 lessons arranged into 15 units, contains instructional material for a one-semester course. In addition, a supplementary problems booklet and a tests booklet are available. Supplementary problems are new material and are similar to textbook problems. Both objective and production tests are included in the tests booklet. Solutions appear in the Teacher's Edition.

Keyboarding skill. Special technique drills are included in nearly every lesson. Speed and control aids are generously placed throughout the book. Exercises progress from simple to complex; copy appears first in print, then in rough draft and script to help students develop keying skill under realistic conditions.

Keyboarding applications. After the alphabetic keyboard has been covered and before the figures and symbols are introduced, a centering unit is given to introduce word processing concepts while reinforcing keying techniques.

Following the introduction of figures and symbols, a unit on short reports precedes a review and skill-building unit.

Personal notes, tabulation with up to four columns and including column headings, and personal-business letters are completed before another review and skill-building unit is given.

Multiple-page reports, including a term paper compiled from the problems in the short reports unit, keying documents for club activities, business letters, and another review/skill-building unit complete the text.

Language arts development. After students have acquired desirable techniques, they are introduced to various language arts activities.

Special Index. This index provides students with easy reference to each activity that can aid them in problem areas. The Special Index lists the locations of

- Language arts skills
- Timed writings (including speed ladder paragraphs)
- Formatting problems
- Key location drills
- Manipulative and preapplication writings
- Technique builders
- Skill builders
- Skill comparison sentences and paragraphs
- Guided writings
- Continuity and fluency practice
- Control builders
- Speed builders
- Rough draft sentences/paragraphs

KEY TO ICONS

Computer terms

Language arts skills

Timed writings

Formatting problems

Technique builders

Speed builders

Extra-time activities

FEATURES

Spacing and arrangement of the drills, problems, and directions provide for attractive appearance and maximum readability.

Color is used effectively throughout to highlight information deserving particular attention.

Special icons make it easy to identify important activities and instructions.

Every fourth lesson in the introductory unit is devoted to key location reviews and technique reinforcement.

A convenient reference section contains a Glossary of Word Processing Terms, as well as other needed explanations and illustrations.

ACKNOWLEDGMENTS

Our sincere appreciation is extended to those who provided encouragement, insight, and suggestions during the writing of this text.

Grace L. Marshall
Berle Haggblade

CONTENTS

MICRO MASTERY WORD PROCESSING CHART

COMMANDS	IBM WORDPERFECT 5.0/5.1	IBM MICROSOFT WORKS 1.05/2.0	APPLEWORKS 3.0	MACINTOSH MICROSOFT WORKS 2.0
CHARACTER FORMATS				
Bold	F6	CTRL + B	CTRL-B OR OPEN-APPLE-0, BB	COMMAND, B
Hard Space	HOME + SPACE BAR	CTRL + SHIFT + SPACE BAR	OPEN-APPLE-SPACE	....
Normal Text	CTRL + F8, N (3)	CTRL + SPACE BAR	....	COMMAND, N
Underline	F8	CTRL + U	CTRL-L or OPEN-APPLE-0, UB	COMMAND, U
PARAGRAPH FORMATS				
Centered Alignment	SHIFT + F6	CTRL + C	CTRL-C or OPEN-APPLE-0, CN	FORMAT MENU, JUSTIFICATION, CENTERED
Double Spacing	SHIFT + F8, L (1), S (6)	CTRL + 2	OPEN-APPLE-O, DS	FORMAT MENU, SPACING
Left & Right Indent	SHIFT + F4	ALT, T, A	OPEN-APPLE-O, IN	FORMAT MENU, SHOW RULER
New Line	....	SHIFT + ENTER	OPEN-APPLE-O, SK	....
Tab Set	SHIFT + F8, L (1), T (8)	ALT, T, T	OPEN-APPLE-T	FORMAT MENU, SHOW RULER, CLICK
Widow/Orphan	SHIFT + F8, L (1), W (9)	ALT, T, A	OPEN-APPLE-O, GB, GE	....
PAGE & DOCUMENT FORMATS				
Hard Page Break	CTRL + ENTER	CTRL + ENTER	CTRL-P or OPEN-APPLE-O, NP	FORMAT MENU, INSERT PAGE BREAK
Header	SHIFT + F8, P (2), H (3)	ALT, O, H or ALT, P, H	OPEN-APPLE-O, HE	FILE MENU, PAGE SETUP
Margin Set	SHIFT + F8, L (1), M (7)	ALT, P, L or M	OPEN-APPLE-O, LM, RM	FILE MENU, PAGE SETUP
Page Numbers	SHIFT + F8, P (2), N (6)	ALT, P, L or M	OPEN-APPLE-O, PN	FORMAT MENU, SET PAGE #
CURSOR MOVEMENT				
Beginning of Line	HOME, ←	HOME	OPEN-APPLE ←	←
End of Line	HOME, →	END	OPEN-APPLE →	→
Beginning of Document	HOME, HOME, ↑	CTRL + HOME	OPEN-APPLE-1	COMMAND, G, 1
End of Document	HOME, HOME, ↓	CTRL + END	OPEN-APPLE-9	COMMAND, G, LAST PAGE #
FILE MANAGEMENT				
Exit	F7	ALT, F, X	MAIN MENU, QUIT (6)	COMMAND, Q
List Files	F5	ALT, F, O	MAIN MENU, OTHER (5), LIST (2)	FILE MENU
Open/Retrieve a File	SHIFT + F10	ALT, F, O	MAIN MENU, ADD FILES (1), GET (1)	FILE MENU
Print	SHIFT + F7	ALT, P, P	OPEN-APPLE-P	COMMAND, P
Print Preview	SHIFT + F7, V (6)	ALT, P, V	OPEN-APPLE-K	FILE MENU, PRINT MENU, PRINT PREVIEW
Save	F10	ALT, F, S	CTRL-S or OPEN-APPLE-S	COMMAND, S
EDIT FUNCTIONS				
Cancel	F1	ESC	ESC	CANCEL BUTTON FROM WINDOW
Copy	CTRL + F4	F8, ALT E, C	OPEN-APPLE-C	COMMAND, C
Go To	CTRL + HOME	F5	OPEN-APPLE-1 to 9, approx. document area	COMMAND, G
Help	F3	F1	OPEN-APPLE-?	COMMAND, ?
Move	CTRL + F4	F8, ALT E, M	OPEN-APPLE-M	COMMAND, X; COMMAND, V
Search	F2	ALT, S, S	OPEN-APPLE-F	COMMAND, F
Search & Replace	ALT + F2	ALT, S, R	OPEN-APPLE-R	COMMAND, R
Spellcheck	CTRL+ F2	ALT, O, C or S	OPEN-APPLE-V	SPELL MENU, DICTIONARY
Undo	....	ALT + BKSP	....	EDIT MENU, UNDO

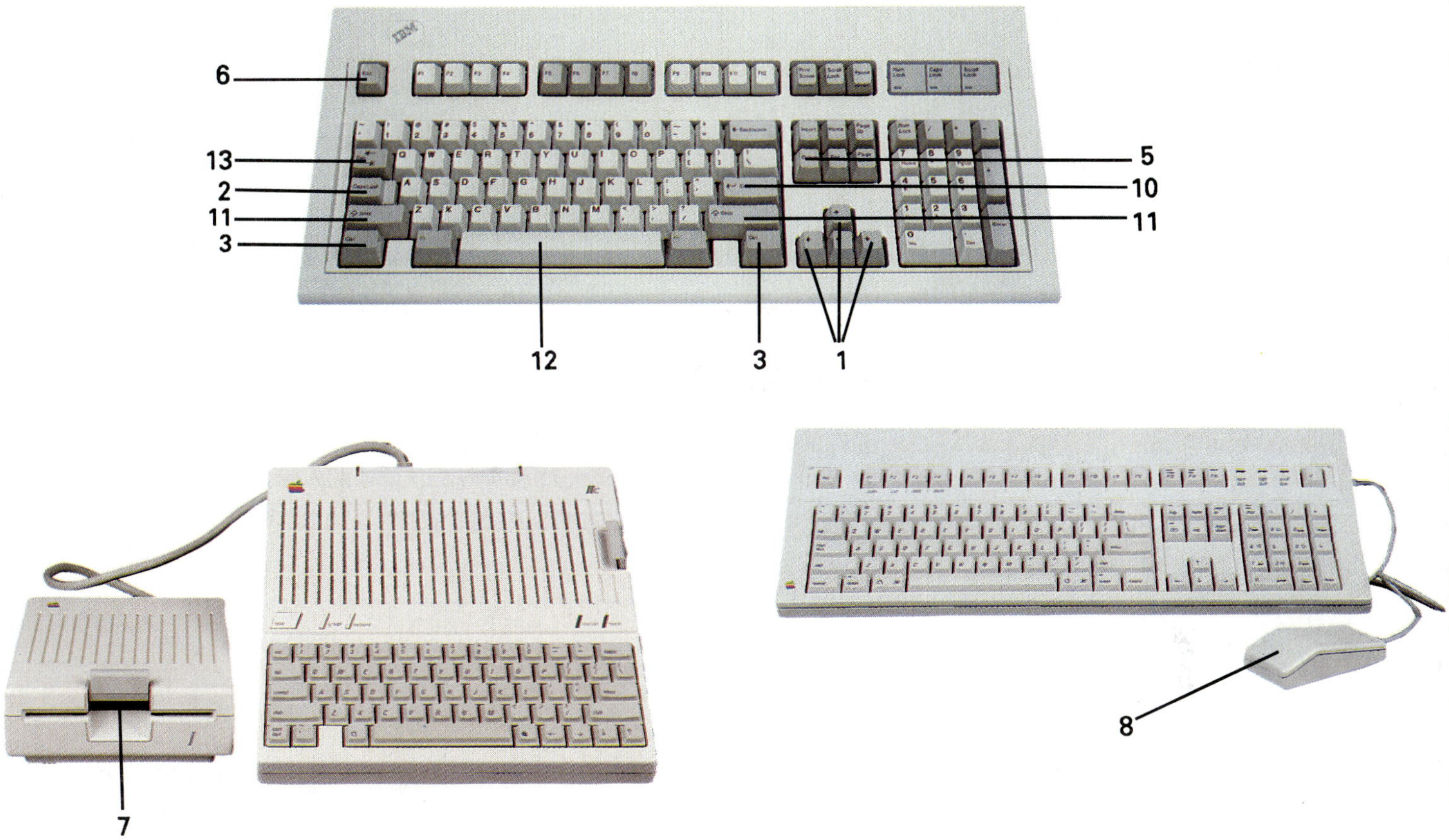

THE APPLE IIC, Macintosh, IBM and Compatible Systems

The diagrams above show the various parts of the keyboards for the **Apple IIc**, **Macintosh**, and **IBM** and **Compatible Systems**. Microcomputers/word processors have similar parts, though the names of these parts and their arrangements may differ. With the help of the User's Manual for your equipment, you should be able to identify each item labeled in the illustration above.

The particular word processing software that you use will determine the specific uses of "function keys." Therefore, you must familiarize yourself with the User's Manual for your software as well as the one for your equipment.

1 "arrow" keys--used to move cursor in the direction of the arrow

2 caps lock key--used to lock shift mechanism for alphabet characters only

3 control (CTRL) key--used with selected function keys to perform certain operations

4 CPU (Central Processing Unit)--the piece of equipment that holds the hardware or the "brain" of the computer (not shown)

5 delete key--used to remove characters from screen one by one

6 escape (ESC) key--used to cancel a function or exit a program section

7 external disk drive--reads information from and writes information to disks, just like the built-in disk drive

8 mouse--moves a marker across the screen

9 ON/OFF control--used to "power up" or "power down" the system (not shown)

10 return/enter key--used to return cursor to left margin and down to the next line; also, to enter system commands

11 shift key--used to key uppercase letters and the upper character on 2-character keys

12 space bar--used to move cursor to right one space at a time or to add space between characters

13 tab key--used to move cursor to tab stops along ruler/format line

14 video monitor--the piece of equipment used to display text, data, and graphic images on screen (not shown)

Care of Your Equipment

1. Wipe monitor screen with soft, clean cloth.
2. Brush the dirt and dust from the keyboard.
3. Keep desk free of dust, especially the area under the keyboard.
4. Shut off power after each use.

Position of Hands

When keying, keep your fingers deeply curved. Fingernails should be neatly trimmed.

Hold your hands directly over the keys. Turn the hands inward slightly to get straight, tapping strokes. Do not permit your hands to turn over on the little fingers.

Keep your forearms in a parallel line with the slope of the keyboard. Hold your wrists down near, but not resting on, the front frame of the machine.

Do not buckle your wrists upward.

Barely touch the home keys with your fingertips. Feel the keys; do not smother them.

When a finger makes a reach from its home position to tap another key, the other fingers remain on or near their home keys. Such reaches are made by the finger without twisting the wrist or moving the arm or elbow.

Forearms parallel to slant of machine

Reach with the finger

Fingers curved

Keep arms and wrists quiet

Keying Rhythm

Your goal is to tap the keys at a steady pace, without breaks or pauses. At first, you will think each letter as you key it. Later, you will think and key short, easy-to-key words and phrases as a whole. You will key longer, hard-to-key words by letters or syllables. Finally, you will combine whole word keying with letter or syllable keying into a smooth, fluent, steady rhythm.

Stroking

Center the stroking action in your fingers. Keep your elbows, arms, and wrists quiet as you key. Your fingers should be deeply curved. Use quick, sharp, tapping strokes. Release the keys quickly by snapping the fingers toward the palm of the hand. Strike the keys squarely with short, quick, straight strokes.

Posture

Good posture is vital in learning to key well. Given below are 10 guides of good form. Study the guides carefully. Observe them whenever you work at your machine.

1. Book at right of keyboard on bookholder or with something under top for easier reading.

2. Table free of unneeded books and papers.

3. Front frame of the keyboard even with the edge of the desk.

4. Body centered opposite the **h** key, 6 to 8 inches from front frame of keyboard.

5. Body seated back in chair, shoulders erect with body leaning forward slightly from waist.

6. Elbows held near the body.

7. Wrists held low with forearms parallel to the slant of the keyboard. Do not rest lower hand on frame of keyboard.

8. Feet flat on the floor, one just ahead of the other.

9. Head turned toward book with eyes on copy.

10. Fingers curved and held over second row of keys.

Spacing Between Words

Almost one in every five strokes is made with the space bar. Learn to operate the space bar correctly.

1. Hold the right thumb curved under the hand just over the space bar.
2. Tap the bar with a quick down-and-in motion of the thumb.
3. Keep the wrist low and quiet as you tap the bar.
4. Keep the left thumb tucked under the hand.

Control of the space bar

Shift and Shift Lock Keys

The left shift key is used when capital letters are keyed with the right hand. Use a one-two count as you shift.

ONE Depress the shift key with the little finger and hold it down.

TWO Tap the capital letter with the opposite hand; then quickly release the shift key and return the little finger to its home row position.

The right shift key is used when capital letters are keyed with the left hand.

To key ALL CAP items, depress the caps/shift lock with the little finger and key. To escape, depress the caps/shift lock.

Control of left shift

Control of right shift

Return/Enter Key

Operate the return/enter key at the end of each drill line and at the end of a paragraph.

Return/Enter

GET READY TO DO WORD PROCESSING

WORD PROCESSING Word processing is a method of writing, editing, and storing letters, reports, etc., on a computer, electronic typewriter, or word processor. It may also include printing of the final document.

MICROCOMPUTER A small, relatively inexpensive computer is called a microcomputer or a personal computer. The "brains" of the microcomputer is a Central Processing Unit (CPU).

WORD PROCESSOR OR MICROPROCESSOR The word processor (or microprocessor) is a microcomputer which contains instructions that allow the user to create, modify, and print documents.

HARDWARE The microprocessor you are using includes the keyboard, monitor, and disk drive. These pieces are called the hardware.

The main part of the keyboard resembles a traditional typewriter keyboard, but also includes a numeric keypad, direction keys, and function keys.

The monitor (CRT or Cathode Ray Tube) displays text, data, and graphic images on a screen.

The disk drive is a device into which a disk is inserted so information can be either retrieved or recorded. Depending upon the system used, the disk drive may be in a horizontal or vertical position.

WORK STATION The desk containing the hardware and the space around the hardware is your work station. You should have an area for your textbook and a secure place for disks not currently in use.

PERIPHERALS Equipment that works with a word processing system, but is not part of it, is called a peripheral. One peripheral is a printer. If a printer is not a part of your work station, you are probably connected to one through a networked system.

A dot-matrix printer uses closely grouped dots to form letters and is good for producing first drafts of letters or reports. For correspondence or final copies, a letter quality printer is desirable. A laser printer produces a clear image that is especially good preparing masters for multiple copies.

Other peripherals, including scanners and modems, are available and may be added as needed.

STAND-ALONE and NETWORKED SYSTEMS If the work station operates independently of all other systems, it is called a stand-alone system.

When the work station is connected to other work stations and/or printers with cables, it is a networked system. All work stations in a networked system are linked to a server. A networked system is also known as a LAN (local area network).

SOFTWARE Software refers to the set of instructions (or programs) for the operation of a word processor, and is housed on a disk (diskette or floppy disk). A disk is a magnetic, mylar-coated, record-like disk encased in a protective envelope that is used for reading and writing by a CPU. Common sizes are 5 1/4" and 3 1/2".

A large disk, housed within a metal case and having a greater storage capacity, is called a hard disk. The hard disk may contain the programs as well as data the operator has entered. The server for a networked system usually contains a hard disk.

FORMATTING or INITIALIZING A DISK Before the user can store information on a data disk, the disk must be prepared to accept the information. The preparation is called formatting or initializing a disk. Refer to the hardware manual or the User's Manual for your software for specific directions on disk formatting.

GET THE SYSTEM READY FOR WORK

When you are ready to work, you will need to prepare or "boot up" the system for use. The computer DOS (Disk Operating System) or start-up program must be in place to cause the microcomputer to operate.

If the system has not been turned on for you, you will need to "cold start or boot" it by turning on all pieces of the microcomputer hardware. The ON/OFF Control is used to "power up" (turn on or start) the system. When the system is on, the power light should be showing for each piece of the work station. If the system has been turned on for you (the power lights are on), you will perform a "warm start or boot."

As soon as DOS is loaded into your work station, remove the DOS disk, insert the program disk, and enter the load command (directions to load the software). When the system has a hard disk or is networked, DOS will be loaded as part of the booting up. The software or program disk will also be on the hard disk, but will have to be loaded into the microcomputer with the load command (see User's Manual). While the disk drive is working (writing to or reading from the disk), the disk use light is on. DO NOT insert or remove a disk when the disk use light is on. DO NOT turn ON/OFF while light is on.

When the software program disk has been loaded, the monitor will show a *main menu* which gives options for using the software.

EXIT/QUIT

At the end of class, or when you are finished using the work station, you will "exit/quit" (leave) the software program and "power down" (turn off all equipment). Carefully remove all disks and place them in protective envelopes for storage.

CHECK YOUR KEYBOARDING POSITION

1. Place this book to the right of your keyboard on a book holder, or put something under the top of the book to raise it for easier reading.

2. Position the keyboard so that the center of the alphabetic keyboard (the space between *G* and *H*) is lined up with the center of your body with the front edge of the keyboard even with the front edge of the desk.

If your keyboard is adjustable, adjust the angle so that the keyboard tilts slightly upward for ease of operation.

3. Your body should be six to eight inches from the front edge of the keyboard.

4. Don't slump; sit erect. Hold your elbows near your body.

5. Place your feet on the floor, one just ahead of the other in order to give you good balance.

GET READY TO KEY

1. Hold the program disk label-side up for a horizontal drive, label to your left for a vertical drive. When directed to insert the disk, hold the disk at the label and insert into the slot of the disk drive.

2. Note whether you are using a single- or a dual-drive system. If there are two disk drives, you will use Drive A which is on the top if the drives are stacked one over the other, on the left if the drives are side by side.

3. Check that the power cords are plugged into the power source outlet.

4. Check that the monitor, keyboard, and printer are connected to the keyboard.

5. Check paper supply and paper feed on the printer if you will be printing.

6. Locate the display controls (contrast and brightness) so that you may adjust them if nothing appears on the screen in the next step.

7. "Power up" (turn on) the equipment according to the brand name of equipment you are using (see below). The power lights for all pieces of equipment should be on.

For the IBM Compatibles, "power up" as follows:

a. Insert the DOS disk into the disk drive and close the door, if using a 5 1/4" disk. The drive for a 3 1/2" disk has no door, so gently insert disk.

b. Turn on the computer by operating the ON/OFF control. Make sure that the monitor (if separate) and printer (if one is connected to your computer) are also on. *If the computer is already on, hold down the control (CRTL) and alternate (ALT) keys and tap the delete (DEL) key at the same time.*

c. When the computer prompts you to enter the date, either do so or tap the return/enter key. When the computer prompts you to enter the time, either do so or tap the return/enter key.

d. The computer will display the message A>. *(If DOS has been installed on the program disk or the server for a networked system, go to step f.)*

e. Remove the DOS disk from Drive A and insert the appropriate program disk in the drive; then close the door (if using the 5 1/4" disk).

f. Key the specific command for the software in use (see User's Manual).

g. Move from screen to screen to follow the on-screen prompts.

For the Apple IIe, Apple IIc, and Apple IIGS computers, "power up" as follows:

a. Turn on the monitor.

b. Open the door of the disk drive; insert the program disk; and close the door if using the 5 1/4" disk.

c. Turn on the computer by operating the ON/OFF control. (*If the computer is already on, hold down the control, "open apple," and reset keys simultaneously.*) The title screen will appear automatically.

d. Move from screen to screen by following the on-screen prompts.

Care of Disks

1. Do not bend or fold a disk or attach a paper clip to it.

2. Keep all disks away from direct sunlight, magnets, and x-ray devices.

3. Do not expose disks to extremely hot or cold temperatures.

4. Do not touch exposed areas of 5 1/4" disks.

5. Leave the metal sliding door on the 3 1/2" disk closed when handling the disk.

6. Use only felt-tipped pens when writing on disk labels—prepare label and then attach it to the disk.

7. Use care when inserting disks into and removing them from the disk drives. Do so only when the disk drive light is off. If the door of the disk drive doesn't close easily, remove the disk and reinsert it. *Never force the door to close.*

8. Store each disk vertically in the envelope when not in use.

LESSON 90

1" side margins

90a • Keyboard Review

5 minutes

Directions: Key each sentence three times SS. DS between 3-line groups.

alphabet Mavis Grable will quickly explain what John made for prizes.

fig/sym Prices--except on 1993 and older models--will increase 6.8%.

easy See if they can do most of their work on these new machines.

| 1 | 2 | 3 | 4 | 5 | 6 | 7 | 8 | 9 | 10 | 11 | 12 |

90b • Timed Writings

15 minutes

Directions: **1.** Take one 1' writing on each ¶ of 86c, page 161. Count errors.

2. Take one 5' writing on all ¶s combined. Count errors. Figure *gwam*.

90c • Format Review

25 minutes

Problem 1 Tabulation Review

Directions: **1.** Retrieve **L89c**.
2. Add the cities, making them the first column and leaving 10 spaces between that column and the column with the stadium names.
3. The heading for the cities column will be "City" (underlined).
4. Save as **L90c1**.

WORLD LEAGUE OF AMERICAN FOOTBALL STADIUMS

1991 Season

City	Stadium	Seating
Birmingham	Legion Field	72,000
Sacramento	Hughes Stadium	23,000
San Antonio	Alamo Stadium	25,000
Montreal	Olympic Stadium	60,000
Rutherford	Giants Stadium	75,000
Orlando	Florida Citrus Bowl	70,000
Raleigh	Carter-Finley at NC State	45,000
Barcelona	Motjiuc Stadium	70,000
Frankfurt	Waldstadion	55,000
London	Wembley Stadium	72,000

Problem 2 Report Review

Directions: **1.** Retrieve **L87c1**.
2. Add the paragraph given below.
3. Cursor down until you are at the beginning of the next page.
4. Import **L90c1**. Center the table on the new page. You may need to insert spaces to move the table right as the margins change from L90c1.

A summary of the cities in which each of the teams was located, the name of the stadium each team played in, and the seating capacity of each stadium follows this report. For ease of reading this summary, it appears on the following page.

Learning to Operate the Letter Keys (Lessons 1-15)

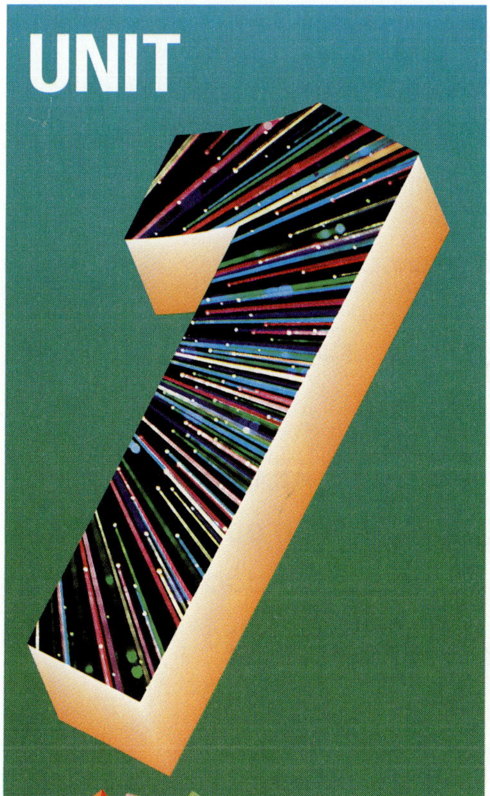

Learning Goals

1. Locate and use the cursor (arrow) keys.
2. Key all letter keys by touch, using correct fingering.
3. Locate and use function keys according to the software directions.
4. Locate and use correctly all the equipment parts introduced in Unit 1.
5. "Power up" equipment and prepare software for use.
6. Key with good techniques and form, paying particular attention to the posture guides and technique goals introduced in Unit 1.
7. Learn one method of naming a file (**Les** for **Lesson**).
8. Learn how to save a file.
9. Exit/quit the software program and "power down" (turn off) equipment used.

Word Processing Concepts Introduced in Unit 1

cursor (arrow) keys	file name	printing a hard copy
default margins	preset tabs	ruler/format line
escape (ESC) key	power down	save
exit/quit	power up	word wrap

LESSON 1

1a • Find the Home Keys, Space Bar, and Return/Enter Key

hands upright over keys

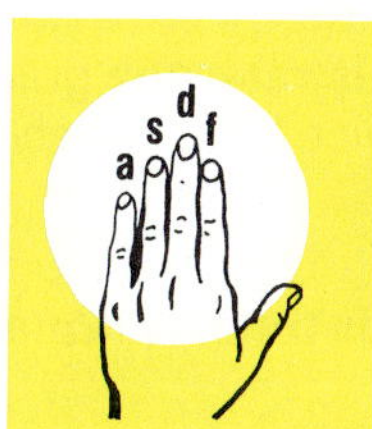

fingers deeply curved

1. Place the fingers of your left hand on **a s d f**.
2. Place the fingers of your right hand on **j k l ;**.
3. Take your fingers off the home keys. Replace them. Say the keys of each hand as you touch them. Repeat several times to get the "feel" of these keys.
4. Hold your right thumb over the middle of the space bar. Tap the bar with a quick, inward motion of your right thumb. Keep the left thumb out of the way.
5. Curve your fingers. Hold them very lightly over the home keys. Key the line below. Say and think each letter as you tap it.

```
ff jj dd kk ss ll aa ;; fj dk sl a; fj dk sl a; fj
```

23 minutes

89c • Format Review

Tabulation Review

Directions: **1.** Retrieve **L44d2**.
2. Format for a DS tabulation problem by uncentering the lines with the stadium names and adding seating capacities.
3. Leave 10 spaces between columns.
4. Add and underline column headings as marked below.
5. Save as **L89b**.

WORLD LEAGUE OF AMERICAN FOOTBALL STADIUMS

1991 Season

Stadium	Seating
Legion Field	72,000
Hughes Stadium	23,000
Alamo Stadium	25,000
Olympic Stadium	60,000
Giants Stadium	75,000
Florida Citrus Bowl	70,000
Carter-Finley at NC State	45,000
Motjiuc Stadium	70,000
Waldstadion	55,000
Wembley Stadium	72,000

12 minutes

89d • Language Arts Skills: Punctuation Guides for Commas

Directions: **1.** The following are punctuation guides and sentences that illustrate the use of commas.
2. Study each guide; key the sentence that illustrates the guide. Key each sentence twice SS. DS between 2-line groups.

Guide:
Use commas to set off interrupting words that are nonessential to the sentence.
Illustration:
We had, of course, planned to attend the concert.

Guide:
Use a comma to set off interjections (yes, no , well) if there is a break in continuity.
Illustration:
Well, we could see if this experiment works out in the same way.

Guide:
Use commas to set off the name of the person addressed.
Illustration:
The game, Ron, is tomorrow. Lee, do you have tickets for all of us?

Guide:
Use commas to separate dates from years and cities from states.
Illustration:
The convention will be in New Orleans, Louisiana, beginning on July 28, 1994.

CURSOR The cursor is a blinking light on the screen that identifies the position where text (copy) will be entered or edited. Arrow keys (cursor keys) used to move the cursor around the screen may be located on your computer's numeric keypad or as a separate group of keys.

LEFT/RIGHT CURSOR (ARROW) KEYS These keys move the cursor one space at a time in a left or right direction.

UP/DOWN CURSOR (ARROW) KEYS These keys move the cursor up or down one line at a time.

FUNCTION KEYS Function keys are keys usually labeled with F and a number, whose specific roles are defined by the software. Their uses include saving and manipulating data.

quick finger stroke

space with right thumb

1b • Use Proper Techniques

Hand Position

Hold your hands directly over the keys, keeping your fingers deeply curved.

Do not permit your hands to turn over on the little fingers. Turn your hands inward slightly to get straight strokes.

Hold your wrists down near, but not resting on, the front frame of the keyboard. Keep your forearms in a parallel line with the slope of the keyboard.

Barely touch home keys with the fingers.

Stroking

Center the stroking action in your fingers. Keep elbows, arms, and wrists quiet as you key. Your fingers should be deeply curved. Use quick, sharp strokes.

Release the keys quickly by snapping the fingers toward the palm of the hand. Tap the keys squarely with short, quick, straight strokes.

return/enter

Spacing Between Words

Hold the right thumb curved under the hand just over the space bar. Tap the bar with a quick down-and-in motion of the thumb. Keep wrist low and quiet as you tap the bar.

Return/Enter Key

Operate the return/enter key at the end of each drill line to bring the cursor to the beginning of the next line.

1. Reach the little finger of your right hand to the return/enter key (No. 10). The left hand remains on home keys.

2. Tap the return/enter key quickly.

3. Return the finger at once to its home key position.

1c • Home-Key Practice

Directions: Key each line with your teacher at least once. Tap return/enter key at end of each line (where you see the **R/E**).

Technique Goal: Think and say each letter as you tap it.

home keys

think and say each letter

```
1  ff jj ff jj ff jj ff jj ff jj fj fj fj fj fj fj fj  R/E
2  dd kk dd kk dd kk dd kk dd kk dk dk dk dk dk dk dk  R/E
3  ss ll ss ll ss ll ss ll ss ll sl sl sl sl sl sl sl  R/E
4  aa ;; aa ;; aa ;; aa ;; aa ;; a; a; a; a; a; a; a;  R/E
5  fj dk sl a; fj dk sl a; fj dk sl a; fj dk sl a; fj  R/E
```

10 minutes

88c • Timed Writings

Directions: **1.** Take two 1' writings on each ¶ DS. Check the one on which you made your best rate; then check the one on which you made the fewest errors.
2. Take a 5' writing on both paragraphs combined. Check errors. Figure *gwam*.
Alternate Procedure: Work for speed as you take one 5' writing on both ¶s combined. Figure *gwam*.

keep your eyes on the copy

all letters used 1.3 si word wrap

	gwam 5'		
Do you know why many people fail in their jobs? Their	2	22	42
spelling, poor as it often is, is not the reason. They get by in	5	25	45
figuring too. The reports of many studies show that they fail	7	27	47
because they do not work with one another as well as they should.	10	30	50
We ask much of other people but give little in return. We	12	32	52
stress their mistakes with the same zest we use in hiding our	15	35	55
own. We are being neither fair to them nor honest with	17	37	57
ourselves. When we do these things, we cannot work as well as we	20	40	60
should.	20	40	60

5' *gwam* | 1 | 2 | 3 |

LESSON 89

1" side margins

5 minutes

89a • Keyboard Review

Directions: Key each sentence three times SS. DS between 3-line groups.

alphabet Joy Brave will squeeze six big limes for the drink of punch.
fig/sym Martie ran the 100-yard dash (91.4 meters) in less that 15".
easy Fix the handle so tight that he will not be able to turn it.

| 1 | 2 | 3 | 4 | 5 | 6 | 7 | 8 | 9 | 10 | 11 | 12 |

5 minutes

89b • Speed Builder

Directions: Key the ¶ below as many times as you can in the given time.

all letters used 1.3 si word wrap

	words
In spite of all we read about the fitness craze, experts say	12
that most folks simply are not in very good shape. Though you	25
see joggers out running almost every day, it is a unique adult	38
who can climb one flight of stairs without becoming short of	50
breath.	51

1d • Technique Builder: Stroking

Directions: Key each line once with your teacher. Repeat the lines a second time by yourself. When you key on each line, you are single spacing (SS). **Technique Goal:** Curve your fingers. Use quick, sharp taps.

home keys

use quick, sharp, tapping strokes

```
1 as ask as ask as ask all all lass lass as all lass   R/E
2 all fall all fall all all fall fall all fall falls   R/E
3 ad lad ad lad ad lad all a lad all a lad all a lad   R/E
4 a lad; a lad asks; a lass; a lass asks; ask a lass   R/E
5 a lass; as a lass; as a lass falls; as a lad falls   R/E
6 a lad asks; a lass asks; ask a lass; ask all lads;   R/E
```

1e • Ending the Lesson

FILE NAME The name you give the work you have completed is called a file name. The file name should give a clue to the contents of the work and should be concise, as you are limited in the number of letters, numerals, symbols, or a combination of them that will be accepted by the software. DO NOT leave any spaces in the file name.

SAVE To save your work means to record it on a formatted (initialized) data disk so that it can be recovered later for additional use. If you are using a system that has a hard disk, or a system that is networked, you will save in the directory that has been created for you.

ESCAPE (ESC) KEY The escape key lets the user cancel a function or leave one segment of a program and go to another.

EXIT/QUIT

After you have saved your work, you will leave (exit/quit) the software program before you walk away from the work station.

1. Remove the program disk, if you need to and have not already done so, and gently return to protective envelope.
2. Insert the formatted data disk, being sure to close the drive door if you are using the 5 1/4" disk. If you are saving to your directory, go to it, then save.
3. Follow the directions in the User's Manual for your software to save the work you did today, using the file name of **Les1** (for Lesson 1).
4. Exit/quit the software program, remove all disks and gently put them in the protective envelopes, and "power down" (turn off) all pieces of equipment as directed in the User's Manual. Return disks to appropriate disk cases and textbook to storage shelf.

87c1, continued

Montreal, Canada; Orlando, Florida; and Raleigh-Durham, North Carolina made up the North American East Division. North American West Division teams were located in Sacramento, California; San Antonio, Texas; and Birmingham, Alabama. Each team played a 10-game, round-robin schedule making one trans-Atlantic trip each season.

For football fans who had been accustomed to NFL exhibition games that begin as early as July, and a season ending with the Super Bowl in January, the WLAF season of about ten weeks was very short. Play began in late March, and the "World Bowl" league championship game was played early in June.

Along with the shorter season WLAF paychecks were much smaller than those of NFL players. At the beginning of the WLAF, kickers were paid $15,000; quarterbacks received $25,000; and everyone else earned $20,000. Incentive clauses were not included in these amounts, but the maximum amount any player could receive was around $100,000.

A new approach to communication was the installation of radios in the helmets of the quarterbacks for talks with coaches on the sidelines. Rather than the National Football League standard of 45 seconds between plays, the WLAF teams were allowed only 35 seconds. In the event of a tie at the end of the regulation period, the one overtime period was a maximum 15 minutes long. In addition to other changes in the rules for the WLAF, the one change that might have been hardest for fans to adjust to was that there was no instant replay during the game.

After the first successful year, NFL owners agreed to a three-year TV contract with two networks. Money was contributed by 28 teams. The contract covered 35 regular-season games, two play-off games, and the World Bowl. The San Antonio team moved to Marcos, Texas, and a new team replaced the dropped Raleigh/Durham Skyhawks.

Problem 2 Personal-Business Letter Review

Directions: **1.** Retrieve **L80c**. **2.** Delete spaces to change the modified block to block style. **3.** Delete the punctuation following the salutation and closing to change from mixed to open punctuation.

LESSON 88

1" side margins

5 minutes

88a • Keyboard Review

Directions: Key each sentence three times SS. DS between 3-line groups.

keep arms and wrists quiet

alphabet	Fred Vasquez again explained why he objected to the remarks.
figure	On July 1 their extension will be changed from 2983 to 6745.
easy	She thinks he will be there to see her when the plane lands.

| 1 | 2 | 3 | 4 | 5 | 6 | 7 | 8 | 9 | 10 | 11 | 12 |

30 minutes

88b • Format Review

Problem 1

Tabulation Review

Directions: **1.** Retrieve **L24c3**. **2.** Arrange into a 3-column table by placing the first five items in Column 1, the second five in Column 2, and the last five in Column 3. Leave six spaces between columns.

Problem 2 Review of Personal Notes

Directions: **1.** Retrieve **L86b1**. **2.** Change to modified block style with open punctuation.

LESSON 2

2a • Keyboard Review

Spacing Guide: Space once after a semi-colon (;) within a sentence.

Directions: **1.** Review the procedure for booting up the computer and for preparing the software program for use explained on page 1. **2.** Key each line once with your teacher.

Posture Goal: Place your feet flat on the floor for balance.

think each key as you tap it

home keys

```
1 ff jj dd kk ss ll aa ;; ff jj dd kk ss ll aa ;; fj R/E
2 fj dk sl a; fj dk sl a; fj dk sl a; fj dk sl a; fj R/E
3 as as; ask a; ask a lass; ask a lad; ask all lads; R/E
4 lad lad lads ask ask lass lass all all fall fall a R/E
5 all lads fall; ask a lass; as a lass falls; a lass R/E
```

2b • Location of E and H

Plan for Learning New Keys

1. Find new key on keyboard chart.

2. Locate key on your keyboard.

3. Place fingers over home keys.

4. Know which finger taps each key.

5. Watch your finger as you make the reach to the new key.

6. Key each short drill twice on the same line. Be sure to use the correct finger.

Reach to E

1. Find **e** on the chart.
2. Find it on your keyboard.
3. Place your fingers over the home keys.
4. Reach to **e** with the **d** finger.
5. Touch **ed** lightly without moving the other fingers from their home position.
6. Key the drill below twice on the same line.

```
ded ded ed ed ed led led
```

Reach to H

1. Find **h** on the chart.
2. Find it on your keyboard.
3. Place your fingers over the home keys.
4. Reach to **h** with the **j** finger.
5. Touch **hj** lightly without moving the other fingers from their home position.
6. Key the drill below twice on the same line.

```
jhj jhj hj hj ha had had
```

LESSON 87

1" side margins

5 minutes

87a • Keyboard Review

Directions: Key each sentence three times SS. DS between 3-line groups.

alphabet May Dick will give the puzzle to Jess Quinn for the old box.

fig/sym Asia's Mount Everest (5 1/2 miles high) was climbed in 1953.

easy Most of us show what we are by what we do with what we have.

| 1 | 2 | 3 | 4 | 5 | 6 | 7 | 8 | 9 | 10 | 11 | 12 |

10 minutes

87b • Sentence Guided Writings

Directions: **1.** Take 1' writings on each sentence SS. Try to key each sentence four times within the minute without error. **2.** Your teacher will call the return each 15" to guide you. **3.** Figure *gwam* and count errors.

		gwam 15"
1	We live in an information age.	24
2	Computers are used for many things.	28
3	Some people are worried about eyestrain.	32
4	A few factories are now making use of robots.	36
5	Most machines are now becoming more user-friendly.	40
6	In some instances you can do your banking by telephone.	44
7	Skill in keyboarding is really important for all of us.	44
8	Persons of every age group are being affected by technology.	48
9	Not everybody will adjust easily to this new computer world.	48

| 1 | 2 | 3 | 4 | 5 | 6 | 7 | 8 | 9 | 10 | 11 | 12 |

30 minutes

87c • Format Review

Problem 1 Multiple-Page Report

Directions: **1.** Format 1 1/2" left margin, 1" right margin, and heading centered on line 13. The second page will be numbered. **2.** Save as **L87c1**.

FOOTBALL PLAYOFFS IN JUNE?

By (Student's name)

Sunday afternoons and Monday nights have long been reserved for watching professional football games on television. Most fans choose their favorite team at an early age, and stick by that team through losing as well as winning seasons. Thousands of items, from clothing to wastebaskets to desk accessories, complete with team name and/or logo entice fans into stores and promote team loyalty.

Soon after Super Bowl XXV and the end of the NFL season in January, 1991, a new football league, sponsored by NFL owners, began its first regular season schedule. Called the World League of American Football, or WLAF, this new league had three divisions. The European Division was comprised of teams in London, England; Barcelona, Spain; and Frankfurt, Germany. Teams in New York/New Jersey;

(continued on next page)

2c • Location Drills: E and H

Directions: Key each line once with your teacher. Repeat the lines a second time by yourself. Tap the return/enter key at the end of each line. **Technique Goal:** Think and say each letter as you tap it.

Reach to e

Reach to h

ded ded ded ded ed ed ed ed led led fled fled fled

e fee fee feed feeds feels feels less less else else

sell sell sale sales deal deal desk desk jade jade

jhj jhj jhj hj hj hj hj ha ha has has had had half

h has ash ash lash flash flash hall hall shall shall

had a half; had a half; has a half; has had a half

he heed heeds she shell shelf held head heads shed

e/h shed shells shade shale leash flesh flashed dashed

hash hall; elf elk; he has shade; she held a leash

2d • Technique Builder: Eyes on Copy

Directions: Key each line two times as shown SS, tapping the return/enter key at the end of each line. To double-space (DS), operate the return/enter key twice. Leave a blank line (DS) between 2-line groups.

single-space (SS) repeated lines

double-space (DS) when you start a new line

1 fjdk sla; fjdk sla; ed hj ed hj ed hj he he she he
fjdk sla; fjdk sla; ed hj ed hj ed hj he he she he

DS

2 she she held held lad lad lass lass she head heads
she she held held lad lad lass lass she head heads

DS

3 as as has has lash lash; flash flash; flask flasks
as as has has lash lash; flash flash; flask flasks

DS

4 sale sale; a sale a sale; lake lake; a lake a lake
sale sale; a sale a sale; lake lake; a lake a lake

DS

5 sea sea sake sake; see see; see a leaf; see a leaf
sea sea sake sake; see see; see a leaf; see a leaf

DS

6 hall halls; sell sells; sells a desk; sells a desk
hall halls; sell sells; sells a desk; sells a desk

DS

7 ash ash; dash dash; he had a sled; she had a sled;
ash ash; dash dash; he had a sled; she had a sled;

86b, continued

Problem 2 Centering Review

Directions: 1. Retrieve **L73c1**.
2. Move the names of those in attendance to the end of the minutes and delete the rest of the problem.
3. Add a heading of ATTENDANCE FOR MEETING OF OCTOBER 18.
4. Center each name horizontally DS.
5. Center the problem vertically on a full sheet of paper.

ATTENDANCE FOR MEETING OF OCTOBER 18

Mali Brakeman

Phil Johnson

20 minutes

86c • Paragraph Guided Writings

Directions: 1. Work on control as you take a 1' writing on ¶ 1. Move to succeeding ¶s when you complete each one within the error limit specified by your teacher. If time allows, repeat any ¶s in which you exceeded the error limit.
2. Take at least one 5' writing on all ¶s combined. Figure *gwam*.

all letters used 1.3 si word wrap

	gwam 5'		
Down through the years, humans have always found a need to	2	30	58
exchange written messages with those who live some distance away.	5	33	61
The first record of a system for doing this goes back to the days	8	35	63
of bronze tablets carried on horseback.	9	37	65
Our own mail service has evolved from the era of the pony	12	39	67
express to the jet age. To handle the expanding volume,	14	42	69
equipment is used that reads ZIP Codes to direct a piece of	16	44	72
mail to one section of a block or one certain building.	18	46	74
No one knows how we will be sending written notes to each	21	49	76
other in the future. Today many firms use some form of	23	51	79
electronic mail, where their letters are sent by means of	25	53	81
telephone lines and no written copies are transported at all.	28	56	83

5' *gwam* | 1 | 2 | 3 |

2e • Fluency Practice

Directions: **1.** Key each line twice SS, tapping the return/enter key at the end of each line. DS after each 2-line group. **2.** Save today's work as **Les2**, following the procedure in Lesson 1. **3.** Exit/quit the software program and power down the program when directed to do so.

Technique Goal: Use quick, sharp taps. Release the keys instantly.

```
1 a lad; a lass; as a lad; as a lass; sell sell else
2 he he held held he held; he held; she has; as she;
3 all fall; all fall; a deal; a deal; a deal; a half
4 fee fee feel feel asked asked; he asked; she asked
5 as a; as a lad; as a lad falls; a lass; as a lass;
6 asked a fee; asked a fee; held a lead; held a sale
7 as he fell; as she fell; has a lease; had a lease;
```

LESSON 3

3a • Keyboard Review

Spacing: Double
Margin: Default

Directions: Key each line once with your teacher. Repeat the lines a second time by yourself. Tap the return/enter key at the end of each line.

Posture Goal: Sit erect. Hold elbows near the body. Keep wrists low and quiet and eyes on copy.

```
e                  ded ded ed ed see feel less see sale else desk see
h                  jhj jhj hj hj he held had has hall half dash shall
e/h                he heads shelf shake flesh she heeds leash flashed
all letters taught add add ask ask less less head head fall fall feel
                   jell jell; she shall see; has a desk; held a sale;
```

DEFAULT MARGINS Default margins are one of several preset specifications in word processing software. Common default margins are 1″ on each side of the text.

3b • Location of T and O

Reach to T

1. Find **t** on the chart.
2. Find it on your keyboard.
3. Place your fingers over the home keys.
4. Reach to **t** with the **f** finger.
5. Touch **tf** lightly without moving other fingers from their home positions.

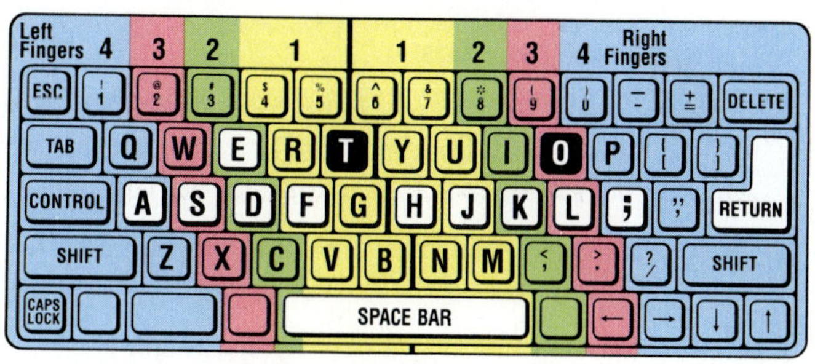

Reach to O

1. Find **o** on the chart.
2. Find it on your keyboard.
3. Place your fingers over the home keys.
4. Reach to **o** with the **l** finger.
5. Touch **ol** lightly without moving other fingers from their home positions.

```
ftf ftf tf tf tf the the          lol lol ol ol ol old old
```

Key twice on same line

15 minutes

85b • Timed Writings

Directions: Take a 1' writing on each ¶ in 81c, page 155. Count errors. Figure *gwam*. Take one 5' writing on all the five ¶s combined. Count errors. Figure *gwam*.

25 minutes

85c • Format Review

Problem 1 Edited Agenda

Directions: **1.** Retrieve **L73c2**. **2.** Make the changes as marked.

STUDENT COUNCIL AGENDA

~~Friday~~ Thursday, October ~~18~~ 17, Period ~~5~~ 4

Library ~~Conference~~ Work Room

Problem 2 Business Letter Review

Directions: **1.** Retrieve **L78d1**.
2. Change from modified block style with mixed punctuation to block style with open punctuation.
3. Change the name and mailing address to: Mr. Stanley T. Ott | Clothing and More | 5412 Kings Road | Lake Charles, LA 70601-2576

Reminder: Change the salutation to match the name of the receiver of the letter.

Problem 3 Business Letter Review

Directions: **1.** Retrieve **L77c**.
2. Change from block style with open punctuation to modified block with mixed punctuation and indented paragraphs.

LESSON 86

1" side margins

86a • Keyboard Review

5 minutes

Directions: Key each sentence three times SS. DS between 3-line groups.

alphabet Gary Wells put five dozen quarts of jam in the box for Jack.

fig/sym Since the tickets sell for $3.50 each, two will cost you $7.

easy Rosa took the lead early in the race and thus won the title.

| 1 | 2 | 3 | 4 | 5 | 6 | 7 | 8 | 9 | 10 | 11 | 12 |

20 minutes

86b • Format Review

Problem 1 Personal Note Review

Directions: **1.** Format for side margins of 2" with the date on line 20. **2.** Use block style with open punctuation. **3.** Save as **L86b1**.

Today's date / Dear Kristin /

Finally! School is over for the summer! Just think--next year we won't be the youngest class in the building. Our science class will never be the same without Mr. Lee, but I hear we will be doing a lot of experiments next year.

The big concert is tomorrow night and we can't miss our favorite group. Do you think that 6:30 is early enough to leave? We don't want to miss the opening act.

Let's get this summer vacation started right.

See you soon.

Reach to t

Reach to o

3c • Location Drills: T and O

Directions: Key each line once with your teacher. Repeat a second time by yourself. Tap the return/enter key at the end of each line.

Technique Goal: Snap the finger toward the palm of the hand after each tap.

ftf ftf ftf ftf tf tf tf tf the the that that that
t the that the that last let last let late late last
late take talk tell take talk tell these these set

lol lol ol ol ol old old told told hold hold holds
o of of of to to to those those too too took took of
do do does does so so; do so; do so; does so; does

toe toes toss toss tot tot toast toast stood stood
t/o dot dots soft soft jot jots hot hot lost lost lots
to jot; too soft; to those lots; to those lots too

3d • Technique Builder: Finger-Action Stroking

Directions: Key each line two times, tapping the return/enter key at the end of each line. DS between each 2-line group.

Technique Goal: Move your fingers, not your arms or wrists.

double-space (DS) after second keying of line

1 fjdk sla; fjdk sla; ed hj tf tf ol ol late late at
2 to to of of too too took took hold hold holds does
3 at at late late look look food food off off let to
4 lot lot left left loss loss felt felt sold sold so
5 foot foot lost lost take take too too set set take

3e • Fluency Practice

Directions: **1.** Key each line three times SS, tapping the return/enter key at the end of each line. DS between 3-line groups. **2.** Save your work as **Les3**. **3.** Exit/quit the software and power down the equipment.

Technique Goal: Key without pauses.

key each line three times

key without pauses

1 she looks; she looks at; he took; he took the desk
2 she does; he does; she has; he has; she has a half
3 a joke; that jet; that lot; the shoe; the old shoe
4 he has a half; had a talk; had a loss; held a sale

84c • Format Review

20 minutes

Directions: Retrieve **L67c1** and make the editing changes marked.

CONSERVING WATER

By (Student's name)

Enough rain falls in most parts of the United States to keep our lawns green, our gardens growing, and our reservoirs full. *satisfy our thirst and keep us clean,*

If you look at a picture taken from outer space, you will notice that water mass exceeds landmass. But ~~the~~ *this* large amount of water mass leads to one of our worries, for less than one percent of that water is drinkable. More than two percent of the water on earth is frozen in glaciers and ice at the North and South Poles. The remaining 97 percent of the water is ~~locked~~ *trapped* in salt water oceans and coastal seas (Stewart, 1990, 225). The fresh water actually available for human use in lakes, rivers, and the accessible ground water amounts to less than half of one percent of the total water supply. The purest, most easily developed supplies of water have already been tapped, and a growing number of users are fighting for access to the shrinking reserves (Coffel, 1989, 13). We don't have enough water to waste.

The average consumer uses about 50 gallons of water a day, or 240 gallons for a family of four (Handbook, 1991, 3). Humans require two to three quarts of water per day just to maintain the crucial liquid balance within the body (Coffel, 1989, 16). Some of that water comes from the food eaten, but much of it is taken in as fluids. Amazingly, water is probably the only drink which is free of calories, sweeteners, caffeine, and alcohol (Stewart, 1990, 225).

The use of large quantities of water is an inescapable part of American life today. How can we reduce the amount of water we use?

Three-quarters of the water is used in the bathroom. As you may have heard in televised commercials, older toilets use more than five gallons with each flush. New toilets may use up to 3.5 gallons--a savings of 25 percent. ~~By inserting a toilet tank dam, an additional half gallon of water is saved. The savings would then be 40 percent!~~

Are you one who likes to take a long shower? ~~Some~~ *Most* shower heads use between five and seven gallons of water per minute*, or 25 to 30 gallons for one 5-minute shower*. Low-flow shower heads that use only 2.5 gallons of water per minute are available. Switching to a new low-flow shower head results in a 35 to 50 percent savings. *Also available are timers to remind the shower taker just how long he/she has had the water running.* And, much as you might enjoy that long shower, five minutes of scrubbing will get you clean.

Other ways to save water include running the dishwasher and washing machine only when full (or adjusting the water level setting), using a vegetable brush to remove dirt from fresh fruit and vegetables, and fixing any leaking pipes or faucets. Simply turning off the water while brushing your teeth saves at least four gallons of water each day.

~~We have been looking at savings on water consumption. It should go without saying that for those who pay for the amount of water measured by the water meter, a reduction in the quantity used means a reduction in the size of the bill.~~

~~Most~~ *Many* of us could adjust our use of water as outlined in the preceding paragraphs and never feel we were *being* deprived. Unless more of us make the adjustments voluntarily, we are likely to find that ~~more~~ *some* drastic measures are imposed upon us by local, state, or even federal agencies so that water for only essential use is available.

LESSON 85

1" side margins

85a • Keyboard Review

5 minutes

Directions: Key each sentence three times SS. DS between 3-line groups.

keep fingers deeply curved

alphabet Major taxes have clearly penalized quite a few bigger banks.

fig/sym Hank is almost 5'8", Mary is 5'10", and Jose is nearly 6'2".

easy Try using your head at a job before you try your hand at it.

| 1 | 2 | 3 | 4 | 5 | 6 | 7 | 8 | 9 | 10 | 11 | 12 |

Spacing: Double
Margin: Default

LESSON 4 REVIEW LESSON

4a • Keyboard Review

Directions: Key each line once with your teacher, tapping the return/enter key at the end of each line. Repeat the lines by yourself.

Posture Goal: Sit back in your chair with body centered opposite **h** key. Keep your eyes on the copy.

Finger-Action Stroking
When one of your fingers reaches from its home position to tap another key, keep the other fingers curved on the home keys. Make the reach without raising the wrist or moving your arm or elbow.

home row fj dk sl a; fj dk sl a; all all fall as ask ad add

e ded ded ed ed fed feed deed deal desk else see led

h jhj jhj hj hj he had has she shall held half heads

t ftf ftf tf tf at that late date let tell the these

o lol lol ol ol of off old told holds look took food

4b • Basic Techniques Review

Directions: Key each line two times, tapping the return/enter key at the end of each line. Strive to achieve the specific goal provided for each set of lines.

Posture Goal: Keep head turned toward book; wrists held low; elbows near body; fingers curved.

keep eyes on copy

1 adds adds fall falls dad dads fad fads asks flasks

2 sales shell asked fled deal sell deed jade lake he

3 had has she he shall held half dash head hall lash

4 take these test last date left fast tell felt talk

5 those look to told took hold loss looked food shoe

Technique Goal: Keep fingers deeply curved; use quick, sharp, tapping strokes.

use quick, sharp keystrokes

1 lass lass lads lads asks flask falls fads jak jaks

2 sales deals lease desks keel flake fled flesh safe

3 she shell shells shall flash flesh head heads half

4 state feet late staff health test sheet east steel

5 holds fold joke soft stood sold food told too took

Technique Goal: Tap space bar with quick down-and-in motion of thumb.

use quick down-and-in motion of thumb

1 a a as as as ask ask ad ad ads ads all all jak jak

2 see eke fee feel less she head he fell fed led she

3 ha had has half he she heads ah ash dash lash sash

4 the at let set jet that at let set jet the at that

5 of old off so do to too hold loss lot toe does oak

20 minutes

83c • Format Review

Directions: 1. Retrieve **L52c3**. **2.** Add the information below. Recalculate for the vertical center. **3.** When all information has been keyed, arrange in alphabetical order according to state name.

Nebraska	Cornhusker
Rhode Island	Ocean State
Washington	Evergreen State
Maryland	Free State
Alaska	Last Frontier
Hawaii	Aloha State
Mississippi	Magnolia State

LESSON 84

1" side margins

84a • Keyboard Review

5 minutes

sit erect

keep feet flat on floor

Directions: Key each sentence three times SS. DS between 3-line groups.

alphabet She laid their keys down here so they would be out of sight.

fig/sym Send a check for $5.98 to 27 West 43rd Street, New York, NY.

easy Those who were in good shape ran down the field at halftime.

| 1 | 2 | 3 | 4 | 5 | 6 | 7 | 8 | 9 | 10 | 11 | 12 |

84b • Timed Writings

20 minutes

Directions: 1. Work on control as you take a 1' writing on ¶ 1. Move to succeeding ¶s when you complete each one within the error limit specified by your teacher. **2.** Take a 5' writing on all ¶s combined. Figure *gwam*.

all letters used 1.3 si

word wrap

use quick, sharp, tapping strokes

	gwam	5'	
As more and more of us work in white collar jobs each year,	2	30	58
we hear increased concern being expressed about real health	5	33	60
hazards which we may face in the office. Two factors often	7	35	63
mentioned are eyestrain and stress.	9	37	64
The fact that so many people must look at their computer	11	39	66
screens all day long has raised questions about the role of	13	41	69
computer screens in causing eyestrain. Some say they think that	16	44	71
computer terminals make their eyes tired and sore.	18	46	73
A few workers even blame the modern office for their back	20	48	76
pains, heart diseases, and other ills that can be caused by	23	50	78
stress. These critics point out that the worst health hazards of	25	53	81
the factory have now been brought to workers who sit behind a	28	55	83
desk.	28	56	83

5' *gwam* | 1 | 2 | 3 |

4c • Check on Keyboarding Techniques

Directions: Read the questions and check yourself as you key.

1. Are your eyes on the textbook as you key?

2. Are you sitting up straight with your back touching the back of the chair as you work?

3. Are both feet flat on the floor, one slightly ahead of the other?

4. Are you tapping the return/enter key at the end of the line without first tapping the space bar?

5. Are you keying without pauses between words?

4d • Fluency Practice

Directions: Key each line three times, tapping the return/enter key at the end of each line.

Technique Goal: Try to achieve fluency by cutting out pauses and wasted movements in your arms, elbows, and wrists.

```
1 she sold; she sold those; she sold those old shoes
2 eat the food; look at that desk; take these tests;
3 he asked; he asked to see the jet; she told a joke
4 he talks to; she talks to; she talks to the staff;
5 to the; to that; to do; do so; at the; at the sale
6 the the that that these these those those that the
```

LESSON 5

Spacing: Double
Margin: Default

5a • Keyboard Review

Directions: Key once; repeat. Tap the return/enter key at the end of each line.

Technique Goal: Use quick, sharp, tapping strokes. Release the keys instantly.

```
home row           fjdk sla; fjdk sla; fj as ask all fall ad had jade
t                  tft ftf tf tf to too took the these that take tell
o                  lol lol ol ol old of off do does hold look do food
all letters taught least staff jet dot test stood foot steel date oak
                   she sold all the old shoes; he looked at the food;
```

5b • Location of W and I

Reach to W

1. Find **w** on the chart.
2. Find it on your keyboard.
3. Place your fingers over the home keys.
4. Reach to **w** with the **s** finger.
5. Touch **ws** lightly without moving other fingers from their home positions.

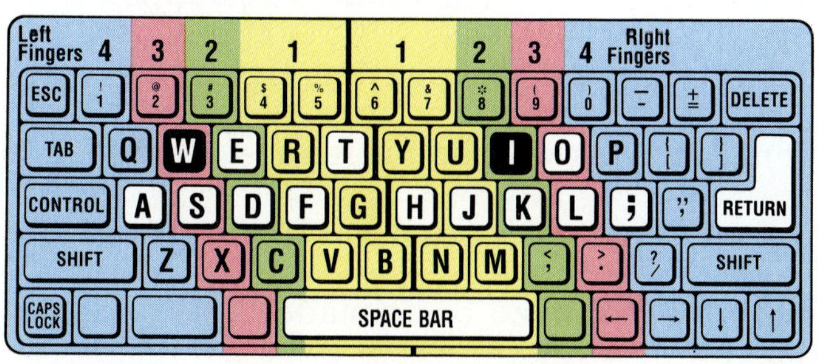

Reach to I

1. Find **i** on the chart.
2. Find it on your keyboard.
3. Place your fingers over the home keys.
4. Reach to **i** with the **k** finger.
5. Touch **ik** lightly without moving other fingers from their home positions.

Key twice on same line

```
sws ws ws wish wish wish
kik kik ik ik id did did
```

23 minutes

82d • Format Review

Problem 1 Centering Review

Directions: 1. Retrieve **L69c**. **2.** Delete all paragraphs, leaving only the heading and the side headings to center horizontally and vertically on a full sheet DS. **3.** Remove the underlining from the side headings.

Problem 2 Tabulation Review

Directions: 1. Retrieve **L81b1**. **2.** Delete the items inside the parentheses. **3.** Change from a centering problem to a tabulation problem by moving every other item to the tab for the second column. Leave 12 spaces between columns. Keep 1" side margins. **4.** Recalculate the top margin to center vertically.

LESSON 83

1" side margins

5 minutes

83a • Keyboard Review

Directions: Key each sentence three times SS. DS between 3-line groups.

alphabet	Jacqueline amazed everyone by fixing these packages of bows.
fig/sym	Paul said, "To get the answer, add 9 1/3, 6 5/8, and 7 3/4."
easy	Use well the gift of learning to add to the things you know.
	1 | 2 | 3 | 4 | 5 | 6 | 7 | 8 | 9 | 10 | 11 | 12

20 minutes

83b • Paragraph Guided Writings

Directions: 1. Take two 5' writings on the ¶s below. Figure your *gwam*. **2.** Submit the better writing.

keep your eyes on the copy

all letters used 1.3 si — word wrap

	gwam 5'		
The subject of energy is now one of the hottest topics	2	21	40
around. Most experts think we are on the edge of a new era, a	5	24	43
new stage of history in which our wasteful way of living will	7	26	45
have to change.	8	27	46
Here are several things that may happen in the next few	10	29	48
years. Our cars will be smaller, lighter in weight, and more	13	32	50
efficient. Houses will be built so as to reduce heating and	15	34	53
cooling costs. A shift from gas and oil to coal, nuclear, or	17	36	55
solar energy will need to be made.	19	38	56

5' *gwam* | 1 | 2 | 3 |

Reach to w

Reach to i

5c • Location Drills: W and I

Directions: Key each line once with your teacher, tapping the return/enter key at the end of each line. Repeat a second time by yourself.

Technique Goal: Reach to **w** and **i** without moving your hands forward. Hold the wrists low and quiet.

```
    sws sws sws sws ws ws ws ws we week week who whose
w   wall wall walk walk well well how how law law laws
    west west show show few few week weeks was was low

    kik kik kik kik ik ik ik ik did did slid slid dike
i   dike is is this this dish dish fish fish fill fill
    its its like likes list list still still life life

    with with wish wish wife wife will wills wide wide
w/i wise wise waits waits wished wished with with will
    wait a while; a wise wish; he waits with his wife;
```

5d • Technique Builder

Directions: Key each line two times, tapping the return/enter key at the end of each line.

Technique Goal: Quick, sharp keystrokes.

double-space (DS) when you start a new line

release the keys instantly

```
1 jfdk sla; ik ik ik ws ws ws did did dike dike wide
2 will will with with wait wait like likes it it its
3 we we well well side sides still was was wash wash
4 if if wife wife wide wide field fields while while
5 who who what what two two said said life life list
6 how how his his few few still still week week show
```

5e • Fluency Practice

Directions: Key each line three times, tapping the return/enter key at the end of each line.

Technique Goal: Keep arms and wrists still.

key steadily

```
1 it was; it will; it will last; it will last a week
2 he was; she was; he said; she said; she saw a show
3 this file; these files; these weeks; all this week
4 at the side; at the west side; is at the east side
5 it is; it is wide; it is white; it is a white wall
6 she will wait; she will wait a few weeks; we will;
```

LESSON 82

1" side margins

82a • Keyboard Review

5 minutes

Directions: Key each sentence three times SS. DS between 3-line groups.

keep fingers deeply curved

alphabet Ava Mudge will quickly explain the fire hazards on this job.

fig/sym That company was in business there for 96 years (1890-1986).

easy You win when you get your mind to stick to a job to the end.

| 1 | 2 | 3 | 4 | 5 | 6 | 7 | 8 | 9 | 10 | 11 | 12 |

82b • Timed Writing

10 minutes

Directions: **1.** Take a 5' writing on the ¶s in 81c, page 155. **2.** Count errors and figure *gwam.*

82c • Language Arts Skills: Capitalization Guides

7 minutes

Directions: Each of the capitalization guides below is followed by a sentence that illustrates it. Study the guide; then key the sentence that illustrates the guide. Key each sentence once.

Guide:
Capitalize the first word of a complete sentence.
Illustration:
Many students take at least one language course in school.

Guide:
Capitalize the first word of a quoted sentence. (A period or comma is keyed before the ending quotation mark.)
Illustration:
Her teacher said, "Finish reading the book before next Wednesday."

Guide:
The names of school subjects, except languages and numbered courses, are not capitalized.
Illustration:
He signed up for music, Science 9, word processing, and English.

Guide:
Do not capitalize a quotation resumed within a sentence.
Illustration:
"Why is it," she asked, "that when I hurry I make mistakes?"

Guide:
Capitalize the pronoun I, both alone and in contractions.
Illustration:
I'd rather go today, if I really must go.

Guide:
Capitalize titles of organizations, institutions, and buildings.
Illustration:
The French Club went to the Balfour Auditorium for one meeting.

Guide:
Capitalize the principal words in titles of articles and plays, except short prepositions, conjunctions, or articles.
Illustration:
Our class saw "Phantom of the Opera" on our field trip.

LESSON 6

6a • Keyboard Review

Spacing: Double
Margins: Default

Directions: Key once; repeat. Tap the return/enter key at the end of each line.

Posture Goal: Sit erect; eyes on copy.

w sws sws ws ws wish wise with was wall walk who how

i kik kik ik ik did did slid slid dike dike hid hide

t/o of to the that let these so do those take last too

all letters taught weeks date fast steel aid jail whole test fit like

she held a safe lead; he looked at the white dish;

6b • Location of R and N

Reach to R

1. Find **r** on the chart.
2. Find it on your keyboard.
3. Place your fingers over the home keys.
4. Reach to **r** with the **f** finger.
5. Touch **rf** lightly without moving other fingers from their home positions.

Reach to N

1. Find **n** on the chart.
2. Find it on your keyboard.
3. Place your fingers over the home keys.
4. Reach to **n** with the **j** finger.
5. Touch **nj** lightly without moving other fingers from their home positions.

frf frf rf rf fo for for

Key twice on same line

jnj jnj nj nj an and and

6c • Location Drills: R and N

Reach to r

Reach to n

Directions: Key each line once with your teacher. Repeat a second time by yourself.

Technique Goal: Tap each key with a quick, sharp, tapping stroke; release quickly.

frf frf frf frf rf rf rf rf for for her here there

r are are here here their their real real work works

were were world world three three first first fire

jnj jnj jnj jnj nj nj nj nj an an and and sand end

n land land ran ran end end lend lend than than then

in in on on one one own owns send sends need needs

near near friend friends nor nor north north learn

r/n learn earn earn warn warn torn torn horn horn fern

fern torn horn nor north friends learns earns warn

81b, continued

Problem 2 Sign-Up Sheet

Directions: 1. Retrieve **L71d**.
2. Change the heading as noted.
3. Delete the secondary heading and the three lines of instruction.
4. Set a tab one space left of the center of the line of writing. At this point, insert a space and then number from 26 to 50 to get a Sign-Up Sheet that will hold 50 signatures.

~~STUDENT COUNCIL ELECTION PETITION~~ SIGN-UP SHEET

~~For the Office of Vice President~~

~~Each signature must be that of a student of this school and must be legible. This petition must be submitted to the Student Council Advisor no later than May 10.~~

```
1. ______________________   26. ______________________
2. ______________________   27. ______________________
3. ______________________   28. ______________________
```

20 minutes

81c • Paragraph Guided Writings

Directions: 1. Take three 1' writings on each ¶ below. Try to make no more than three errors on the first writing, one error on the second, no errors on the third. Compare *gwam* on the three writings of each ¶.
2. Take a 5' writing on both ¶s combined. Figure *gwam*.

all letters used 1.3 si — word wrap

	gwam 5'		
One sure method people can use to save both gasoline and	2	25	47
money is to crowd extra miles per gallon into their driving.	5	27	49
Good mileage depends on more than just the make and model of a	7	30	52
car. It is also a direct result of the grade of gas used, the	10	32	54
way the car is driven, and the condition of the engine.	12	34	57
Those who pay heed to these hints will be amazed at the	14	37	59
results. Avoid quick starts and jerky driving. Have the engine	17	39	61
tuned at regular intervals. Check tire pressure at least once a	19	42	64
month and watch the pattern of wear to see if your wheels are	22	44	66
properly aligned.	23	45	67

5' *gwam* | 1 | 2 | 3 |

6d • Technique Builder

Directions: Key each line two times SS, tapping the return/enter key at the end of each line. DS between each 2-line group.

Technique Goal: Use quick, sharp keystrokes.

1 nj nj rf rf an and and hand hands than than thanks

2 in in kind kind one one done done far far her hers

3 here here there there first first air air red read

4 no no not not note notes think thinks thank thanks

5 near near own own down down front front word words

6 were were their theirs where where free free rates

7 now now know knows known when when fine fine finds

8 trend trends rain rain train trains worn worn rind

6e • Fluency Practice

Directions: Key each line two times SS, tapping the return/enter key at the end of each line. DS between each 2-line group.

Technique Goal: Key steadily without pauses between strokes.

1 if he is; if he is here; if she is; if she is here

2 we went; we went to the store; it was; it was fine

3 on the land; on the road; in the air; in the world

4 two or three; two or three lines; one or two words

5 it is; it is on the north side; it was for her son

6 on the trains; in their hands; near the front door

7 there were ten art shows; read all this; fine rain

8 she wrote her two friends; he ran down that street

LESSON 7

Spacing: Double
Margin: Default

7a • Keyboard Review

Directions: Key once; then repeat. Tap the return/enter key at the end of each line.

Posture Goal: Curve fingers over keys.

r frf frf rf rf for far nor nor hear hard fire start

n jnj jnj nj nj an an and land need need new new now

all letters taught when know send want line free join sent rate shown

needs a loan; wrote his friend; sent her the news;

Format Review and Skill Building (Lessons 81-90)

Learning Goals

1. Review the formats for all types of problems presented in Units 1-14.
2. Improve technique in keying skills.
3. Improve technique in language arts skills.

General Directions

Use 1" side margins for all lessons in this unit unless otherwise directed. SS sentences and drill lines. DS between repeated groups of lines. DS paragraph copy for timed writings. Proofread and correct all errors in the problems.

LESSON 81

1" side margins

81a • Keyboard Review

5 minutes

Directions: Key each sentence three times SS. DS between 3-line groups.

use quick, sharp, tapping strokes

alphabet Four experts quickly amazed the crowd by juggling five axes.

fig/sym Barbara's score was 84%, Tim's was 89%, and Nancy's was 91%.

easy The folks to get even with are the ones who have helped you.

| 1 | 2 | 3 | 4 | 5 | 6 | 7 | 8 | 9 | 10 | 11 | 12 |

81b • Format Review

20 minutes

Problem 1 Centering Review

Directions: **1.** Format to center the problem below vertically and horizontally in a single column on a full sheet of paper DS. **2.** Save as **L81b1**.

PRODUCTS USING PETROCHEMICALS

Plexiglas
Antifreeze
Fire extinguisher foam
Teflon
Plastic laser disks
Aspirin
Plastic wrap
Synthetic fibers (nylon, rayon, orlon, dacron)
Artificial body parts (tissue, bones, arteries)
Rugs
Furniture
Wall coverings
Puncture-proof tires
Bulletproof vests
Parts in cars, planes, trains
Waterproof rain gear
Batteries & solar electric cells
Ropes

7b • Location of C, . (period), and Shift

Reach to C

1. Find **c** on the chart.
2. Find it on your keyboard.
3. Place your fingers over the home keys.
4. Reach to **c** with the **d** finger.
5. Touch **cd** lightly without moving other fingers from their home positions.

Reach to . (period)

1. Find **.** on the chart.
2. Find it on your keyboard.
3. Place your fingers over the home keys.
4. Reach to **.** with the **l** finger.
5. Touch **.l** lightly without moving other fingers from their home positions.

```
dcd dcd cd cd ca car car
```

Key twice on same line

```
l.l .l .l .l fell. fell.
```

Reach to c

Reach to . (period)

7c • Location Drills: C and . (period)

Directions: Key each line once with your teacher, tapping the return/enter key at the end of each line. Repeat the lines a second time by yourself.

Technique Goal: Reach to the new keys without moving your hands out of position.

```
  dcd dcd dcd dcd cd cd cd cd car car cars call call
c can can care care cards cards call calls cost cost
  each each class class act acts force force car car

           l.l l.l l.l .l .l .l fill. fell. sell. call. hall.
(period) . ill. ail. all. wall. well. hail. fail. real. seal.
           tell. will. fall. feel. deal. cool. shell. school.
```

Spacing Guide
Space twice after a period that ends a sentence.
When the period comes at the end of a line, return/enter without spacing.
Space only once after a period following an initial or abbreviation.

7d • Shifting for Capitals: Left Shift Key

1. The left shift key (No. 11) is used to key capital letters with the right hand.
2. Use a one-two count.

One Depress the shift key with the **a** finger. Hold it down.
Two Tap the capital letter; then quickly release the shift key and return the **a** finger to its home position.

Reach to left shift key

Directions: Key each line two times. DS between each set of two lines.

Posture Goal: Hold shoulders erect with body leaning slightly forward.

```
1 Ha Ha Hal Hall La La Lane Ja Ja Jan Jan Ka Ka Karl
2 Lee ran.  Lee ran here.  I see it.  I can see Kit.
3 H. J. Hill had a hat.  Jo will write ft. for feet.
```

15 minutes

80b • Timed Writings

Directions: **1.** Take a 1' writing on each ¶ in 78b, page 150. Count errors. Figure *gwam*.

2. Take a 5' writing on all three ¶s combined as you work for control. Count errors. Figure *gwam*.

25 minutes

80c • Formatting Problem: Business Letter

Modified Block Style Letter with Mixed Punctuation

Directions: **1.** Same format as L78d1 EXCEPT put the date on line 12. This letter is in response to L77c. **2.** Save as **L80c**.

Today's date | Mr. Walter Nielsen, Manager | Purchasing Department | Choctaw Manufacturing Company | 818 High Point Road | Choctaw, OK 73020-1190 | Dear Mr. Nielsen:

We are pleased to respond to your letter of (date of L77c letter). We believe that our company stands behind our products and offers prompt service to our customers.

You may place your orders by mail or, if you prefer, use our toll-free number (1-800-555-9272). Most orders are shipped within two weeks and the most economical ground transportation is used. Because our prices are the lowest we can possibly offer, we must add a $3.00 processing charge to each order. In addition, the shipping charge for each item is indicated in each description section of our catalog.

To keep our prices low, payment must be made at the time of the order. We accept checks, money orders, and major bankcards.

In the event an order is damaged in shipment, we ask that you securely repack the merchandise and return it to us with an explanation enclosed. The same procedure is used for returning any unsatisfactory items.

Thank you, Mr. Nielsen, for giving us the opportunity to answer your questions. We look forward to filling your computer supplies needs.

Sincerely, | Derek Van Kleeck | Shipping Manager | urs

7e • Technique Builder: Shift Key Control

space twice after period at end of a sentence.

Directions: Key each line two times SS, tapping the return/enter key at the end of each line.

Technique Goal: Hold the shift key down until you tap the capital letter; then release it quickly.

1 It is here. Nan hit it. Jeff can see it. I ran.

2 He can sell it. I can take it. Jo will tell her.

3 I ran fast. I ran to school. Lane ran to school.

4 Joan went there. Joe called. Nan called for her.

5 Jake has a friend. He is her friend. He is late.

6 I like to work. Jo works hard. He needs to work.

LESSON 8 REVIEW LESSON

8a • Keyboard Review

Spacing: Double
Margin: Default

Directions: Key once, then repeat. Tap the return/enter key at the end of each line.

Posture Goal: Wrists held low; elbows near body.

hold wrists low

keep elbows near body

w sws sws ws ws who whose how laws week was what few

i kik kik ik ik it its with this side file fill life

r frf frf rf rf for are were there three works world

n jnj jnj nj nj in fine fan one soon known when than

c dcd dcd cd cd costs close clean chief child chance

. l.l l.l .l .l .l ill. fill. will. all. call. fall.

Shift Hi Hi Hill Lil Lil; Lil Kine; Kate Kate; Kate Kane

8b • Basic Techniques Review

Directions: Key each line two times; concentrate on the technique goal. Tap the return/enter key at the end of each line.

Technique Goal: Keep fingers curved; make quick, sharp, tapping strokes.

1 we week well west who what was how few two law low

2 is this it with will his if its like life said did

3 for are were here there where their her first work

4 and in on one not an than thank then when own need

5 can call case card cost check which each since act

quick, sharp strokes

20 minutes

79b • Language Arts Skills: Punctuation Guides

Directions: The following are punctuation guides and sentences that illustrate those guides. Study each guide; then key the line that illustrates the guide. Key each sentence two times SS. DS between 2-line groups.

Guide:
Use a comma after each item in a series, except the last one.
Illustration:
Be sure to bring your book, paper, and pencil to class tomorrow.
Guide:
Use a comma to separate consecutive adjectives when the *and* has been omitted.
Illustration:
The tall, slender player could reach the top of the goal.
Guide:
Use a comma to separate a dependent clause that precedes the main clause.
Illustration:
When you have finished the test, I will check your answers.
Guide:
Use a comma to separate two complete clauses separated by *and, but, for, or, so, yet.*
Illustration:
The forecast was for snow, but we had cold rain instead.
Guide:
Use a comma to set off day from year, city from state, and hundreds from thousands.
Illustration:
All 3,245 of them plan to meet on May 21, 1994, in Chicago, Illinois.
Guide:
Use a comma to set off a short direct quotation from the rest of the sentence.
Illustration:
The timer of the race said, "Begin at the signal."

20 minutes

79c • Formatting Problem: Business Letter

Change from One Letter Style to Another

Directions: **1.** Retrieve **L76b2**. **2.** Insert spaces to change from block style to modified block. Add punctuation to change from open to mixed punctuation.

LESSON 80

1" side margins

5 minutes

80a • Keyboard Review

Directions: Key each sentence three times SS. DS between 3-line groups.

alphabet Fay quoted six or seven major zoning laws checked by police.

symbol Tom delivered my papers (<u>Los Angeles Times</u>) in half an hour.

easy He tried to learn to keep his eyes on the ball at all times.

| 1 | 2 | 3 | 4 | 5 | 6 | 7 | 8 | 9 | 10 | 11 | 12 |

Reach to left shift key

8b, Continued

Directions: Key each line two times. Concentrate on the technique goal. Tap the return/enter key at the end of each line.

Technique Goal: Depress shift key with the **a** finger. Tap the capital letter; quickly release shift key.

```
1 Jane Noakes and Karl Hicks; Lane Katt and Nan Hale
2 Jill North and Keith Halls; Jo Lind and Kent Hart;
3 John called Lil Nolan.  He called Joan Noakes too.
4 Jon wrote to Joan Lands.  Jeff wrote to Kate Haak.
```

Technique Goal: Tap return key quickly with **;** finger.

return/enter

```
1  I said she
2  ran there.

3  Jan took a ride
4  in the new jet.

5  He went to the lakes
6  in her fine old car.

7  I will walk to that store
8  if I need dark red shoes.

9  Kent starts to work there as a
10 clerk at the end of this week.
```

Computing Gross Words a Minute (*gwam*)
Each letter or space is referred to as a character. Five characters/spaces are counted as one word. Each line in 8c has 50 strokes, or 10 words. For each full line keyed, give yourself 10 *gwam*. For a partially keyed line, note the scale under the sentences. Add the figure below the last character or space keyed to your complete sentence score. This total is your gross words a minute (*gwam*).

8c • Sentence Skill Builder

Directions: Key a 1' (minute) writing on each line below. Compute your gross words a minute (*gwam*).

Technique Goal: Use quick, crisp, sharp, tapping strokes.

```
1 I was asked to look at the north side of the door.
2 Jan wants to trade her old car for a nice new one.
3 One word in the line was too hard for her to read.
4 He saw lots of fine artwork at the fair this week.
5 Lil said that she was not late to her first class.
  | 1 | 2 | 3 | 4 | 5 | 6 | 7 | 8 | 9 | 10 |
```

25 minutes

78d • Formatting Problems: Business Letters in Modified Block Style

Problem 1 Model of Modified Block Letter with Mixed Punctuation

Directions: 1. Format for side margins of 1 1/2", date on line 16, tab at center of line of writing.
2. Key the letter below, putting your initials where you see *urs*. Choose the correct pronoun from the choices in parentheses.
3. Save as **L78d1**.

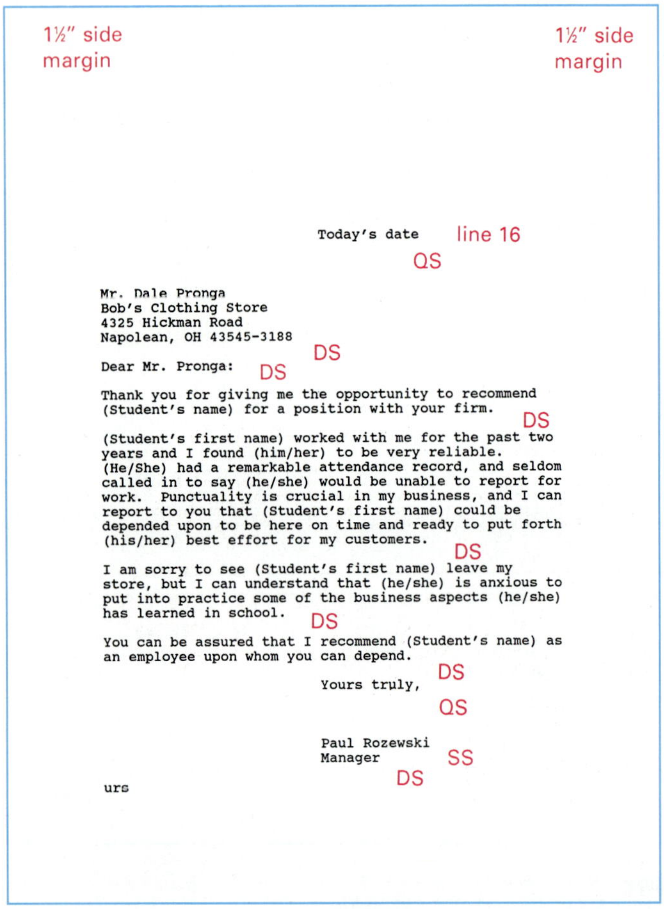

Today's date

Mr. Dale Pronga
Bob's Clothing Store
4325 Hickman Road
Napoleon, OH 43545-3188

Dear Mr. Pronga:

Thank you for giving me the opportunity to recommend (Student's name) for a position with your firm.

(Student's first name) worked with me for the past two years and I found (him/her) to be very reliable. (He/She) had a remarkable attendance record, and seldom called in to say (he/she) would be unable to report for work. Punctuality is crucial in my business, and I can report to you that (Student's first name) could be depended upon to be here on time and ready to put forth (his/her) best effort for my customers.

I am sorry to see (Student's first name) leave my store, but I can understand that (he/she) is anxious to put into practice some of the business aspects (he/she) has learned in school.

You can be assured that I recommend (Student's name) as an employee upon whom you can depend.

Yours truly,

Paul Rozewski
Manager

urs

Problem 2

Directions: Retrieve **L76b1**. Insert spaces to change the letter style from block to modified block. Add punctuation to change from open to mixed punctuation.

LESSON 79

1" side margins

5 minutes

79a • Keyboard Review

Directions: Key each sentence three times SS. DS between 3-line groups.

keep wrists and elbows quiet

alphabet Jerry Diamond packed the fine quartz in twelve larger boxes.
symbol Their boss shouted out, "Someone will have to pay for this."
easy It may pay you to learn what you are to do before you start.

| 1 | 2 | 3 | 4 | 5 | 6 | 7 | 8 | 9 | 10 | 11 | 12 |

LESSON 9

Spacing: Double
Margin: Default

9a • Keyboard Review

Directions: Key once; then repeat. Tap the return/enter key at the end of each line. **Posture Goal:** Sit erect; eyes on copy.

keep eyes on copy

```
c      cd cd check checks card cards face face cost costs
.      l.l l.l .l .l .l .l. ill. ital. kil. dal. Lt. Ill.
shift  Lance Jones and Jane Keel; Jack Halls and Nan Ides
all letters taught
       He asked her if she knew where to send the checks.
       Jets will take off at the rate of three each week.
       | 1 | 2 | 3 | 4 | 5 | 6 | 7 | 8 | 9 | 10 |
```

9b • Location of G and U

Reach to G

1. Find **g** on the chart.
2. Find it on your keyboard.
3. Place your fingers over the home keys.
4. Reach to **g** with the **f** finger.
5. Touch **gf** lightly without moving other fingers from their home positions.

Reach to U

1. Find **u** on the chart.
2. Find it on your keyboard.
3. Place your fingers over the home keys.
4. Reach to **u** with the **j** finger.
5. Touch **uj** lightly without moving other fingers from their home positions.

Key twice on same line

```
fgf fgf gf gf go got got          juj juj uj uj us use use
```

Reach to g

Reach to u

9c • Location Drills: G and U

Directions: Key once with your teacher, a second time by yourself.

Technique Goal: Reach your fingers, not your hands, to the new keys.

```
   fgf fgf fgf fgf gf gf gf gf go good good gone gone
g  got got sign sign light light right right get gets
   eight eight age age girl girls green green gas gas

   juj juj juj juj uj uj uj uj us use used hour hours
u  out out our our could could should should due dues
   just just such such full full four four hour hours
```

LESSON 78

1" side margins

5 minutes

78a • Keyboard Review

Directions: Key each sentence three times SS. DS between 3-line groups.

keep your eyes on the copy

alphabet Jeff Long experienced a quick shave with my razor and brush.

fig/sym My new 4-door model had over 59.8 cubic feet of cargo space.

easy Their problem was to enter the figures right the first time.

| 1 | 2 | 3 | 4 | 5 | 6 | 7 | 8 | 9 | 10 | 11 | 12 |

10 minutes

78b • Timed Writings

Directions: Take two 1' writings on each ¶; try to increase speed on the second writing. Figure *gwam*.

Alternate Procedure: Work for speed as you take one 5' writing on all three ¶s combined. Figure *gwam*.

keep fingers deeply curved

all letters used 1.3 si

word wrap

	gwam 1'	5'	
Though many of us may not be aware of it, most hazards to our	12	2	27
health may be found in the home. Millions of people are injured	25	5	30
or killed in home accidents each year.	33	7	32
Falls are to blame for a great number of these mishaps. They	12	9	34
don't have to be from one level to another. They often happen on	25	12	37
the floor, ground, or sidewalk. Sometimes, people fall off	37	14	39
ladders because they try to reach too far.	46	16	41
The next leading cause of accidents around the home is fire.	12	18	43
To guard against fire danger, be sure never to leave the house	25	21	46
while something is cooking on the range. It is also a good idea	38	23	48
to equip your home with smoke detectors.	46	25	50

5' gwam | 1 | 2 | 3 |

5 minutes

78c • Skill Builder

Directions: Take two 1' writings on each sentence. Figure *gwam*. Work for speed as you key this exercise.

keep arms and wrists quiet

1 Those things you learn after you know it all count the most.

2 No test was graded. You sat on my seat. Sew my extra vest.

| 1 | 2 | 3 | 4 | 5 | 6 | 7 | 8 | 9 | 10 | 11 | 12 |

9d • Technique Builder: Wrists Low and Steady

Directions: Key each line two times SS, tapping the return/enter key at the end of each line. DS between 2-line groups.

Technique Goal: Curve your fingers. Hold your wrists low and steady.

curve your fingers

keep wrists and elbows still

1 uj gf uj gf such such glad glad long long run runs

2 four four though though thought thought turn turns

3 just just would would sound sounds through through

4 to do; to do the; to go; to go to the; to go there

5 if he; if she; if he can; if she can; if we do the

6 I can go. He will go there. He can go there too.

7 He will need four hours. He will go in two hours.

8 One of their goals is to hold the wrists down low.

| 1 | 2 | 3 | 4 | 5 | 6 | 7 | 8 | 9 | 10 |

Keep wrists low.

Position of Wrists
Keep your wrists low, but do not allow them to touch the machine. Keep forearms parallel to the slant of the keyboard.

Forearms parallel to slant of keyboard.

9e • Sentence Skill Builder

Directions: Key two 1' writings on each sentence. Figure your *gwam*.

Posture Goal: Keep the wrists low.

1 I can do the work if I find the tools that I need.

2 He will learn the rules that she has on the cards.

3 I know that he and she can gain a good high skill.

4 Kate thought that the chair was not right for her.

5 Jack said he likes to eat fast food for his lunch.

6 Ned told us a good joke that he heard at the show.

7 Lu will walk to that new store with all the girls.

8 Half of the words on the last test were hard ones.

9 It was the sort of chance we knew she had to take.

10 One thing he needs to do is take care of his cars.

| 1 | 2 | 3 | 4 | 5 | 6 | 7 | 8 | 9 | 10 |

77b, continued

Guide:
Use a period after a sentence making a statement or giving a command.
Illustration:
Each student was assigned a report to write for Thursday.
Guide:
Use a period after an initial.
Illustration:
Juan A. Santos was named to fill the post vacated by Maria T. Perez.
Guide:
Do not use a period after a nickname.
Illustration:
Tom and Joe planned to meet Dan and Al after the game.
Guide:
Use a period after most abbreviations.
Illustration:
Dr. Alma Johnson wrote a paper for the Wallace Co., Tulsa, Oklahoma.
Guide:
Use a question mark after a direct question.
Illustration:
Did you make the reservation for this weekend?
Guide:
Use a period after requests and indirect questions.
Illustration:
Will you please return my call at your convenience.
Guide:
Use an exclamation mark to express strong or sudden feeling.
Illustration:
No! Never! There is nothing you can do to change my mind!

20 minutes

77c • Formatting Problem: Business Letter in Block Style, Open Punctuation

Directions: **1.** Format 1 1/2" side margins, date on line 16.
2. Key the letter below in block style with open punctuation.
3. Save as **L77c**.

Today's date | Western Computer Supply Co. | 1020 Whalley Avenue | Gladstone, OR 97027-0752 | Ladies and Gentlemen

Your company has been recommended as a firm that stands behind the products it sells. Before I place an order, however, I would like answers to some questions.

Must I order by mail or do you have a toll-free number I could use? How quickly are orders shipped after they have been received? What shipping company do you use for small items such as ribbons and disks? Is your shipping charge based on weight or number of items being shipped?

Do you accept purchase orders or must payment be made at the time the order is placed? Can payment be made by bankcard or do you accept only checks and money orders?

What is your policy for items that are damaged in shipping? Should an item be unsatisfactory for our use, what steps must be taken to return it to you?

Thank you for taking the time to answer my questions.

Sincerely yours | Walter Nielsen, Manager | Purchasing Department | urs

Spacing: Double
Margin: Default

LESSON 10

10a • Keyboard Review

Directions: Key once; repeat. Tap the return/enter key at the end of each line.

Posture Goal: Keep eyes on copy.

use quick, sharp, tapping strokes

g great great light lights large large charge charge

u would would south south course course thing things

all letters taught I will join their staff as soon as I get a chance.

Kids who work here are out of class for that hour.

| 1 | 2 | 3 | 4 | 5 | 6 | 7 | 8 | 9 | 10 |

10b • Location of V, Y, and Shift

Reach to V

1. Find **v** on the chart.
2. Find it on your keyboard.
3. Place your fingers over the home keys.
4. Reach to **v** with the **f** finger.
5. Touch **vf** lightly without moving other fingers from their home positions.

Reach to Y

1. Find **y** on the chart.
2. Find it on your keyboard.
3. Place your fingers over the home keys.
4. Reach to **y** with the **j** finger.
5. Touch **yj** lightly without moving other fingers from their home positions.

fvf fvf vf fiv five five

Key twice on same line

jyj jyj yj yj ja jay jay

10c • Location Drills: V and Y

Directions: Key each line once with your teacher, tapping the return/enter key at the end of each line. Repeat by yourself.

Technique Goal: Think the letters as you key. Use quick, sharp, tapping strokes.

Reach to v

Reach to y

fvf fvf fvf fvf vf vf vf vf five fives lives lives

v have have five five give give dive dive hive hives

save saves gave gave wave waved raves leave leaves

jyj jyj jyj jyj yj yj yj yj jay jays lay lays slay

y sly sly fly fly try try jay jay ray ray stay stays

the they eye eyes try tray fry fray lay lays yells

very very every every vinyl vinyl navy navy vanity

v/y vainly vainly vaguely vaguely convey convey savory

valley valley verify verify varsity varsity vanity

5 minutes

76c • Folding Business Letters for Large Envelopes

Directions: Review the steps for folding letters for large envelopes described in L56e.

10 minutes

76d • Speed Ladder Sentences

Directions: Key each sentence for 1'. Your teacher will call the guide at 15" and 12" intervals. As time permits, repeat sentences on which you were not able to complete a line with the call of the guide.

		gwam 15" guide	12" guide
1	Time will not wait for anyone.	24	30
2	Every day gives you another chance.	28	35
3	You are worth what you make of yourself.	32	40
4	Every time you speak, your mind is on parade.	36	45
5	Do not look for jobs that are equal to your skill.	40	50
6	Look, instead, for skills that are equal to your tasks.	44	55
7	The only time people dislike gossip is when it's about them.	48	50

| 1 | 2 | 3 | 4 | 5 | 6 | 7 | 8 | 9 | 10 | 11 | 12 |

LESSON 77

1" side margins

5 minutes

77a • Keyboard Review

Directions: Key each sentence three times SS. DS between 3-line groups.

keep feet flat on the floor

alphabet Max Cady just loves a big frozen pie after he quits working.

fig/sym Even sums like $580 or $476 don't require decimals or zeros.

easy Wait for your ship to come in only if you have sent one out.

| 1 | 2 | 3 | 4 | 5 | 6 | 7 | 8 | 9 | 10 | 11 | 12 |

20 minutes

77b • Language Arts Skills: Punctuation Guides, Period, Question Mark, and Exclamation

Directions: Each of the punctuation guides on the next page is followed by a sentence that illustrates it. Study each guide; then key the sentence that illustrates the guide. Key each sentence twice SS. DS between 2-line groups.

Note: A space follows each period after initials. No space is needed after a period within an abbreviation. Space once after a period that ends an abbreviation unless that period ends a sentence, in which case, space twice.

10d • Shifting for Capitals: Right Shift Key

Spacing Guide: Remember to space twice after a period that ends a sentence (except at the end of a line).

1. The right shift key (No. 11) is used to capitalize letters keyed with the left hand.

2. Use a one-two count.

One Depress the shift key with the **;** finger. Hold it down.

Two Tap the capital letter; then quickly release the shift key and return the **;** finger to its home position.

Reach to right shift key

Directions: Key each line two times SS.

Posture Goal: Use a quick, firm reach to the shift key.

```
1  Ted Ted Fran Fran; Ted and Fran; Fran and I; Frank
2  Ted is here.  Fran can see Ted.  She can see Fran.
3  Frank is ill.  I need Art here.  She and I see it.
```

10e • Technique Builder: Shift Key Control

Directions: Key each line three times SS, tapping the return/enter key at the end of each line. DS after the third line.

Technique Goal: Hold the shift key down until you tap the capital letter; then release quickly.

return/enter without spacing after . at end of line

```
1  vf yj vf yj day day dry dry say say stay stay days
2  yes yet hear the they ray gray tray sly slay style
3  She can.  She can have her turn.  I can give five.
4  Jan and I can stay.  Jan can stay there five days.
5  Ann and Karl are here.  Jan left her friend there.
6  I can learn.  She can get all the funds she needs.
```

LESSON 11

Spacing: Double
Margin: Default

11a • Keyboard Review

Directions: Key once; repeat. Tap the return/enter key at the end of each line.

Posture Goal: Sit back in chair. Keep eyes on copy.

return/enter quickly

```
v            give give live live gave gave view views save save
y            you you years years way way ways says says why why
shift        Fred Sills and Ann Shields; Rick Weld and Sue Todd
all letters  You will have to judge the facts in each new case.
taught       Kris needs to work hard if she wants a good grade.
             | 1 | 2 | 3 | 4 | 5 | 6 | 7 | 8 | 9 | 10 |
```

76b, continued

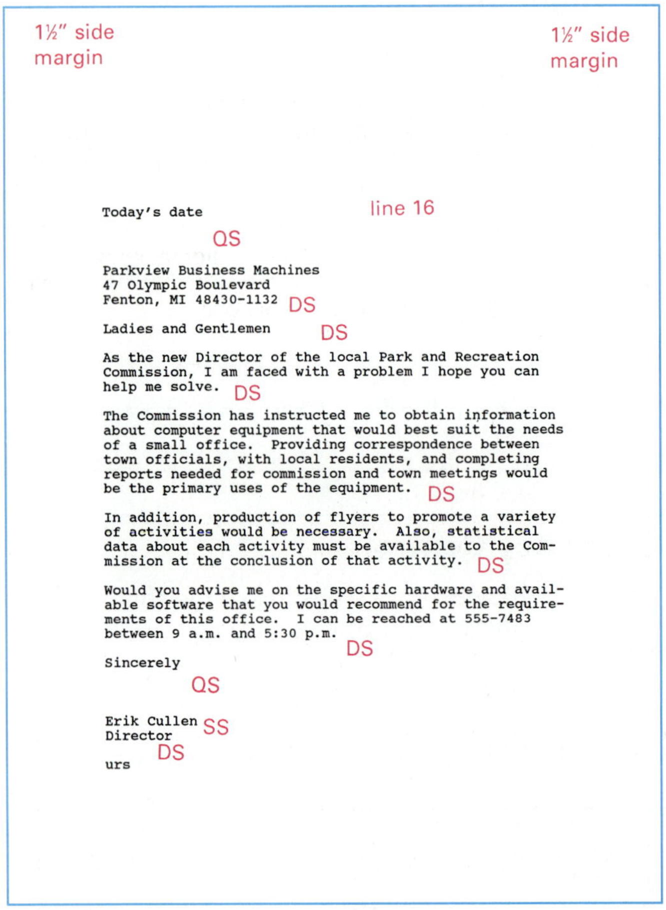

1½" side margin

1½" side margin

Today's date line 16

QS

Parkview Business Machines
47 Olympic Boulevard
Fenton, MI 48430-1132 DS

Ladies and Gentlemen DS

As the new Director of the local Park and Recreation Commission, I am faced with a problem I hope you can help me solve. DS

The Commission has instructed me to obtain information about computer equipment that would best suit the needs of a small office. Providing correspondence between town officials, with local residents, and completing reports needed for commission and town meetings would be the primary uses of the equipment. DS

In addition, production of flyers to promote a variety of activities would be necessary. Also, statistical data about each activity must be available to the Commission at the conclusion of that activity. DS

Would you advise me on the specific hardware and available software that you would recommend for the requirements of this office. I can be reached at 555-7483 between 9 a.m. and 5:30 p.m. DS

Sincerely

QS

Erik Cullen SS
Director
DS
urs

Today's date

QS

Parkview Business Machines
47 Olympic Boulevard
Fenton, MI 48430-1132

DS

Ladies and Gentlemen

DS

As the new Director of the local Park and Recreation Commission, I am faced with a problem I hope you can help me solve.

DS

The Commission has instructed me to obtain information about computer equipment that would best suit the needs of a small office. Providing correspondence between town officials, with local residents, and completing reports needed for commission and town meetings would be the primary uses of the equipment.

DS

In addition, production of flyers to promote a variety of activities would be necessary. Also, statistical data about each activity must be available to the Commission at the conclusion of that activity.

DS

Would you advise me on the specific hardware and available software that you would recommend for the requirements of this office. I can be reached at 555-7483 between 9 a.m. and 5:30 p.m.

DS

Sincerely | Erik Cullen | Director | urs

Problem 2 Business Letter in Block Style, Open Punctuation

Directions: **1.** Same format as Problem 1. **2.** Save as **L76b2**.

Today's date | McCormick Audio Store | 879 Tyvola Road | Jennings, MO 63136-2209

Ladies and Gentlemen

The Jennings Park and Recreation Commission purchased a sound system for the Centennial Park from your store last July. Your employees installed the system soon after the purchase. The system provided clear, distinct sound for the park for the remainder of the summer season.

At the end of the season, employees from your store returned to disconnect the system and to store it for the winter.

We are ready to begin activities for this summer and will, of course, need the sound system for many of the events. Will you send someone to the park to prepare the system for use this year.

If you will let me know when someone will be available for this task, I will arrange to meet that person at Centennial Park. I can be reached at 555-7483 between 9 a.m. and 5:30 p.m.

Sincerely | Erik Cullen | Director | urs

11b • Location of B, M, and Tab

Reach to B

1. Find b on the chart.
2. Find it on your keyboard.
3. Place your fingers over the home keys.
4. Reach to b with the f finger.
5. Touch bf lightly without moving other fingers from their home positions.

Reach to M

1. Find m on the chart.
2. Find it on your keyboard.
3. Place your fingers over the home keys.
4. Reach to m with the j finger.
5. Touch mj lightly without moving other fingers from their home positions.

```
fbf fbf bf bf ib fib fib
```

Key twice on same line

```
jmj jmj mj mj ja jam jam
```

Reach to b

Reach to m

Tabulation

11c • Location Drills: B and M

Directions: Key each line once with your teacher, tapping the return/enter key at the end of each line. Repeat a second time by yourself.

Technique Goal: Use finger, not hand, motions as you reach for these keys.

```
  fbf fbf fbf fbf bf bf bf bf buff buff job job jobs
b big big both both boy boy boys blue blue ball ball
  bus bus by by buy buy but but hub hub lab lab burn

  jmj jmj jmj jmj mj mj mj mj jam jam make make made
m men men mean mean them them come come much much am
  same same game games more more most most from from

    boom boom bomb bombs comb combs brim brim blossoms
b/m beam beam blame blame broom broom bloom bloom balm
    become become became became member member basement
```

11d • Indenting for Paragraphs and Location of Tab Key

RULER/FORMAT LINE The line at the top or bottom of the screen (or accessible within a document) is the ruler/format line. It is used to set the document format consisting of left and right margins, tab stops, text alignment, and line-spacing.

TABS Tabs are stops set in the ruler/format line that allow you to indent paragraphs and lists and to align columns in tables. When you tap the TAB key, the cursor moves to the desired tab stop.

WORD WRAP (WRAPAROUND) Word wrap is an automatic feature that determines whether the word being keyed will extend beyond the right margin. If so, the program automatically "wraps the text around" to the beginning of the next line while the user continues keying. A return/enter is used only when mandatory, such as at the end of a paragraph or a line of statistical copy.

PRINTING When a printed (hard copy) is desired, directions to print must be given to the word processor. If you are using a stand-alone work station, check to see that the paper is in place and that the printer is turned on. If you are using a networked system, also check to see that no one else in the system is printing. Follow the directions in the User's Manual and the screen-to-screen displays to print.

Formatting and Keying Business Letters (Lessons 76-80)

Learning Goals

1. Format and key business letters in block style and modified block style with open and mixed punctuation.
2. Learn proper placements of reference initials and enclosure notations.
3. Continue to build keying skills.

Word Processing Concept Introduced in Unit 14

letter stationery reference initials

General Directions

Use 1" side margins, unless otherwise directed, for all lessons in this unit. SS sentences and drill lines. DS between repeated groups of lines and paragraph copy. Proofread and correct all errors in the problems.

LESSON 76

1" side margins

5 minutes

76a • Keyboard Review

Directions: Key each sentence three times SS. DS between 3-line groups.

alphabet Please pack my boxes with five dozen jugs of liquid varnish.

symbol Place added information (such as a date) within parentheses.

easy Most of the tires on the bus are worn down and out of shape.

| 1 | 2 | 3 | 4 | 5 | 6 | 7 | 8 | 9 | 10 | 11 | 12 |

25 minutes

76b • Business Letters in Block Style; Open Punctuation

LETTER STATIONERY Most business letters are processed on standard-size letterheads (8 1/2" x 11") with the company name, address, and telephone number printed at the top.

Problem 1 Model of Block Letter with Open Punctuation

Directions: **1.** Review format for block style letters with open punctuation.
2. Key the letter on page 147 in block style with open punctuation. Format for side margins of 1 1/2", date on line 16. Put your initials where you see *urs*.
3. Save as **L76b1**.

REFERENCE INITIALS Business letters are usually keyed by one person and signed by the person actually writing the letter. When the keyboard operator is not the writer of the message, the operator's initials (in lowercase) are keyed a DS below the writer's name or title.

11e • Paragraph Keying

Using the Tab Key and Word Wrap

1. Your tabs are preset. Check the User's Manual for your software to learn the proper procedure to clear and reset tabs.

2. Tap the tab key with your little finger to indent for paragraphs, then quickly return to the home key.

3. In keying paragraphs, tap the return/enter key only at the end of the paragraph.

Directions: Using the preset tab, key the paragraphs below twice DS. Repeat if time permits. If your software allows you to key with double spacing, your teacher will explain how to select this option. If your software requires you to select double spacing at the point of printing, your teacher will explain how you are to key the paragraphs and then print with double spacing.

Computing Gross Words a Minute (*gwam*).
To figure *gwam* on paragraph copy, note the figure at the end of the last complete line keyed in the column at the right. For a partially keyed line, note (in the scale at the bottom of the paragraphs) the last stroke keyed. Add this figure to the figure at the end of the last complete line keyed. The total is your *gwam*.

all letters used — word wrap — *gwam 1'*

tab → Kids who want to have good health try to stay fit. They 12
like to walk a lot or jog in the fresh air. Most of them ride 25
bikes too. 26

(reach to tab key with little finger)

tab → Yet these same boys and girls may find it hard to eat what is 38
good for them. A few will buy much more junk food than they 51
should. 52

(quickly return to home key)

| 1 | 2 | 3 | 4 | 5 | 6 | 7 | 8 | 9 | 10 | 11 | 12 | 13 |

Note: Work that is to be given to your teacher must have your name on it (your teacher will tell you where to key your name).

LESSON 12 REVIEW LESSON

Spacing: Double
Margin: Default

12a • Keyboard Review

Directions: Key once; repeat. Tap the return/enter key at the end of each line.

Posture Goal: Elbows in; wrists low.

```
g  fgf fgf gf gf get great glad gone long light right
u  juj juj uj uj out our hour four would should could
v  fvf fvf vf vf five give have save gave leave drive
y  jyj jyj yj yj yes yet you yours years days way say
b  fbf fbf bf bf be been back best bill both board by
m  jmj jmj mj mj more most much means mind some homes
   | 1 | 2 | 3 | 4 | 5 | 6 | 7 | 8 | 9 | 10 |
```

75b, continued

Problem 2 Questionnaire

Directions: Use 1" margins; and key the questionnaire, which is arranged for ease of completion by the responders as well as ease of recording responses. Set a tab at center for the second column of dates in the questionnaire. DS entire problem.

1" margin | 1" margin

STUDENT COUNCIL CONFERENCE — line 13

Name of school____

School address____

City____

State and ZIP Code____

Advisor's name____

Number of students attending_________________________________

Number of advisors attending_________________________________

Indicate preferred time for conference.

_____ September   _____ November

_____ February   _____ April

Suggestions for keynote speaker_______________________________

List successful activities your group has organized.

____

____

List unusual activities that other groups might want to try.

____

____

How do you involve the entire student body in activities?

____

____

---

5 minutes

75c • Technique Builder: Stroking

quick return; no pauses

Directions: Key each sentence three times SS. DS between 3-line groups.

1 John gave Lynn my extra red cards. We saw Barb waste water.

2 Pop quizzes, although appropriate, are always unappreciated.

3 Colleen takes bookkeeping and programming classes at school.

| 1 | 2 | 3 | 4 | 5 | 6 | 7 | 8 | 9 | 10 | 11 | 12 |

12b • Basic Technique Review

Directions: Key each line two times, tapping the return/enter key at the end of each line. Concentrate on the technique goal.

Posture Goal: Shoulders erect with body leaning slightly forward.

Technique Goal: Keep the fingers deeply curved; make quick, sharp, tapping strokes.

1 sign large length charge change eight wrong strong
2 source just due such thus thought runs found house
3 view voice have gives five serve gave leave drives
4 style young years yet eyes stays try why ways gray
5 brought bank book club blue big doubt job base buy
6 farm whom make made film from times them same name

Technique Goal: Depress right shift key with the ; finger. Tap the capital letter; quickly release the shift key.

1 Dee Smith and Ray Brown; Deb Green and Frank Sands
2 Sue Thoms and Bob Arndt; Barb Vance and Thane Eads
3 Ana saw Don Reese. Rosa Ramos rode with Sam Weld.

Technique Goal: Tap return/enter key quickly with ; finger.

1 Both girls
2 came late.

3 Their class met
4 once each week.

5 Each girl will bring
6 a gift for her date.

7 We thought our team would
8 lose the game that night.

9 They can all stay at school so
10 no one will have to walk home.

12c • Paragraph Skill Builder: Tabulation Stops

Directions: **1.** Use the preset tab.
2. Tab to begin a ¶.
3. Key the paragraph (¶) once for practice; then take three 1' writings on it. Figure your *gwam* on the best writing.
4. Print if your teacher directs you to do so.

word wrap *gwam* 1'

tab → Set your goals if you want to make the best use of your time. 12
This is true for your work at home as well as what you do at your 25
school. You will get more work done when you know what it is you 38
want to do. 41

| 1 | 2 | 3 | 4 | 5 | 6 | 7 | 8 | 9 | 10 | 11 | 12 | 13 |

20 minutes

74c • Formatting Problem: Document for Club Activities

Flyer for Food Drive

Directions: Prepare a flyer to be distributed to all students in homeroom. Format 1" margins on all sides. Use your judgement to leave spaces between the lines for attractive placement on the page. Leave one space between letters and three spaces between words for the spread arrangement.

COMING SOON!

T H E   D R I V E   T O

F I G H T   H U N G E R

BRING NON-PERISHABLE FOOD ITEMS TO STUDENT COUNCIL OFFICE

DO YOUR PART TO HELP OTHERS

NOVEMBER 18 TO NOVEMBER 22

LESSON 75

1" side margins

5 minutes

75a • Keyboard Review

Directions: Key each sentence three times SS. DS between 3-line groups.

alphabet Oakmont citizens have explored ways of quieting the big jet.

fig/sym I quoted three sources: Time, Newsweek, and The New Yorker.

easy They thought there should be goals at each end of the field.

| 1 | 2 | 3 | 4 | 5 | 6 | 7 | 8 | 9 | 10 | 11 | 12 |

75b • Formatting Problems: Documents for Club Activities

35 minutes

Problem 1 Personal-Business Letter

Directions: **1.** Format for side margins of 1 1/2" with return address on line 14. **2.** Complete in modified block style with indented paragraphs and open punctuation.

ENCLOSURE NOTATION An enclosure notation indicates that something other than the letter is included in the envelope. When appropriate, key the word *Enclosure* or *Enclosures* a DS below the name (or title) of the writer.

65 Emmons Lane | Norton, MA 02766 | Today's date | Mrs. Yvonne Gunn | Student Council Advisor | Westfield Central School | 1410 Cavalier Court | Westfield, MA 01085 | Dear Mrs. Gunn |

The Student Council at (Your school) is exploring the possibility of hosting a one-day conference for Student Councils in our area.

Our current plans call for a keynote speaker for the general session in the morning, followed by small group discussion sessions. Following lunch in our school cafeteria, we believe workshops on activities would be beneficial to those attending.

In order to make definite plans, we need some input from your organization. Would your group be interested in participating? How many students and advisors would be in the group? Would your group be able to provide leadership for one or more of the discussion sessions?

Please complete and return the enclosed form so that we can continue with our early planning.

Sincerely | (Your name) | Corresponding Secretary | Enclosure

LESSON 13

Spacing: Double
Margin: Default

13a • Keyboard Review

Directions: Key once; repeat. Tap the return/enter key at the end of each line.

Posture Goal: Keep feet flat on the floor, one ahead of the other.

use quick, sharp, tapping strokes

```
b            fbf fbf bf bf board board doubt doubts bring bring
m            jmj jmj mj mj him him room room my my month months
v/y          yj vf yj vf voice voice leave leave you your young
in           in fine find kind line mine thin think thing since
all letters  June is the best month to hold the race this year.
taught       We gave them the names of the four books he needs.
```

| 1 | 2 | 3 | 4 | 5 | 6 | 7 | 8 | 9 | 10 |

13b • Location of X and P

Reach to X

1. Find **x** on the chart.
2. Find it on your keyboard.
3. Place your fingers over the home keys.
4. Reach to **x** with the **s** finger.
5. Touch **xs** lightly without moving other fingers from their home positions.

Reach to P

1. Find **p** on the chart.
2. Find it on your keyboard.
3. Place your fingers over the home keys.
4. Reach to **p** with the **;** finger.
5. Touch **p;** lightly without moving other fingers from their home positions.

```
sxs sxs xs xs ix six six
```

Key twice on same line

```
;p; ;p; p; p; pa par par
```

13c • Location Drills: X and P

Directions: Key each line once with your teacher, tapping the return/enter key at the end of each line. Repeat a second time by yourself.

Technique Goal: Reach to the new keys with your fingers. Keep your wrists low.

Reach to x

Reach to p

```
     sxs sxs sxs sxs xs xs xs xs six six fix fix ox box
x    lax lax flax flax flex flex next next fox fox hoax
     excel excel flux flux hex hex relax relax axe axes

     ;p; ;p; ;p; ;p; p; p; p; p; par par part pass pass
p    past past page page pay pay put put trip trip kept
     flip flip slip slip pile pile play play spar spare

     expect expect expand expands expert experts extent
x/p  explain explains expense expenses explore explores
```

LESSON 74

1" side margins

5 minutes

74a • Keyboard Review

Directions: Key each sentence three times SS. DS between 3-line groups.

alphabet Max delivered the wrong size pack to Jeff quite by accident.

fig/sym Use a diagonal for fractions such as 2 7/8, 6 2/3, or 5 3/4.

easy I asked them to print their names to the right of the title.

| 1 | 2 | 3 | 4 | 5 | 6 | 7 | 8 | 9 | 10 | 11 | 12 |

20 minutes

74b • Language Arts Skills: Capitalization Guides

Directions: The following are capitalization guides and sentences that illustrate those guides. Study each guide. Key the sentences that illustrate the guides two times SS; DS between 2-line groups.

Guide:
Capitalize days, months, years, and holidays, but not seasons.
Illustration:
Thanksgiving is celebrated on a Thursday in November, late in the fall.

Guide:
Capitalize names of rivers, oceans, and mountains.
Illustration:
We studied the Connecticut River and the White Mountains.

Guide:
Capitalize North, South, etc., when they name particular parts of the country, but not when they refer to directions.
Illustration:
Those who came from the East drove north to cross the bridge.

Guide:
Capitalize names of religious groups, political parties, nations, nationalities, and races.
Illustration:
The Republicans met in St. Louis while the Democrats chose Denver.

Guide:
Capitalize all proper names.
Illustration:
Keith and Flip went to the mall in Providence.

Guide:
Capitalize the names of stars, planets, and constellations except sun, moon, or earth, unless they are used with astronomical names.
Illustration:
Jupiter and Venus were nearly as bright as the moon.

Guide:
Capitalize a title when used with a person's name.
Illustration:
Senator Dodd met with Senator Moyers before the hearing.

13d • Technique Builder: Down-and-in Motion of Right Thumb

Directions: Key each line two times SS, tapping the return/enter key at the end of each line. DS between 2-line groups.

Technique Goal: Tap space bar with quick down-and-in motion.

curve right thumb over space bar;

use quick down-and-in motion of thumb

```
1  xs p; sx p; sx p; flax flax help help cap caps six
2  fox tax fox lax six jinx box hex coax hoax vex axe
3  top stop lot lay play plan plus post nap hope ship
4  fix the step; keep the box; pay the tax; six steps
5  I can pay it.  He can pay for it.  She can pay it.
6  I paid six of the girls for the good job they did.
   | 1 | 2 | 3 | 4 | 5 | 6 | 7 | 8 | 9 | 10 |
```

13e • Paragraph Keying

Directions: Use the preset tab. Key the ¶ two times DS. Repeat if time permits.

Technique Goal: Reach to the tab key; release and quickly return to home key position.

keep wrists and elbows still

all letters used — word wrap — *gwam* 1'

We know that those who hit the most home runs in a ball game 12
strike out a great deal too. Keep this fact in mind the next time 26
you do not do a job as well as you should have. 35

| 1 | 2 | 3 | 4 | 5 | 6 | 7 | 8 | 9 | 10 | 11 | 12 | 13 |

LESSON 14

14a • Keyboard Review

Spacing: Double
Margin: Default

Directions: Key once; repeat. Tap the return/enter key at the end of each line.

Posture Goal: Keep fingers deeply curved.

```
x                sxs sxs xs xs six six lax flax next next flex flex
p                ;p; ;p; p; p; par part pal pail plan pain tip trip
b/m              bf mj bf mj mail mail best best name names bad bad
an               an and can man change chance plan plant stand want
all letters      Their next big job is to pave all the new streets.
taught           He could key the words on the form at a high rate.
                 | 1 | 2 | 3 | 4 | 5 | 6 | 7 | 8 | 9 | 10 |
```

73c, continued

The Drive to Fight Hunger committee reported that arrangements have been made for collecting non-perishable food items the week prior to Thanksgiving. Posters have been made and morning announcements will list the locations of the collection boxes.

Plans for the Kindergarten Costume Party are complete and the committee expects a large group of children to participate.

The date for the Semi-Formal Dance was announced for January 26 in the school library. Campus Clean-Up Day is set for April 30.

Speakers are being contacted for the National Freedom Day assembly on February 1.

No other business was brought up, so the meeting adjourned with a motion by Andrea McKinney, seconded by Pat Chandler.

(At center) Respectfully submitted,

QS

(Key underline from center to right margin) ______________________________
Sabrine Lesmarie, Secretary SS

Problem 2 Agenda for Student Council Meeting

Directions: **1.** Format for 1 1/2" side margins; center heading on line 13. **2.** Follow the directions below as a guide for spacing. DS items 1-7. **3.** Save as **L73c2**.

STUDENT COUNCIL AGENDA line 13
DS
Friday, October 18, Period 5
DS
Library Conference Room
QS

1. Call to Order
2. Record of Attendance
3. Reading of Minutes from October 4 Meeting
4. Committee Reports
    A. Talent Show
    B. Drive to Fight Hunger
    C. Costume Party for Kindergarteners
5. New Business
    A. Semi-Formal Dance
    B. Campus Clean-Up Day
    C. National Freedom Day
6. Other Items
7. Adjournment

14b • Location of Q and , (comma)

Reach to Q

1. Find q on the chart.
2. Find it on your keyboard.
3. Place your fingers over the home keys.
4. Reach to q with the a finger.
5. Touch qa lightly without moving other fingers from their home positions.

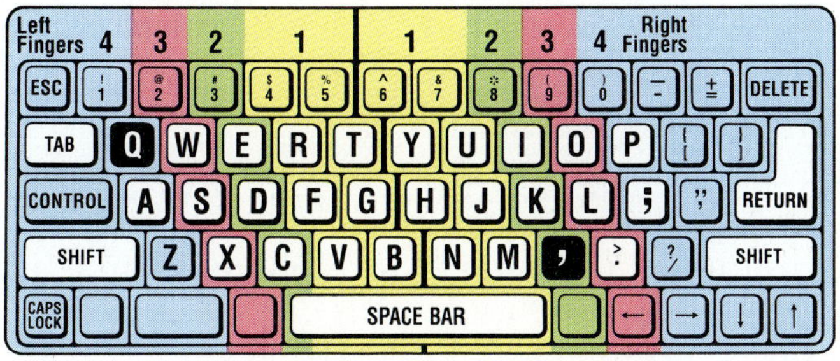

Reach to , (comma)

1. Find , on the chart.
2. Find it on your keyboard.
3. Place your fingers over the home keys.
4. Reach to , with the k finger.
5. Touch ,k lightly without moving other fingers from their home positions.

```
aqa qa qa quit quit quit
```

Key twice on same line

```
k,k k,k ,k rk, irk, irk,
```

14c • Location Drills: Q and , (comma)

Reach to q

Reach to , (comma)

Directions: Key each line once with your teacher, tapping the return/enter key at the end of each line. Repeat the lines again by yourself.

Spacing Guide: Space once after a comma within a sentence.

q

```
aqa aqa aqa qa quit quite quiet quills quips equip
pique quilt square quench queen quart quote quotes
quaint quake quick queue squid squeak equal plaque
```

, (comma)

```
k,k k,k k,k ,k ,k work, rock, broke, trick, truck,
fork, forks, sock, socks, dock, dike, lock, clock,
kick, choke, steak, rake, kale, king, chock, soak,
```

q/,

```
quack, quad, quell, quest, lacquer, opaque, qualm,
```

14d • Technique Builder

Directions: Key each line two times SS; then key 1' writings on the last three lines.

Technique Goal: Do not look from the copy to the keyboard and back again. Keep eyes on copy at all times.

space once after a comma within a sentence

```
1 qa ,k qa ,k qa ,k quit, qualm, quip, quite, squeal
2 quick, quill, queen, quotes, qualms, quilt, quench
3 to quote, to quit, the quick, the queen, the quilt
4 I was quick to quote the girls with the red quilt.
5 Drive right, as the life you save may be your own.
6 As you key, use quick, short, quiet, sure strokes.
7 We can gain the high skills we need for this work.
  | 1 | 2 | 3 | 4 | 5 | 6 | 7 | 8 | 9 | 10 |
```

10 minutes

73b • Timed Writings

Directions: Take two 1' writings on both ¶s; try to increase speed on the second writing. Figure *gwam*.

Alternate Procedure: Work for speed as you take one 5' writing on both ¶s combined. Figure *gwam*.

keep fingers curved and upright

all letters used 1.3 si — word wrap

	gwam 1'	5'	
No matter whether it is a trip of several miles or just a	12	2	21
jaunt to the local grocery store, many people are traveling by	24	5	24
bike these days. While kids still account for the greatest share	37	7	26
of all bike sales, quite a few adults now whiz around on two	49	10	29
wheels.	50	10	29
In a commuter race staged in one major city a few years back,	12	13	32
a bicycle rider covered a distance of four miles in less time	25	15	34
than two competitors. The cyclist beat a sports car by one	37	18	37
minute and a city bus by five.	43	19	38

5' gwam | 1 | 2 | 3 |

30 minutes

73c • Formatting Problems: Documents for Club Activities

Problem 1 Minutes of Student Council Meeting

Directions: **1.** Format for 1" side margins; center heading on line 13. **2.** SS and indent paragraph copy; leave a DS between paragraphs. **3.** Save as **L73c1**.

STUDENT COUNCIL MINUTES line 13

DS

October 18, Period 5

QS

The Student Council met in the Library Conference Room on Friday, October 18, during Period 5.

President Mali Brakeman called the meeting to order. Others in attendance were: Phil Johnson, Robert Hillmann, Andrea McKinney, Tara Pryce, John Schmidt, Cheyenne Parish, Kasey Moore, Deborah Baker, Kym Stock, Jen Verona, Irene Duntz, Matt Saparoso, Sabrine Lesmarie, Pat Chandler, and advisor Miss Komm.

Minutes of the October 4 meeting were read and approved.

The Talent Show committee reported that ten groups have been auditioned and that the selection of the six acts to perform at the show will be named next week.

(continued on next page)

14e • Paragraph Skill Builder

Directions: **1.** Use the preset tab. Key the ¶ DS once for practice; then take three 1' writings on it. Figure *gwam* on the best writing. **2.** Print if your teacher directs you to do so.

all letters used — word wrap — *gwam* 1'

tab → Do not punch or mash the keys when you work. Just tap them 12
with a quick stroke and then get off. Be sure to give this plan 25
a try the next time you sit down at your desk or in front of 38
a screen. 39

| 1 | 2 | 3 | 4 | 5 | 6 | 7 | 8 | 9 | 10 | 11 | 12 | 13 |

LESSON 15

Spacing: Double
Margin: Default

15a • Keyboard Review

Directions: Key once; repeat. Tap the return/enter key at the end of each line.

Technique Goal: Wrists low and still.

q — aqa aqa qa qa quit quits quote quotes quart quarts

, (comma) — k,k k,k ,k ,k work, all, fork, fill, dark, squall,

x/p — xs p; xs p; tax tax box box up up group group keep

he — he he she she held held the them these their there

all letters taught — She was quick to point out the tax we have to pay.
My friends would like to play big jokes on me too.

| 1 | 2 | 3 | 4 | 5 | 6 | 7 | 8 | 9 | 10 |

15b • Location of Z and ? (question mark)

Reach to Z

1. Find **z** on the chart.
2. Find it on your keyboard.
3. Place your fingers over the home keys.
4. Reach to **z** with the **a** finger.
5. Touch **za** lightly without moving other fingers from their home positions.

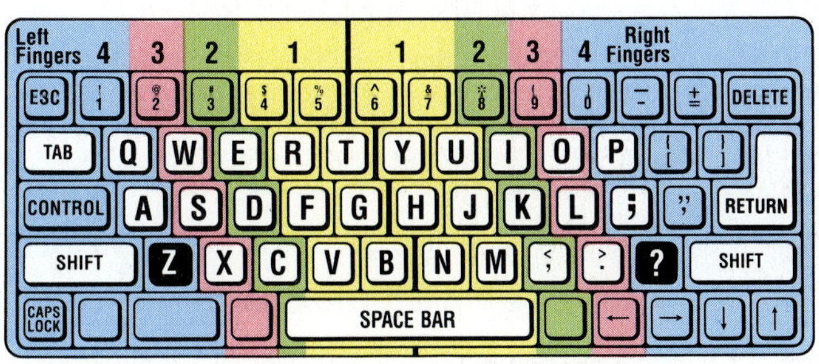

Reach to ? (question mark)

1. Find **?** on the chart.
2. Find it on your keyboard.
3. Place your fingers over the home keys.
4. Reach to **?** with the **;** finger.
5. Hold down left shift key as you reach your right little finger to the question mark.

aza za za zone zone zone — Key twice on same line — ;?; ?; ;?; ?;? Why? Why?

72b, continued

MORNING ANNOUNCEMENT

Please include the following in the morning announcements for October 16 and October 17:

The Student Council will meet Period 5 on October 18 in the Library Conference Room. See the Activities Bulletin Board for the agenda.

MORNING ANNOUNCEMENT

Please include the following in the morning announcements for October 18:

The Student Council will meet Period 5 today in the Library Conference Room. See the Activities Bulletin Board for the agenda.

10 minutes

72c • Timed Writings

Directions: 1. Take 1' writings on each ¶ below. Count errors and figure *gwam*. **2.** When you key a ¶ within the error limit specified by your teacher, move to the next ¶. Use control as you key this exercise.

all letters used 1.2 si — word wrap — *gwam* 5'

use quick, sharp, tapping strokes

There is little doubt that more and more people today are 2 | 27
concerned about keeping fit. We are being warned not to gain too 5 | 30
much weight or to let our blood pressure rise. 7 | 31

Some people lift weights in the executive suite, jog on their 9 | 34
lunch break, or work out with a rowing machine on the back porch. 12 | 37
They ride bikes, hike on trails, and swim laps in greater numbers 14 | 39
than ever before. 15 | 40

Whether you like to zoom down a roaring river on a raft or 17 | 42
whack a ball with a racquet, you will be wise to stay in shape. 20 | 45
If we sit behind a desk every day, we need some kind of exercise 23 | 48
to keep our bodies strong and our minds alert. 24 | 49

gwam 5' | 1 | 2 | 3 |

LESSON 73

1" side margins

5 minutes

73a • Keyboard Review

Directions: Key each sentence three times SS. DS between 3-line groups.

alphabet Pamela gave Nick exquisite old jewelry for the bazaar today.

fig/sym The 269 3/4 acres of land sold for more than $1,875 an acre.

easy They came with the chain to see if we had made a first down.

| 1 | 2 | 3 | 4 | 5 | 6 | 7 | 8 | 9 | 10 | 11 | 12 |

15c • Location Drills: Z and ? (question mark)

Reach to z

Reach to ? (question mark)

Directions: Key once with your teacher, tapping the return/enter key at the end of each line. Repeat by yourself.

Technique Goal: Reach to the shift key without moving your arms or wrists.

z
aza aza aza za za za zone zones zero zip zeal zinc
zoo size maze maze gaze graze doze quiz quiz froze

?
;?; ;?; ;?; ?; ?; ?; Is it? Can they go? Why go?
Can he tell them how? or why? Whom will she take?
space once — space twice

z/?
Did it buzz? Is this a quiz? Who won that prize?
Did they freeze? Was I in a daze? Had she dozed?

15d • Technique Builder

Directions: Key each line one time. Take three 1' writings on the sentences below. Print if your teacher directs you to do so.

Technique Goal: Hold shift key down; release it quickly. Try to keep a steady, even pace.

home row	Ada has a flask; dad has a salad; lads shall fall;
e/h	Jake had a desk. She had a sale. He asked a fee.
t/o	Take these foods too. He told jokes to the staff.
w/i	This is what we did with the saws while we waited.
r/n	Rhonda and her friends ran down there in the rain.
c/.	Face facts. Carl can choose. Each school closed.
g/u	Our group thought all the ground was rough though.
v/y	On your drive you will have views of every valley.
b/m	Both members seemed to blame them for the bad job.
x/p	I expect to pay a tax on the six extra parts next.
q/,	Quinn, not one to quit, quickly drew a new square.
z/?	Was Zane amazed? What size is their frozen pizza?
left shift	Hired were P. O. Yang, Lee Isaac, and N. K. Jones.
right shift	Beth and Ron Eads live on Gem Avenue in San Diego.
all letters	Have Jack quit buying sox; Pam will find a blazer.
all letters	Danny Flammon saw Bix give the prize a quick jerk.
	1 | 2 | 3 | 4 | 5 | 6 | 7 | 8 | 9 | 10

Spacing Guide
Space twice after a question mark at the end of a sentence; space once after a question mark within a sentence.

15e • Paragraph Skill Builder

Directions: Use the preset tab. Key the ¶s DS once for practice; then take three 1' writings on them. Figure *gwam* on the best writing.

all letters used — word wrap — *gwam* 1'

Now that you know where to find each of the keys, your job 12
is to work hard and learn to key well. This is a goal that all 25
of you can reach. 28

There is no quiz you can take that will prove your skill. 40
You must do more than read your text. If you try, you are bound 53
to gain a high speed. 57

1 | 2 | 3 | 4 | 5 | 6 | 7 | 8 | 9 | 10 | 11 | 12 | 13

71d, continued

STUDENT COUNCIL ELECTION PETITION

For the Office of Vice President

Each signature must be that of a student of this school and must be legible. This petition must be submitted to the Student Council Advisor no later than May 10.

1.____

2.____

3.____

COPY Copy is an editing feature that allows you to define a block of text (word, phrase, sentence, paragraph, or document) in one location of a document and copy (repeat) it in another location of the same document or in a different document. The original block remains intact. First you identify the copy command by tapping a specific keystroke combination (such as *the shift and F4 keys*). Next you identify the block to be copied. Then you position the cursor in the location where the copied text will appear. To complete the copy function, tap the return/enter key or a special function key as directed in your User's Manual.

LESSON 72

1" side margins

5 minutes

72a • Keyboard Review

Directions: Key each sentence three times SS. DS between 3-line groups.

reach with your fingers

alphabet	Pete B. Mavy forgot he was required to sell six dozen jacks.
fig/sym	John keyed a 5-minute writing on page 127 with 98% accuracy.
easy	I know she can see most of the fish if she sits on the dock.
	1 | 2 | 3 | 4 | 5 | 6 | 7 | 8 | 9 | 10 | 11 | 12

30 minutes

72b • Formatting Problems: Documents for Club Activities

Announcements

Directions: **1.** Put each announcement on page 140 on a separate sheet. Format 1" margins (top and side) for the request. Leave a DS between lines.

2. Set temporary left and right margins (indent) of 2" for the body of the announcement. Leave a DS between lines.

INDENT The indent, or temporary margin, is a special tab stop set in the ruler/format line to mark the position where every line of text (paragraph or column) will begin from the left margin (and end for the right margin). When word wrap is on, tap a specific key (such as *F4*) and the indent feature remains in effect until you remove it.

Improving Your Keying Techniques (Lessons 16-20)

Learning Goals

1. Reinforce proper stroking techniques, using the goals stressed in the text.
2. Stroke difficult, awkward, and long reaches smoothly with a minimum of hand, wrist, and arm movements.
3. Key short, common, balanced-hand words by word response; that is, by thinking and keying whole words rather than individual letters.
4. Key one-hand words by letter response, and combine word response with letter response into a flowing, rhythmic pattern.
5. Identify keying errors.
6. Learn to correct keying errors.
7. Operate the shift/caps lock.
8. Learn to retrieve previously saved documents.
9. Learn to move selected text from one part of the document to another.
10. Increase the keying rate on sentences and short paragraphs by approximately one word each lesson.

Word Processing Concepts Introduced in Unit 2

backspace erase	delete	resave
clipboard	edit	strikeover/replacement
command	file retrieval	
cut and paste	move	

General Directions

Use the default margins for all lessons in this unit. SS sentences and drill lines. DS between repeated groups of lines. DS paragraph copy if your software permits. Use preset tab for keying paragraphs.

Practice time is given for each section of a lesson in this unit. If it seems best to vary the schedule, do so with the approval of your teacher.

LESSON 16

16a • Keyboard Review

7 minutes

Directions: Key each line two times SS. DS between 2-line groups.

sit erect
feet flat
on floor

```
z         aza aza za za zeal zones doze quiz maze graze zest
?         ;?; ;?; ?; ?;  Who?  When?  How many?  Is she here?
ou        our four found house south though course out doubt
alphabet  Chris asked me what my grade was on the math quiz.
          Rick plans to move to Texas if he finds a new job.
          | 1 | 2 | 3 | 4 | 5 | 6 | 7 | 8 | 9 | 10 |
```

16b • Technique Builder: Keying Whole Words

8 minutes

Directions: Key each line as your teacher dictates SS. DS between 2-line groups.

Do not key the lines between words.

think and key whole words

```
1 if|if|it|it|is|is|if it|if it|it is|it is|if it is
2 to|to|do|do|so|so|to do|to do|do so|do so|to do so
3 he|he|is|is|he is|he is|she|she|is|is|she is|he is
4 if|if|he|he|if he|if he|if he is|she|she|if she is
```

10 minutes

71c • Language Arts Skills: Number Expression and Spacing Guides

Directions: The following are examples of number expressions. The guides give the rule; the remaining lines illustrate it. Key each illustration once.

Note: When referring to the time of day, spell out the hour with *o'clock*; use figures with *a.m.* or *p.m.*

Guide:
With "o'clock," spell out the hour. Use figures with "a.m." or "p.m."
Illustration:
We plan to leave at ten o'clock, not two o'clock.
Illustration:
Classes start at 7:54 a.m. and end at 2:01 p.m.

Guide:
All numbers used at the beginning of a sentence must be keyed in full.
Illustration:
Fourteen students are enrolled in the word processing class.

Directions: **1.** Each of the spacing guides below is followed by a sentence that illustrates it. **2.** Study the guides; key each line that illustrates the guide once.

keep your eyes on the copy

think as you key

Guide:
Space twice after a period at the end of a sentence.
Illustration:
Drew came to the door. Silvia is not here. We plan to leave soon.

Guide:
Space once after a semicolon or comma.
Illustration:
Rob went to class Thursday; therefore, he did not need the assignment.

Guide:
Space twice after a question mark at the end of a sentence.
Illustration:
How did you do on the test? Are you sure? When will we know?

Guide:
Space twice after a colon except when stating time.
Illustration:
You may attend any session: 1:30 p.m., 3:00 p.m., or 4:45 p.m.

Guide:
Space twice after an exclamation mark that ends a sentence.
Illustration:
That is terrific! We did it! This is the best one yet!

Guide:
Key the dash with two hyphens. Do not space before or after.
Illustration:
Nancy--not Kelly--plans to work after school.

---

25 minutes

71d • Formatting Problem: Document for Club Activities

Petition

Directions: **1.** Design a petition form to include signatures for student council election.
2. Format 1" side margins; format top and bottom margins to fit on one page DS.
3. Copy the signature lines on page 139 so that you have 20 lines on the sheet. Key in the correct number for each line.

13 minutes

16c • Sentence Skill Builder

Directions: Key each sentence two times; then take a 1' timed writing on each sentence. Figure your *gwam*.

key short easy words as a whole

```
1 Sherri asked me to tap each key as if it were hot.
2 You should keep your eyes on the book as you work.
3 I hope he can key the whole word some of the time.
4 They can store a great deal more on the hard disk.
5 Check all words on the screen; then you can print.
  | 1 | 2 | 3 | 4 | 5 | 6 | 7 | 8 | 9 | 10 |
```

7 minutes

16d • Proofreading Your Work

Directions: Some common keying errors are listed below. Read for errors, counting only one error to a word. As you read each description, note the circled examples.

1. A wrong letter.	Now thar you knoe where all
2. An incorrect or omitted punctuation mark.	can watch your speed climb, If
3. Failure to space between words.	one once in a while, donot let it
4. Failure to capitalize a letter.	be sure to keep your mind on
5. An omitted or added word.	work ^or as you key words on on your
6. A repeated or missing stroke.	to get llax in you quest for a hi

PROOFREADING When you have finished keying the text, you need to read it over carefully, comparing it with the original copy. This careful reading is called proofreading. Note the errors, and make the corrections necessary so that your copy matches the original copy.

10 minutes

16e • Continuity Practice

Directions: Key the copy below one time. Print your work and circle your errors if your equipment is attached to a printer; otherwise proofread from your screen and note your errors. Take a 1' writing on each ¶. Try to make fewer errors.

The syllable intensity (si) is given for the ¶s below. It is a guide to the difficulty of the material. Copy of average difficulty has an si of 1.5. The material in these ¶s is rated easy.

key without pauses

all letters used 1.0 si word wrap — *gwam* 1' | total words

Now that you know where all the keys are, you can watch your 12 | 12
speed climb. If you hit the wrong one once in a while, do not 25 | 25
let it faze you. 28 | 28

Be sure to keep your mind on the job as you work or as you 12 | 40
key words on your screen. Vow not to get lax in your quest for a 25 | 53
high rate. 27 | 55

| 1 | 2 | 3 | 4 | 5 | 6 | 7 | 8 | 9 | 10 | 11 | 12 | 13 |

Formatting and Keying Documents for Clubs (Lessons 71-75)

UNIT 13

Learning Goals

1. Review and apply the rules for spacing after punctuation.
2. Format and key a variety of documents related to the activities of a school club.
3. Review the process of selecting files listed in the directory for later use and removing those that will not be needed.

Word Processing Concepts Introduced in Unit 13

copy	indent (temporary margins)
enclosure notation	word processing art

General Directions

Use 1" side margins for all lessons in this unit unless otherwise directed. SS sentences and drill lines. DS between repeated groups of lines. DS paragraph copy for timed writings. Proofread and correct all errors in the problems.

LESSON 71

1" side margins

71a • Keyboard Review

5 minutes

Directions: Key each sentence three times SS. DS between 3-line groups.

keep arms and wrists quiet

alphabet Ken Gumpy will acquire a deluxe razor just before he leaves.

fig/sym High Spirits (Viking/Penguin) was $14.95 cloth, $5.95 paper.

easy Please have them fix the sign on the left side of the field.

| 1 | 2 | 3 | 4 | 5 | 6 | 7 | 8 | 9 | 10 | 11 | 12 |

71b • Remove Unneeded Files from Directory

5 minutes

LEAVE THESE FILES:

L24c3	L52c3	L67c1 L69c
L43c L44d2	L64c1	

LESSON 17

default margins

7 minutes

17a • Keyboard Review

Directions: Key each line two times SS. DS between 2-line groups.

keep eyes on copy; sit erect

```
n        jnj jnj nj nj no noon none note one once nine nice
t        ftf ftf tf tf fit fight tune tunes then thin think
er       hers here there were where ever every other serves
         Juan did not expect to win first prize so quickly.
alphabet
         Beth told him to give more help to those who lost.
         | 1 | 2 | 3 | 4 | 5 | 6 | 7 | 8 | 9 | 10 |
```

14 minutes

17b • Technique Builder: Keying Whole Words

Directions: Key each line three times SS. DS between 3-line groups.

key short words as a whole

```
1 He told us how to hold our forks in the right way.
2 At least half of them knew she had paid the bills.
3 Write all of their names on the front of the form.
4 Most girls will want to ride the bus to the games.
5 The name of that town was shown right on the sign.
6 It was their turn to lend us a hand with our work.
7 Both men did lay their pens down at the same time.
  | 1 | 2 | 3 | 4 | 5 | 6 | 7 | 8 | 9 | 10 |
```

10 minutes

17c • Continuity Practice

Directions: Key the copy below; proofread for errors. Repeat.

Use the 1' column at right and the 1' scale underneath the ¶s to figure your 1' rate. Use the 2' column and scale to figure your 2' rate.

all letters used 1.0 si word wrap

	gwam 1'	2'
A small car may not have quite as much zip as you would like,	12	6
and you know that it will not have room for six or eight of your	25	12
friends.	27	13
It will do some good things, though. It will use just half	12	19
as much gas as a great big car, and you will not need to look so	25	26
far to find a spot to park it.	31	29

gwam 1' | 1 | 2 | 3 | 4 | 5 | 6 | 7 | 8 | 9 | 10 | 11 | 12 | 13 |
2' | 1 | 2 | 3 | 4 | 5 | 6 |

70c • Completing the Multiple-Page Report

Problem 1 Table of Contents

Directions: **1.** Prepare a table of contents for L69c, using the same format as for the multiple-page report (left margin 1 1/2", right margin 1", heading centered on line 13).

2. The page numbers must match your printout; therefore, your numbers may not be the same as shown below.

3. Print the table of contents.

LEADERS

Leaders are a series of periods and spaces (. . .) that are keyed between two items in tabulated material to make reading easier. They "lead the reader's eye" from one columnar item to another.

Leaders are made by alternating the period (.) and a space. The lines of leaders should be aligned in vertical rows and should end at the same point at the right.

To align leaders, key all periods on either the odd or the even numbers on the ruler/format line. Begin the first line of leaders on the second space after the first item in the column and end the leaders two or three spaces to the left of the beginning of the next column.

1 1/2" margin

TABLE OF CONTENTS line 13

1" margin

QS

```
Microprocessor Hardware ..............................1

Microprocessor Software ..............................1

Disk Drives ..........................................2

Operating the Cursor Direction Keys ..................3

Function Keys ........................................3

Special Word Processing Functions ....................4

The Insert and Delete Keys ...........................5

File Names ...........................................5

Menus and Directories ................................6

Headers and Footers ..................................6

Document Formatting ..................................7

Proofreading the Document ............................7

Printing the Document ................................8
```

Problem 2 Model of a Title Page

Directions: **1.** Prepare a title page for L69c. Formats for the title page are the same as L69c (left margin 1 1/2", right margin 1").

2. Center the heading on line 16.

3. Space down 16 lines (8 DS). Center your name and DS. Center the name of the school and class, or teacher's name.

4. Space down 16 lines (8 DS). Center the date of the paper.

5. Assemble the pages in order: title page, table of contents, report. Staple evenly two or three times along the left side of the packet 1/2" from the left edge.

Note: This arrangement for the cover page is only one of several acceptable arrangements. Your teacher may prefer another arrangement; if so, follow those directions.

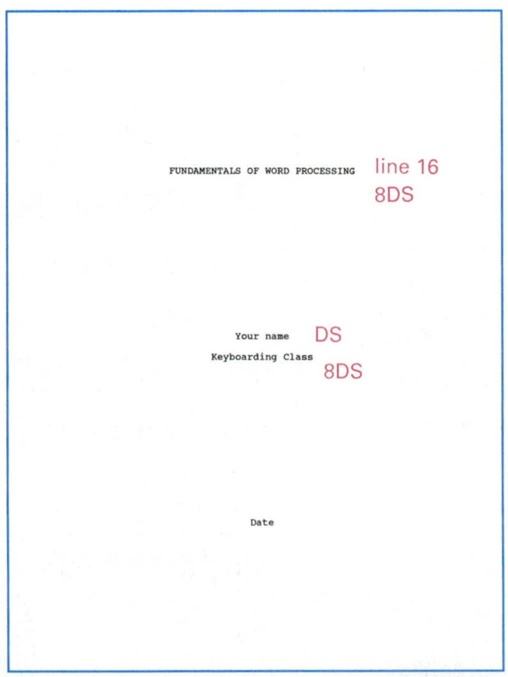
FUNDAMENTALS OF WORD PROCESSING line 16

8DS

Your name DS

Keyboarding Class

8DS

Date

14 minutes

17d • Retrieving a Document Previously Filed

Directions: **1.** Save your work as **Les17**. **2.** Clear your screen. **3.** Retrieve **Les16**, following the directions in the User's Manual. **4.** Cursor to the end of the lesson and key the five lines in L16c one time. Repeat if time permits. **5.** Resave **Les16**.

COMMAND A command is a direction to the word processor that enables the operator to perform a certain task.

RETRIEVE To retrieve means to recover a file from the directory so that it may be altered or reused in another file.

LESSON 18

default margins

7 minutes

18a • Keyboard Review

Directions: Key each line two times SS. DS between 2-line groups.

keep eyes on copy

```
b         bfb bfb bf bf bad back be been big bill both books
p         ;p; ;p; p; p; page part plan plant play post point
re        red real rest reach are care great green sure free
alphabet  Six big rocks jut out right there beside the pier.
          Van said they were quite hard to film in the haze.
          | 1 | 2 | 3 | 4 | 5 | 6 | 7 | 8 | 9 | 10 |
```

10 minutes

18b • Technique Builder: Keying Whole Words

Directions: Key lines 1-5 two times SS as your teacher dictates the words. DS between 2-line groups. Then take two 1' writings on the paragraphs that follow.

Do not key the lines between words.

think and key whole words

```
1 for|for|the|the|for the|and|and|this|this|and this
2 as|as|you|your|as you|as your|she|she|is|is|she is
3 I|I|have|have|I have|they|they|will|will|they will
4 at|at|their|their|at their|are|are|not|not|are not
5 this|this|did this|you|you|are|are|you are|you are
```

all letters used 1.0 si word wrap *gwam* 1'

A lot of the time you will find that you can think and key 12
whole words. This means you will not key all of them at the same 25
exact rate. 27

If a word is long or hard, of course, you can just slow down 12
quite a bit. Your speed is bound to zoom if you learn to key in 25
this way. 27

| 1 | 2 | 3 | 4 | 5 | 6 | 7 | 8 | 9 | 10 | 11 | 12 | 13 |

LESSON 69

1" side margins

5 minutes

69a • Keyboard Review

Directions: Key each sentence three times SS. DS between 3-line groups.

alphabet Tammy Planck will squeeze five or six juicy oranges by hand.

fig/sym We sent a check for $56.80 to Box #174 on February 23, 1994.

easy They came with the chain to see if we had made a first down.

| 1 | 2 | 3 | 4 | 5 | 6 | 7 | 8 | 9 | 10 | 11 | 12 |

10 minutes

69b • Sentence Guided Writings

Directions: **1.** Try to key each sentence in 67b, page 133, 4 times in 1' without error. **2.** Your teacher will call the return each 15" to guide you.

30 minutes

69c • Multiple-Page Report

Directions: **1.** Retrieve **L68c** and continue until all short reports have been linked to form the multiple-page report and all changes have been completed.
2. Check page breaks. Insert hard returns as necessary to avoid widows/orphans. Also check on locations of side headings and insert hard returns as necessary to place side heading on the same page as the paragraph which follows it.
3. Save the complete multiple-page report as **L69c** and print all pages of the report.

LESSON 70

1" side margins

5 minutes

70a • Keyboard Review

Directions: Key each sentence three times SS. DS between 3-line groups.

alphabet Four experts quickly amazed the crowd by juggling five axes.

fig/sym Two tickets (priced at $18.75 each) will be offered for $35.

easy Please have them fix the sign on the left side of the shelf.

| 1 | 2 | 3 | 4 | 5 | 6 | 7 | 8 | 9 | 10 | 11 | 12 |

10 minutes

70b • Timed Writings

Directions: Take two 3' writings on both ¶s combined. Count errors. Figure *gwam*. Submit the better of the two writings.

all letters used 1.3 si

keep wrists and arms still

word wrap *gwam* 3'

The idea of flying flags is quite old. Their use can be 4 | 36
traced to ancient times, when soldiers fixed some kind of emblem 8 | 40
to long poles. Doing this enabled them to see where their leader 13 | 45
was as they followed him into battle. 15 | 47

Their size and design keep changing. One of the largest 19 | 51
flags ever attempted was larger than a football field and had 23 | 55
stars that were more then ten feet across. Whether they are 27 | 59
large or small, flags express an eloquent message for the nation 31 | 64
they represent. 32 | 65

gwam 3' | 1 | 2 | 3 | 4 |

10 minutes

18c • Sentence Guided Writings

Directions: **1.** Take a 1' writing with the call of the guide each 20". Try to complete each sentence as the guide is called. (Your teacher will tell you how the guide will be called.) **2.** Take two 1' writings on the last sentence without the call of the guide.

keep arms and wrists quiet

		words in line	gwam 20"
1	Listen to the guide call.	5	15
2	Sit up straight in your chair.	6	18
3	Do not take your eyes off the book.	7	21
4	Hold your thumb close to your space bar.	8	24
5	Try to raise your rate by one word each line.	9	27
6	Be sure to keep your mind on your work as you key.	10	30

| 1 | 2 | 3 | 4 | 5 | 6 | 7 | 8 | 9 | 10 |

8 minutes

18d • Continuity Practice

Directions: Key both ¶s DS. Proofread for errors. Repeat.

all letters used 1.1 si word wrap

	gwam 1'	2'
All of us ought to take better care of our earth than we have	12	6
in the past. Unless we do so, it will no longer be such a good	25	12
place to live.	28	14
Trash piles up so fast that soon there may be no more places	12	20
to put it. Maybe we should hire a waste czar whose job would be	25	26
to make us quit being so lax in our trash habits.	35	31

gwam 1' | 1 | 2 | 3 | 4 | 5 | 6 | 7 | 8 | 9 | 10 | 11 | 12 | 13 |
2' | 1 | 2 | 3 | 4 | 5 | 6 |

10 minutes

18e • Keying in All Capital Letters

Directions: Key the sentences below two times SS. DS between 2-line groups.

She wrote her report on THE SWISS FAMILY ROBINSON.

Read their DAILY BULLETIN during the FIRST period.

CAPS/SHIFT LOCK The caps/shift lock is a key that causes all letters to be capitalized without having to depress a shift key for each stroke. Use all capital letters for names of books or newspapers or to emphasize a word.

LESSON 68

1" side margins

5 minutes

68a • Keyboard Review

Directions: Key each sentence three times SS. DS between 3-line groups.

alphabet Please pack my boxes with five dozen jugs of liquid varnish.

fig/sym Dale is almost 5'8", Anne is 5'10", and Jose is nearly 6'2".

easy They thought there should be goals at each end of the field.

| 1 | 2 | 3 | 4 | 5 | 6 | 7 | 8 | 9 | 10 | 11 | 12 |

10 minutes

68b • Skill Comparison

Directions: **1.** Take two 1' writings on the *easy* sentence SS. Figure *gwam*.
2. Take two 1' writings on each of the other sentences.
3. Try to match or exceed your *easy* sentence *gwam* on each of the other sentences.

		words
easy	She said that their big problems are due to a lack of goals.	12
fig/sym	Our Model 368 (about $25,000) has a high-performance engine.	12
script	*It's hard to climb a ladder with your hands in your pockets.*	12
rough draft	When the going seems to easy you may wellbe going down hill.	12

30 minutes

68c • Multiple-Page Report

Directions: **1.** Retrieve **L36c1**.
2. Delete your identification of the problem (your name/initials and the problem number).
3. Place your cursor at the beginning of the line below the problem. Import L36c2.
4. Delete your name under each heading after L36c1, then go to the end of the problem and delete your identification of the problem.
5. Repeat Step 3 in sequence for L37c1, L37c2, L37c3, L38c1, L38c2, L39c1, L39c2, L39c3, L40b1, L40b2, and L40b3.
6. Format for a bound report: Left margin will now be 1 1/2", top margin will be 1", right margin and bottom margin stay at 1". A header should be added to number each page after page 1. The page number appears at the right margin on line 7.
7. Add a new heading on line 13: FUNDAMENTALS OF WORD PROCESSING. Uncenter each of the headings to form side headings (they begin at the left margin).
8. As side headings, rekey each, capitalizing only the first letter of important words and underlining the entire side heading.
9. Save what you have completed as **L68c**.

SIDE HEADINGS Long reports are often broken into sections to make them easier to read. These sections are marked by side headings--descriptions of the material to follow Side headings begin at the left margin, have only the first letter of each important word capitalized, and are underlined. A side heading should appear on the same page as the paragraph which follows it.

LESSON 19

default margins

7 minutes

19a • Keyboard Review

Directions: Key each line two times SS. DS between 2-line groups.

keep fingers deeply curved

y	jyj jyj yj yj you your yes yet year eye cycle city
q	aqa aqa qa qa quit quiet quart quote squire square
nd	end send find found friend land hand window second
alphabet	Please wake me if I doze past six on that morning.
	Joy now lives in a quaint house near a good beach.
	1 | 2 | 3 | 4 | 5 | 6 | 7 | 8 | 9 | 10

15 minutes

19b • Sentence Guided Writings

Directions: **1.** Use lines 1-12 for 1' writings with the call of the guide each 20". **2.** Use lines 13-16 for 1' writings without the call of the guide.

return quickly; do not pause

		words in line	gwam 20"
1	Read your theme in class.	5	15
2	*Speak up so all can hear.*	5	15
3	I plan to work out in the gym.	6	18
4	*It is a great way to keep fit.*	6	18
5	My new phone can record your voice.	7	21
6	*Please tell me to return your call.*	7	21
7	These drills will help you learn to key.	8	24
8	*Use the new skill each day in your work.*	8	24
9	We joined the drive to keep our street clean.	9	27
10	*Our club wants to find ways to aid the group.*	9	27
11	Kathy left her bike in the stand next to our room.	10	30
12	*When she came back after class, one tire was flat.*	10	30
13	One thing they had to learn was how to read a map.	10	30
14	*He told us to work all three of the math problems.*	10	30
15	The lunch break seems way too short to most of us.	10	30
16	*Chris thought he would be late for class that day.*	10	30

10 minutes

67b • Sentence Guided Writings

Directions: **1.** Take 1' writings on each sentence SS. Try to reach the end of the sentence as the guide is called.
2. Your teacher will call the return each 15" or 12" to guide you. If you complete each sentence as the guide is called, you will key the sentence four times with the 15" call of the guide or five times with the 12" call of the guide.
3. Figure *gwam* and count errors.

		gwam 15" guide	12" guide
1	A new world era has now begun.	24	30
2	Today's economy is global in scope.	28	35
3	Products come from many different lands.	32	40
4	Be aware of the changes happening around you.	36	45
5	These trends will greatly influence your own life.	40	50
6	An information age requires a well-educated work force.	44	55
7	You should continue to work hard to upgrade your job skills.	48	60

| 1 | 2 | 3 | 4 | 5 | 6 | 7 | 8 | 9 | 10 | 11 | 12 |

30 minutes

67c • Formatting Multiple-Page Reports

Problem 1 Multiple-Page Report

Directions: Retrieve **L66c** and continue keying from where you stopped. Save completed report as **L67c1**.

Problem 2 Report Bibliography

Directions: **1.** Format for the bibliography is the same as for the multiple-page report: 1 1/2" left margin, 1" right margin, and center the heading on line 13.
2. Key the information for the bibliography in the order given below.
3. Proofread, save as **L67c2**, and print all pages of the report and the bibliography. Arrange the pages in order, with the bibliography last. Staple and give to your teacher.

BIBLIOGRAPHY ____ line 13

QS

margin

indent 5 spaces

Coffel, Steve. <u>But Not a Drop to Drink!</u> New York: Rawson
     Associates, MacMillan Publishing Company, 1989.

DS

Connecticut Department of Health Services. <u>Connecticut Water
     Conservation Handbook</u>. Hartford: American Water Works
     Association, Connecticut Section, 1991.

DS

Stewart, John Cary. <u>Drinking Water Hazards</u>. Hiram, Ohio:
     Envirographics, 1990.

10 minutes

19c • Continuity Practice: Correcting Keying Errors

Directions: Key the ¶s below. Proofread for errors. Cursor to each error in the paragraphs and make the necessary correction(s).

The figures indicate the word count every four words. The dots mark every second word between the four-word groups.

all letters used 1.1 si word wrap *gwam* 2' 3'

	2'	3'	
A few surveys have found that students do not learn as much	6	4	21
as they should in school these days. At least one study of this	12	8	26
kind showed that some could not find major bodies of water on a	19	13	30
world map, for example, or get the right answers on a simple math	25	17	34
quiz.	26	17	35
You could claim, though, that this practice of pointing out	6	4	23
what kids do not know is not new. It seems that each generation	12	8	27
is quick to tell what is wrong with the next one. Chances are	18	12	31
good that in a few years those in school now will be the ones	24	18	35
making these kinds of comments.	28	19	37

gwam 2' | 1 | 2 | 3 | 4 | 5 | 6 |
3' | 1 | 2 | 3 | 4 |

EDIT Edit means to read existing text and rearrange, reword, and correct all errors. Editing includes proofreading, but is not limited to it.

DELETE Delete is a word processing feature that allows the operator to remove a defined block of text (such as a character, a word, a line, a sentence, etc.).

BACKSPACE ERASE The backspace erase is an editing tool that allows you to backspace and delete a previously keyed character (or characters). Every time you tap the backspace erase key, the character to the left of the cursor is automatically erased (deleted).

STRIKEOVER/REPLACEMENT MODE The strikeover/replacement mode is an editing feature that allows the operator to position the cursor and key over (strikeover) characters. The existing text is automatically erased and replaced by the new text.

66c, continued

CONSERVING WATER line 13

DS

By (Student's name)

QS

Enough rain falls in most parts of the United States to keep our lawns green, our gardens growing, and our reservoirs full.

If you look at a picture taken from outer space, you will notice that water mass exceeds landmass. But the large amount of water mass leads to one of our worries, for less than one percent of that water is drinkable. More than two percent of the water on earth is frozen in glaciers and ice at the North and South Poles. The remaining 97 percent of the water is locked in salt water oceans and coastal seas (Stewart, 1990, 225). The fresh water actually available for human use in lakes, rivers, and the accessible ground water amounts to less than half of one percent of the total water supply. The purest, most easily developed supplies of water have already been tapped, and a growing number of users are fighting for access to the shrinking reserves (Coffel, 1989, 13). We don't have enough water to waste.

The average consumer uses about 50 gallons of water a day, or 240 gallons for a family of four (Handbook, 1991, 3). Humans require two to three quarts of water per day just to maintain the crucial liquid balance within the body (Coffel, 1989, 16). Some of that water comes from the food eaten, but much of it is taken in as fluids. Amazingly, water is probably the only drink which is free of calories, sweeteners, caffeine, and alcohol (Stewart, 1990, 225).

The use of large quantities of water is an inescapable part of American life today. How can we reduce the amount of water we use?

Three-quarters of the water is used in the bathroom. As you may have heard in televised commercials, older toilets use more than five gallons with each flush. New toilets may use up to 3.5 gallons--a savings of 25 percent. By inserting a toilet tank dam, an additional half gallon of water is saved. The savings would then be 40 percent!

Are you one who likes to take a long shower? Some shower heads use between five and seven gallons of water per minute. Low-flow shower heads that use only 2.5 gallons of water per minute are available. Switching to a new low-flow shower head results in a 35 to 50 percent savings. And, much as you might enjoy that long shower, five minutes of scrubbing will get you clean.

Other ways to save water include running the dishwasher and washing machine only when full (or adjusting the water level setting), using a vegetable brush to remove dirt from fresh fruit and vegetables, and fixing any leaking pipes or faucets. Simply turning off the water while brushing your teeth saves at least four gallons of water each day.

We have been looking at savings on water consumption. It should go without saying that for those who pay for the amount of water measured by the water meter, a reduction in the quantity used means a reduction in the size of the bill.

Most of us could adjust our use of water as outlined in the preceding paragraphs and never feel we were deprived. Unless more of us make the adjustments voluntarily, we are likely to find that more drastic measures are imposed upon us by local, state, or even federal agencies so that water for only essential use is available.

LESSON 67

1" side margins

5 minutes

67a • Keyboard Review

Directions: Key each sentence three times SS. DS between 3-line groups.

alphabet Peggy Klem was acquitted of tax evasion by the dozen jurors.

fig/sym A & R Mfg. has been on E. 76th St. for 58 years (1936-1994).

easy The firms will not pay us for the pens if they are worn out.

| 1 | 2 | 3 | 4 | 5 | 6 | 7 | 8 | 9 | 10 | 11 | 12 |

13 minutes

19d • Sustained Skill Building

Directions: **1.** Take one 1' writing on each paragraph in 19c. Proofread for errors; figure *gwam*.
2. Use these paragraphs for 2' and 3' writings as time permits.
3. To figure *gwam* on the 1' writing, use the nearest figure above the copy. For the 2' and 3' writings, use the columns and scales to figure *gwam*.

LESSON 20

default margins

7 minutes

20a • Keyboard Review

Directions: Key each line two times SS. DS between 2-line groups.

curve fingers; not wrists

```
x        sxs sxs xs xs tax tax mix mix fix fix box axe axle
p        ;p; ;p; p; p; plan plan plant plant play play pray
to       to too took top told town toward touch total today
         Quite a few boys just came back from the zoo trip.
alphabet
         Dawn wants all of us to go in their van next time.
         | 1 | 2 | 3 | 4 | 5 | 6 | 7 | 8 | 9 | 10 |
```

15 minutes

20b • Technique Builder: Keying Whole Words

Directions: Key each line two times SS. DS between 2-line groups. Take a 1' writing on each sentence. Figure *gwam*.

key each word as a unit, not letter by letter

```
1 in|in|our|our|in our|for|for|an|an|and for|and for
2 will|will|be|be|will be|of|of|of|that|that|of that
3 with|with|us|us|with us|has|has|been|been|has been
4 we|we|can|can|we can|on|on|the|on the|that|on that
5 for the|and the|did the|in their|for their|at this
6 Go with us to their game if you can find the time.
7 They will all be there by the first of this month.
8 I think he will have to wait for the rest of them.
9 She wants to send notes to those who are not here.
  | 1 | 2 | 3 | 4 | 5 | 6 | 7 | 8 | 9 | 10 |
```

30 minutes

66c • Formatting Multiple-Page Reports

WIDOW/ORPHAN The widow/orphan feature prevents the printing of the last line of a paragraph at the top of a new page (widow) and the first line of a paragraph at the bottom of a page (orphan). The widow/orphan feature "protects" documents from containing these undesirable features.

Before the widow/orphan feature is turned on, the cursor must be at the beginning of the text to be protected--usually at the beginning of the document. The feature may be turned on and off within a document. Use widow/orphan protection for proper page breaks in all documents of two or more pages.

HEADER/FOOTER A header/footer is the text line (or lines) printed consistently in the top margin (header) or bottom margin (footer) of multiple-page documents. A header/footer may include such information as the document title, page number, and date. Rarely does a single document contain both a header and a footer. The header is preferred by most writers, with the page number appearing at the center or at the right margin of the page.

PAGE BREAK A page break is the point (generally a given line count) at which a page ends. When the printer reaches a page break, it automatically advances a new sheet or allows the user to insert paper.

AUTOMATIC (SOFT/NONREQUIRED) PAGE BREAKS The automatic page break (sometimes called page format) is a feature that allows the user to select the number of lines allowed on the page (generally, 54). When the program recognizes the given number of lines, it automatically inserts a soft page break. When repagination occurs (a paragraph is added or deleted, for example), all soft page breaks are deleted and new ones are inserted automatically.

CONTROLLED (HARD/REQUIRED) PAGE BREAKS Controlled page breaks are accomplished by using a special command inserted by the user to ensure that a page remains intact during automatic pagination. When the program recognizes the special command, it breaks the page at that point. Usually hard page breaks must be deleted by the user.

RUN-IN REFERENCES (INTERNAL CITATIONS) Sources of specific information or lengthy quotes are listed in the sentence with the information as opposed to footnotes or endnotes which were used in the recent past. The correct order for each reference is: name(s) of author(s), the year of publication, and the page number of the source (Jones, 1992, 275).

Leftbound Multiple-Page Report

Directions: **1.** Format for a 1 1/2" left margin, 1" right margin, and 1" top margin.
2. Center the heading on line 13 from the top of the page.
3. Using the header capabilities, number pages (after page 1) in the upper right corner of the page on line 7. Refer to page RG2 for model.
4. Key in *w* each time *water* appears, then use search and replace to change the *w* to *water*.
5. Check on page breaks, inserting hard returns as necessary to avoid widows and/or orphans.
6. Save as **L66c**.

10 minutes

20c • Continuity Practice

Directions: 1. Key both ¶s two times DS. Repeat if time permits. **2.** Save **Les20**.

all letters used 1.1 si word wrap

use quick, sharp strokes

	gwam 2'		3'
We now know quite a lot about which jobs in life are apt to	6	4	28
cause the most stress. As a rule, those which require one to	12	8	32
meet and deal with the public each day head the list.	18	12	36
You need to give some extra thought to how you may want to	23	16	40
spend your working years. As you will soon learn, the size of	30	20	44
your paycheck each month is not the only thing to think about.	36	24	48
gwam 2' — 1 2 3 4 5 6			
3' — 1 2 3 4			

5 minutes

20d • Moving Copy Within the Document

Directions: Following the directions below, select the text you completed in 20c and move it to the end of 20a.

Consult the User's Manual for the function keys to use to complete moving the text.

MOVE Move is an editing feature commonly called "cut and paste" that allows you to move (cut) a block of text from one location in a document and place (paste) it in a different location within the same document. The original block is removed. First you identify the move command by tapping a specific keystroke combination (see the User's Manual). Next you identify the block to be moved (cut out). Then you position the cursor in the location where the moved text will be retrieved (pasted). Finally, tap the return/enter key or a special function key to place the block of text.

CLIPBOARD The clipboard is the section or area of the computer's memory where information that is being moved is temporarily held during the cut-and-paste operation.

8 minutes

20e • Sustained Skill Building

Directions: 1. Move the cursor to the beginning of the line below the last keyed line on your screen.

2. Take a 1' writing on each ¶ in 20c DS. Proofread for errors and figure *gwam* on each writing.

3. Resave **Les20**.

Formatting and Keying Multiple-Page Reports (Lessons 66-70)

Learning Goals

1. Format and key multiple-page reports.
2. Key related materials, including bibliography, table of contents, and cover page.
3. Develop additional basic skills, such as formatting for header/footer commands and page breaks.

Word Processing Concepts Introduced in Unit 12

automatic page break	import (review)
change format of report	page break
controlled page break	widow/orphan
header/footer	

General Directions

Use 1" side margins for all lessons in this unit unless otherwise directed. SS sentences and drill lines. DS paragraph copy. Proofread and correct all errors in the problems.

LESSON 66

1" side margins

5 minutes

66a • Keyboard Review

Directions: Key each sentence three times SS. DS between 3-line groups.

keep wrists and elbows quiet

alphabet	We have quoted him fairly as a recognized junk bonds expert.
fig/sym	Leave 18 spaces for left margins of 1 1/2 inches (12-pitch).
easy	It looks as if six or eight giant signs were then torn down.
	1 2 3 4 5 6 7 8 9 10 11 12

10 minutes

66b • Technique Builder: Stroking

Directions: Key each line three times SS. DS between 3-line groups.

keep your eyes on the copy

hyphen	Joan Lucas-Homan installed high-quality, low-volume faucets.
double letters	Manny Dunne will keep that fellow from passing the football.
direct reaches	Under no circumstances can my younger brother receive money.
one-hand	Teresa read up only on car races. Dad bragged on my grades.
balanced-hand	She paid the rich man for one half of the fish kept at the dock.
combination	We got the rebate as a reward for the work that we did then.
	1 2 3 4 5 6 7 8 9 10 11 12

Learning to Center Horizontally and Vertically (Lessons 21-25)

Learning Goals

1. Format/key copy that is centered vertically and horizontally on full sheets.
2. Use basic correction procedures in correcting keying errors.
3. Increase keying skills by further refining basic techniques.
4. Learn another way to name a file when saving a document (**L21c1** for **Lesson 21, Section c, Problem 1**).

Word Processing Concepts Introduced in Unit 3

automatic centering
document
format
another pattern for file name (for problems)
hard copy
import
integrate

General Directions

Margins refer to the blank space on the left and right sides and at the top and bottom of a page. Left and right margins can be adjusted to the desired line space; top and bottom margins can be adjusted to the desired line.

Use 1″ margins for all lessons in this unit. SS sentences and drill lines. DS between repeated groups of lines. Proofread and correct all errors in the problems.

Save practice as **Les21, Les22, Les23,** etc. Save problems individually as directed in each (**L21c1, L21c2,** etc.).

LESSON 21

1" side margins

21a • Keyboard Review

7 minutes

sit erect; keep arms and wrists quiet

Directions: Key each sentence two times SS. DS between 2-line groups.

alphabet
```
I have a good ink jet printer and a laser one too.
He was amazed how quickly copy can be sent by fax.
```
at
```
at great water rather matter attend nation station
```
easy
```
Their goal is to make a high profit with no risks.
```
| 1 | 2 | 3 | 4 | 5 | 6 | 7 | 8 | 9 | 10 |

21b • Learn to Center Horizontally and Vertically

18 minutes

Centering material so there will be equal left and right margins is called horizontal centering.

HORIZONTAL CENTERING

Step 1 Format equal left and right margins (1" margins are suggested for now).

Step 2 Clear all preset tabs. Set a tab at the center point of the paper you will use (12-pitch center is 51; 10-pitch center is 42).

Step 3 Backspace from center point once for every two characters, punctuation, or spaces in the line to be centered. If there is one character left, do not backspace for it. Begin to key at the point where you complete the backspacing.

(continued on next page)

LESSON 65

1" side margins

5 minutes

65a • Keyboard Review

Directions: Key each sentence three times SS. DS between 3-line groups.

alphabet Jeff Long experienced a quick shave with my razor and brush.

fig/sym Luis said, "To get the answer, add 6 1/2, 9 5/8, and 7 3/4."

easy Jena took the lead early in the race and thus won the title.

| 1 | 2 | 3 | 4 | 5 | 6 | 7 | 8 | 9 | 10 | 11 | 12 |

20 minutes

65b • Sentence Guided Writings

Directions: **1.** Take a 1' writing on each sentence. Try to key the sentence four times within the minute. **2.** Your teacher will call the return each 15" to guide you. **3.** Figure *gwam* and count errors.

	15" guide	*gwam*	words
1	Do you sit erect in the seat as you key?	32	8
2	Do you look at the copy and not your fingers?	36	9
3	Do you strike each key with a quick, sharp stroke?	40	10
4	Do you think and key every easy combination as a whole?	44	11
5	Do you hold the wrists low and quiet as you strike the keys?	48	12

| 1 | 2 | 3 | 4 | 5 | 6 | 7 | 8 | 9 | 10 | 11 | 12 |

20 minutes

65c • Timed Writings

Directions: **1.** Key two 1' writings on each ¶ DS. Check the one on which you made the better rate; then check the one on which you made fewer errors. **2.** Take two 3' writings on both ¶s combined. Count errors. Figure *gwam*. Submit the better of the two writings.

all letters used 1.3 si word wrap

	gwam 3'	
The one thing that most of us never have quite enough of is	4	38
time. At least that's the excuse we usually fall back on	8	42
whenever we do not get a job finished as soon as we or the boss	12	46
wanted. Time is a precious commodity that always seems to be in	17	51
short supply.	17	52
Whether we use primitive means of telling time or rely on	21	56
modern clocks and watches, the time available for us remains	25	60
constant. No matter how rich or poor we might be, or what time	30	64
zone we live in, the number of hours in each day stays exactly	34	68
the same.	34	69

gwam 3' | 1 | 2 | 3 | 4 |

21b, continued

Note: The paper you will print on is 8 1/2" wide. A 12-pitch printer will print 12 characters per inch; therefore, 8 1/2 times 12 equals 102 characters. Half of 102 (51) is the center. A 10-pitch printer will print 10 characters per inch; therefore, 8 1/2 times 10 equals 85 characters, and the center is 42 with the fraction being disregarded.

Directions: **1.** Center each of the following lines, using the backspace-from-center method. **2.** Save **Les21**. **3.** Clear the screen.

```
                 ANNOUNCEMENT
               1| 2| 3| 4| 5| 6
              AN|NO|UN|CE|ME|NT
               Class Meetings
             1| 2| 3| 4| 5| 6| 7
           Cl|as|s |Me|et|in|gs
          During Homeroom Tomorrow
    1| 2| 3| 4| 5| 6| 7| 8| 9| 10| 11| 12
    Du|ri|ng| H|om|er|oo|m |To|mo|rr|ow
```

Note: Once you understand the horizontal centering process, you will be directed to follow the User's Manual to use the automatic centering process for word processing.

VERTICAL CENTERING

Centering material so that it will have uniform top and bottom margins is called vertical centering.

Step 1 Count the lines in the copy to be centered. If your copy is to be double-spaced, remember to count the spaces between the lines. There is only 1 line space following each line of copy when material is double-spaced.

Step 2 Subtract the total lines to be used from the lines available on the paper you are using. (There are *6* lines per inch; your paper is *11* inches long; there are *66* lines on a full sheet. *All problems in this book will be formatted on a full sheet of paper.)*

Step 3 Divide the number of lines that remain by two (half will go above the text, half below); this will give you the number of lines in the top margin. If the result contains a fraction, disregard it.

---

20 minutes

21c • Formatting Problems: Centering

AUTOMATIC CENTERING Automatic centering is a word processing feature that eliminates the calculations in the backspace-from-center method. To center automatically, position the cursor at the left margin. Hold down the designated key or combination (such as *Code* and *c* or *Shift F6*); the cursor moves to the center of the line. As you key, the cursor backs up (but may not print). To print the centered copy, tap the return/enter key. You may find that you must first key in the copy to be centered, then give the center command. Check the User's Manual for complete directions.

DOCUMENT A document is any formatted information such as practice work, a letter, a report, a tabulation, a form.

(continued on next page)

63d, continued

Problem 2 Review of Short Report

Directions: **1.** Retrieve **L43d** and add the paragraphs below. **2.** Keep the format used for L43d.

You will be alerted to a condition or a modification coming in the next part of the class discussion when you hear words like *because*, *therefore*, *unless*, and *consequently*. It is helpful to underline or circle these words when reviewing your notes.

For subjects that invite comparisons, listen for words such as *either*, *opposite*, *best*, and *rather*. These words are really saying that Idea A is going to be compared to Idea B and that one idea might be preferred to another equally sound idea.

When you hear terms like *as a result*, *in conclusion*, *hence*, and *finally*, you know that the discussion is ending and that a summary of what has been said is coming. The summary may hold all the really important facts in a few sentences, so write as much of it as you can.

Staying alert and focused during the entire class will help you in taking clear, concise, and meaningful notes. Writing these notes in a good handwriting will make reviewing the notes for a test a worthwhile step toward a good grade on that test.

Problem 3 Tabulation Review

Directions: **1.** Retrieve **L54d2.** **2.** Arrange in sequence by date. **3.** Save, print, and give to your teacher.

LESSON 64

1" side margins

64a • Keyboard Review

5 minutes

Directions: Key each sentence three times SS. DS between 3-line groups.

use quick, sharp strokes

alphabet Brian knew when Jacques played the fine new sax Roz gave me.

fig/sym Asia's Mount Everest (5 1/2 miles high) was climbed in 1953.

easy All of us think she would be wise to visit the island today.

| 1 | 2 | 3 | 4 | 5 | 6 | 7 | 8 | 9 | 10 | 11 | 12 |

64b • Tabulation Format Review

40 minutes

Problem 1

Directions: Center the problem below on a full sheet of paper DS. Leave 14 spaces between columns.

Reminder: Line up the colons in the times by spacing before keying single-digit hours.

BELL SCHEDULE
Normal Day

Period	Beginning Time	Ending Time
Homeroom	7:40	7:45
1	7:49	8:34
2	8:38	9:23
3	9:27	10:12
4	10:16	11:01
Lunch	11:05	11:35
5	11:39	12:24
6	12:30	1:15
7	1:19	2:04

Problem 2

Directions: Retrieve **L53c3** and change format to 10 spaces between columns, maintaining the DS.

FORMAT The format of a problem refers to the layout of the document and includes line length, spacing, and top and bottom margins. Figuring each of these is referred to as formatting.

HARD COPY A computer printout on paper of the screen display is called the hard copy.

Problem 1

Directions: **1.** Center the listing below horizontally and vertically on a full sheet of paper, following the backspace-from-center directions on page 38. Leave a DS between lines. In the problem, you can see that 35 lines are used. Subtract 35 from 66 to get 31 lines that are not used for the problem. Divide 31 by two (half of the lines not used are above the problem and half below) and get 15 (disregard the fraction). Your top margin will be 15 lines, begin keying on line 16.

2. Label the problem with your name and problem number, following directions from your teacher for placement.

3. Proofread and correct all errors.

4. Save the problem under the name of **L21c1** (for Lesson 21, Section c, Problem 1).

5. Print a hard copy of the problem and give it to your teacher for grading.

6. Clear your screen for formatting and keying the next problem.

Note: If your software limits the size of the top margin, determine whether you can use the default top margin and cursor down enough to get the correct line for the heading or whether you must approach it in another manner.

1" side margin — tab set at center — 1" side margin

```
SOME WORD PROCESSING TERMS

Command

Cursor

Default

Disk

Delete

Document

Hard Copy

Menu

Insert

Software

Function Keys

Pagination

Directory

Hardware

Microprocessor

Spreadsheet

Database
```

(continued on next page)

LESSON 63

1" side margins

5 minutes

63a • Keyboard Review

Directions: Key each sentence three times SS. DS between 3-line groups.

alphabet Gail required me to fix every brown jacket with new zippers.

fig/sym On April 1 the Cota-Lee extension changed from 2530 to 6847.

easy I know she can see most of the fish if she sits on the dock.

| 1 | 2 | 3 | 4 | 5 | 6 | 7 | 8 | 9 | 10 | 11 | 12 |

5 minutes

63b • Skill Comparison

Directions: **1.** Take a 1' writing on the *easy* sentence. Figure *gwam.*
2. Take a 1' writing on each of the other sentences.
3. Try to match or exceed your *easy* sentence *gwam* on each of the other sentences.

do not pause between words

		words
easy	She did not want us to visit with the rich widow on the bus.	12
script	*You know that when the going gets tough the tough get going.*	12
rough draft	one who ~~was~~ is a shal low thinker never leaves adeep impresion.	12

5 minutes

63c • Language Arts Skills: Keying from Dictation and Spelling Checkup

Directions: **1.** Your teacher will dictate the words in 62b, page 125. Key the words from dictation.
2. Check your work for correct spelling. Rekey any words in which you made an error.

30 minutes

63d • Format Review of Personal Notes, Short Report, and Tabulation

Problem 1 Review of Personal Notes

Directions: **1.** Key the personal note below in block style, open punctuation. Format 2" side margins, date on line 20.
2. When the note has been keyed, position the cursor at home position and use search to find each **G**. Replace with **Grandma**.

September 28, 19--

Dear G

Thank you for the birthday check. I went shopping for something extra special to buy with the money. G, I can't wait to show you the shirt I found!

My family treated me to dinner at my favorite pizza restaurant and had the best chocolate cake for me when we came home. It was fun to open the gifts they had for me.

Thanks again, G, for the gift. I'm anxious to see you and am glad I have only one week to wait for your visit.

Love | (Your name)

21c, continued

Problem 2

Directions: **1.** Rekey Problem 1, using the same vertical and horizontal margins. Use the automatic centering procedure according to the User's Manual for your software.

2. Label the problem with your name and problem number.

3. Proofread and correct all errors.

4. Save the problem as **L21c2**.

5. Print the problem and give to your teacher for grading.

LESSON 22

1" side margins

22a • Keyboard Review

7 minutes

Directions: Key each line two times SS. DS between 2-line groups.

key with a steady rhythm

```
alphabet  Our store stocks frozen orange juice by the quart.
          Do not expect her to move more than one mile away.
      ha  has had hand hard have chance change happy perhaps
    easy  Sit down right there when the chief says to do so.
          | 1 | 2 | 3 | 4 | 5 | 6 | 7 | 8 | 9 | 10 |
```

22b • Paragraph Guided Writings

16 minutes

Directions: **1.** Take a 1' writing on ¶ 1. Figure *gwam.* Add four words to your *gwam* for a new goal.

2. Take two 1' writings on the same ¶ as you strive to reach your new goal.

3. Repeat Steps 1 and 2 for ¶ 2.

4. Take a 3' writing on both ¶s combined. Figure *gwam.* Compare your new rate to your 1' writing.

Your teacher may call the 1/2' guide on the 1' writings to aid you in checking your rate.

all letters used | 1.2 si | word wrap | *gwam* 3'

¶ 1 1.2 si

More than you are aware, you are likely to judge people by | 4 | 32
the way they shake your hand. The same thing happens the other | 8 | 36
way around, of course. They tend to size you up that way too. | 12 | 40

¶ 2 1.2 si

As thosc kinds of special treatment which are based on gender | 16 | 44
have now gone out of style, the rules for shaking hands apply | 20 | 48
equally to both sexes. No more is it proper for women to stay in | 25 | 53
their seats when others stand to shake hands. | 28 | 56

gwam 3' | 1 | 2 | 3 | 4 |

5 minutes

62c • Paragraph Guided Writings

Directions: 1. Take one 3' writing on the ¶s below. Proofread for errors. Figure *gwam*.
2. Key each word that you have keyed incorrectly three times with the word that precedes and follows it (ex. humans *habe* always . . . humans *have* always).
3. Take two 1' writings on each ¶. Try to increase your speed. Figure *gwam* and count errors.

keep your wrists low and still

all letters used 1.3 si word wrap

	gwam 3"	
Down through the years, humans have always found a need to	4	50
exchange written messages with those who live some distance away.	8	55
The first record of a system for doing this goes back to the days	13	59
of bronze tablets carried on horseback.	15	62
Our own mail service has evolved from the era of the pony	19	65
express to the jet age. To handle the expanding volume,	23	69
equipment is used that reads ZIP Codes to direct a piece of mail	27	74
to one section of a block or one certain building.	31	77
No one knows how we will be sending written notes to each	35	81
other in the future. Today many firms use some form of	38	84
electronic mail, where their letters are sent by means of	42	88
telephone lines and no written copies are transported at all.	46	92

gwam 3' | 1 | 2 | 3 | 4 |

30 minutes

62d • Review Formatting a Short Report

Directions: 1. Retrieve **L21c1**.
2. Uncenter the terms listed and delete the other terms. Terms to uncenter: *Command, Cursor, Default, Document, Pagination.*
3. Add the following short definitions to form a short report. Underline as shown. Format for 1" side margins. Center the heading on line 13. DS and add your name, then QS.

SOME WORD PROCESSING TERMS

Command is an instruction given to the computer, usually by using the keyboard.

Cursor is a blinking block or underline that indicates where the next character that is keyed in will appear.

Default refers to the automatic use of a format that is incorporated into the software or microprocessor that is being used. This built-in format will be used unless you decide to change it.

Document is any written communication; it could be a letter, a business form, or an interoffice memorandum (correspondence that will stay within the company).

Pagination is the process of breaking the document into pages. You could use the default pagination or force pagination by inserting or deleting blank lines. When headers or footers are used in the document, the pagination includes the numbering of the pages.

22 minutes

22c • Formatting Problems: Centering

Problem 1

Directions: **1.** Format 1" side margins with the top and bottom margins to center the problem below DS on a full sheet of paper.

2. Clear all preset tabs and set one at the center of the paper (12-pitch center is 51; 10-pitch center is 42).

3. Key the announcement below, using the backspace-from-center method.

4. Label the problem with your name and problem number.

5. Proofread and correct all errors.

6. Save the problem as **L22c1**.

7. Print the problem and give it to your teacher for grading.

8. Clear your screen so that you are ready to format and key the next problem.

Vertical Centering Calculation Review

Lines available 66
Less lines required .... __
Lines remaining .... __
Top margin .... __
Begin on line .... __

ATTENTION

Soccer Team Tryouts

Meade Field

Varsity and Junior Varsity

Check Sign on Gym Door

for Date and Time

Problem 2

Directions: **1.** Format 1" side margins with top and bottom margins to center the problem below DS on a full sheet of paper.

2. Use the automatic centering procedure according to the User's Manual for your software.

3. Label the problem with your name and problem number.

4. Proofread and correct all errors.

5. Save as **L22c2.**

6. Print the problem and give it to your teacher for grading.

SUGGESTED READING LIST

The Call of the Wild

Tom Sawyer

My Side of the Mountain

Lilies of the Field

Roots

All Creatures Great and Small

The Old Man and the Sea

The Diary of Anne Frank

Of Mice and Men

61d, continued

Problem 2 Formatting a Centering Problem into a Tabulation

Directions: **1.** Retrieve **L61d1**.
2. Rearrange as a 2-column table. Leave 14 spaces between columns. Add column headings of <u>City</u> and <u>Country</u>.
Hint: Using the automatic centering feature make a *sample line*. Key the longest item in each column, delete the comma, and insert 14 spaces between the two items. Determine where to set the tabs based on the *sample line*, and align the other line items with the tabs.

SELECTED CAPITAL CITIES

Ankara, Turkey

Cairo, Egypt

Damascus, Syria

Dublin, Ireland

Madrid, Spain

Managua, Nicaragua

Nicosia, Cyprus

Paris, France

Tripoli, Libya

(longest item in column 1) `Damascus, Nicaragua` (longest item in column 2)

14 spaces

LESSON 62

1" side margins

5 minutes

62a • Keyboard Review

Directions: Key each sentence three times SS. DS between 3-line groups.

alphabet The quiz show Jack Palm entered had six girls and five boys.

fig/sym Janine ran the 100-yard dash (91.4 meters) in less than 15".

easy Kate tossed the ball right to him as she ran down the court.

| 1 | 2 | 3 | 4 | 5 | 6 | 7 | 8 | 9 | 10 | 11 | 12 |

5 minutes

62b • Language Arts Skills: Spelling and Proofreading Aid

keep arms and wrists quiet

Directions: Key each line three times SS. DS between 3-line groups.

1 machinery endeavor faculty assistant ninth necessity equally
2 appropriate ninety knowledge career truly pamphlet Wednesday
3 doctor completely enthusiasm since occur accurate beneficial

LESSON 23

1" side margins

23a • Keyboard Review

7 minutes

Directions: Key each line two times SS. DS between 2-line groups.

alphabet The woman spoke on the subject of the ozone layer.
Sixth and seventh graders were required to attend.

is is his list miss wish visit discuss furnish island

easy They did not spend their time working at the firm.

| 1 | 2 | 3 | 4 | 5 | 6 | 7 | 8 | 9 | 10 |

23b • Paragraph Guided Writings

16 minutes

Directions: **1.** Take a 1' writing on ¶ 1. Figure *gwam*. Add four words to your *gwam* for a new goal.
2. Take two 1' writings on the same ¶ as you strive to reach your new goal.
3. Repeat steps 1 and 2 for ¶ 2.
4. Take a 3' writing on both ¶s combined. Figure *gwam*. Compare your new rate to your 1' writing.

all letters used 1.2 si word wrap *gwam* 3'

One of these days, the experts say, we may drive cars that 4 | 40
know right where they want to go. They will be equipped with 8 | 44
computer systems that keep them out of traffic jams, space them 12 | 48
evenly on the roads, and find them places to park. Cars will 16 | 52
almost think, it seems. 18 | 54

Most of us will have to admit that this sounds a bit crazy 22 | 58
now, but it is fun to contemplate. If cars can really be made to 26 | 62
do these things, we may not have to build any more new highways 31 | 66
and use up precious land. We would not run into each other 35 | 70
so often either. 36 | 71

gwam 3' | 1 | 2 | 3 | 4 |

10 minutes

61c • Sentence Guided Writings

Directions: **1.** Take 1' writings on each sentence SS. Try to key each sentence four times within the minute without error.
2. Your instructor will call the return each 15" to guide you.
3. Figure *gwam* and count errors.

		gwam 15" guide
1	Key all these facts carefully.	24
2	A fact is a statement that is true.	28
3	Television helps make the world smaller.	32
4	English is now becoming a universal language.	36
5	Today you are truly living in the information age.	40
6	Computers are a real force driving change in the world.	44
7	*They certainly affect the ways in which all of us live.*	44
8	Talking to someone almost anywhere on earth is quite simple.	48
9	*Even words in written form can now be transmitted instantly.*	48

25 minutes

61d • Formatting and Keying Review

Problem 1 Centering Review

Directions: **1.** Key the problem below DS, centered vertically and horizontally on a full sheet of paper.
2. Save the problem, then move the lines so that the cities are in alphabetical order.
3. Resave the problem and print.

Vertical Centering Calculation Review
Lines available 66
Less lines required............__
Lines remaining ....__
Top margin..........................__
Begin on line ....__

SELECTED CAPITAL CITIES

Cairo, Egypt

Tripoli, Libya

Ankara, Turkey

Damascus, Syria

Nicosia, Cyprus

Paris, France

Dublin, Ireland

Managua, Nicaragua

Madrid, Spain

22 minutes

23c • Formatting Problems: Centering

Problem 1

Directions: **1.** Format 1" side margins with the top and bottom margins to center the problem below DS in a single column on a full sheet of paper.

2. Use the automatic centering procedure according to the User's Manual for your software.

3. Label the problem with your name and problem number.

4. Proofread and correct all errors.

5. Save as **L23c1**.

6. Print the problem and give it to your teacher for grading.

7. Clear your screen so that you are ready to format and key the next problem.

Vertical Centering Calculation Review

Lines available 66
Less lines required............__
Lines remaining ....__
Top margin........................__
Begin on line ....__

NATIONAL HOCKEY LEAGUE TEAMS

Boston Bruins

Calgary Flames

Detroit Red Wings

Hartford Whalers

Minnesota North Stars

New Jersey Devils

New York Rangers

Pittsburgh Penguins

St. Louis Blues

Vancouver Canucks

Winnipeg Jets

Problem 2

Directions: Same as for Problem 1; save as **L23c2.**

RECENT FIRST LADIES OF THE UNITED STATES

Barbara Bush	Claudia Johnson
Nancy Reagan	Jacqueline Kennedy
Rosalynn Carter	Mamie Eisenhower
Elizabeth Ford	Bess Truman
Patricia Nixon	Eleanor Roosevelt

Format Review and Skill Building (Lessons 61-65)

Learning Goals

1. Continue refining stroking skills and operating techniques.
2. Continue reinforcing the operation of the tab, shift/caps lock, and return/enter key.
3. Review the formatting and keying of vertical and horizontal placement of centered text.
4. Review the formatting and keying of short reports.
5. Review the formatting and keying of columnar data.
6. Review the formatting and keying of block and modified block letter styles with open and mixed punctuation.

Word Processing Concepts Introduced in Unit 11

changing a centering problem into a tabulation
using a centering problem as a base for a short report

General Directions

Use 1" side margins, unless otherwise directed, for all lessons in this unit. SS sentences and drill lines. DS between repeated groups of lines. DS paragraph copy. Proofread and correct all problems.

LESSON 61

1" side margins

61a • Keyboard Review

5 minutes

Directions: Key each sentence three times SS. DS between 3-line groups.

alphabet Jim was very excited by that big, powerful Santa Cruz quake.

fig/sym All prices--except on Model 1927--will increase 5.6% June 4.

easy I asked them to print their names to the right of the title.

| 1 | 2 | 3 | 4 | 5 | 6 | 7 | 8 | 9 | 10 | 11 | 12 |

61b • Remove Unneeded Files from Directory

5 minutes

Remove files that are no longer needed from your directory.

LEAVE THESE FILES:

L21c1	L37c1	L39c1	L43c	L60c1
	L37c2	L39c2	L43d	
L24c3	L37c3	L39c3	L44d2	
L36c1	L38c1	L40b1	L52c3	
L36c2	L38c2	L40b2	L53c3	
		L40b3	L54d2	
			L59b3	

LESSON 24

1" side margins

7 minutes

24a • Keyboard Review

Directions: Key each line two times SS. DS between 2-line groups.

keep fingers curved; arms and wrists still

alphabet She entered the main office through the back door.
Judy now plans to take her driving quiz next week.

it it its city permit unit profit write either little

easy The world fuel crisis is a problem for most of us.

1 2 3 4 5 6 7 8 9 10

8 minutes

24b • Technique Builder

Directions: Key each line two times from dictation SS. DS between 2-line groups. Tap the return/enter key quickly at the end of each line.

1 and it|and it is|and it is the|and she|and she did

2 if it is|if it is the|if the duty is|if they do go

3 to do the|to do the work|and it did|and it did the

4 and it|and it is|and it is the|and she|and she did

5 she is|she is there|he is|he is there|she is there

6 we are|we are the|they are|they are the|we are the

7 you can|you can have|you have|you did|you did have

8 I will|I will|I will save|I will sign|I will spend

30 minutes

24c • Formatting Problems: Centering

Problem 1

Directions: **1.** Format 1" side margins with top and bottom margins to center the problem below DS on a full sheet of paper.

2. Use the automatic centering procedure according to the User's Manual for your software.

3. Label the problem with your name and problem number.

4. Proofread and correct all errors.

5. Save as **L24c1**.

6. Print the problem and give it to your teacher for grading.

7. Clear your screen so that you are ready to format and key the next problem.

Vertical Centering Calculation Review

Lines available 66
Less lines required .... __
Lines remaining .... __
Top margin .... __
Begin on line .... __

MORE NATIONAL HOCKEY LEAGUE TEAMS
Buffalo Sabres
Chicago Black Hawks
Edmonton Oilers
Los Angeles Kings
Montreal Canadiens
New York Islanders
Philadelphia Flyers
San Diego Sharks
Quebec Nordiques
Toronto Maple Leafs
Washington Capitals

LESSON 60

1" side margins

5 minutes

60a • Keyboard Review

Directions: Key each sentence three times SS. DS between 3-line groups.

key steadily; do not pause between letters or words

alphabet Jack expects to be in Quincy for a visit with Zelda Goodman.

fig/sym The 692 3/4 acres of land sold for more than $1,578 an acre.

easy Make sure that the fuel is kept where there will be no risk.

| 1 | 2 | 3 | 4 | 5 | 6 | 7 | 8 | 9 | 10 | 11 | 12 |

15 minutes

60b • Timed Writings

Directions: **1.** Take two 3' writings on all paragraphs. Figure *gwam*.
2. Take two 1' writings on each ¶; take the first for speed, the second for control.
3. Take another 3' writing on all the paragraphs. Figure *gwam*. Compare your *gwam* and number of errors on this writing to those of your first 3' writing.

all letters used 1.2 si word wrap

	gwam	3'
You may not know what one of our major pastimes is these	4	45
days. It's going shopping. You will be amazed to learn that	8	49
adults spend six hours a week looking for things to buy.	12	53
This is more time than they spend at work in the garden or in	16	56
a chair with a book. It is way ahead of golf or time with their	20	61
kids. Only those hours spent in front of the tube exceed those	24	65
that are devoted to shopping.	27	67
No one is quite sure why all this is true, but here are two	30	71
possible reasons. Some people shop when they are bored. Others	35	75
treat this activity as a sport, to see if they can't win out in a	39	80
contest with the stores.	41	82

gwam 3' | 1 | 2 | 3 | 4 |

25 minutes

60c • Formatting Personal-Business Letters

Problem 1 Changing from Modified Block Style to Block Style

Directions: **1.** Retrieve **L58c3**.
2. Delete spaces to change from modified block to block. Delete punctuation after the salutation and closing for open punctuation.
3. Change the mailing address and salutation to the ones below: Miss Jean Rousseau / Jewell Regional School / 134 Trenton Road / Lawton, OK 73501 / Dear Miss Rousseau /

Problem 2 Changing from Modified Block Style to Block Style

Directions: **1.** Retrieve **L58c1**.
2. Delete spaces to change from modified block to block. Delete punctuation after the salutation and closing for open punctuation.

24c, continued

Problem 2

Directions: Same as for Problem 1: save as **L24c2**.

```
INTRAMURAL SPORTS

   Volleyball
  Floor Hockey
 Indoor Soccer
   Badminton
   Basketball
     Tennis
    Baseball
    Softball
      Golf
   Wrestling
  Racquetball
 Cross Country
```

Problem 3

Directions: Same as for Problem 1: save as **L24c3**.

```
NAMES OF POLYGONS

       Octagon
       Hexagon
       Pentagon
    Quadrilateral
   Scalene Triangle
  Isosceles Triangle
 Equilateral Triangle
    Right Triangle
    Acute Triangle
   Obtuse Triangle
    Parallelogram
      Trapezoid
      Rectangle
       Rhombus
        Square
```

LESSON 25

1" side margins

7 minutes

25a • Keyboard Review

Directions: Key each line two times SS. DS between 2-line groups.

keep wrists low and still

alphabet
```
Your taxi driver avoided the biggest traffic jams.
He knew which plaza would be quiet at that moment.
```
he
```
he her here head help she when where neither other
```
easy
```
Eight chairs were left in this field by the girls.
```

| 1 | 2 | 3 | 4 | 5 | 6 | 7 | 8 | 9 | 10 |

10 minutes

25b • Timed Writings

Directions: Take two 3' writings on the ¶ below DS. Proofread for errors. Figure *gwam*. Submit the better writing.

all letters used 1.2 si — word wrap

	gwam 1'	3'	
It has been said that the only sure and safe way for people	12	4	30
to double their money is to fold it. While this remark was	24	8	34
likely made in jest, there is more than a little truth in it.	37	12	39
Before you decide where to invest the money you earned, give a	50	17	42
good deal of thought to the task. You may want to quiz an expert	63	21	47
in these matters. Money comes too hard for you to squander it in	76	25	52
the wrong place.	79	26	53

gwam 1' | 1 | 2 | 3 | 4 | 5 | 6 | 7 | 8 | 9 | 10 | 11 | 12 | 13 |
3' | 1 | 2 | 3 | 4 |

LESSON 59

1" side margins

5 minutes

59a • Keyboard Review

Directions: Key each sentence three times SS. DS between 3-line groups.

key with your fingers; keep wrists and arms still

alphabet Jeff expects to have two dozen big aprons made very quickly.

symbol Underline magazine titles (The Futurist, Vogue, and People).

easy Their problem was to enter the figures right the first time.

| 1 | 2 | 3 | 4 | 5 | 6 | 7 | 8 | 9 | 10 | 11 | 12 |

40 minutes

59b • Formatting Personal-Business Letters

Problem 1 Block Style, Open Punctuation

Directions: Format for side margins of 1 1/2". Begin return address on line 14.

416 Shady Oak Lane | Sandy, UT 84092 | Today's date |
Ms. Tina Zweig | Northwestern Historical Society | 886 Woodlawn Drive |
Medford, OR 97504

Dear Ms. Zweig

The social studies classes at Sandy Intermediate School will soon be studying the development of northwestern states from early exploration to statehood. Our teacher, Miss Komm, has suggested that you might have information we could use for a report that will be assigned as a part of this unit.

We are particularly interested in events and people of Utah, but we are willing to include a larger area if the events selected for study were typical of the whole region. Folklore about trappers and early settlers would also contribute to our overall presentation.

If you know and could recommend local residents as possible speakers to our classes, we would be pleased to invite them to contribute to our study.

We shall be grateful for any assistance you can give us.

Sincerely | (Your name)

Problem 2 Changing from Block Style to Modified Block Style

Directions: **1.** Retrieve **L56d1**.

2. Change the return address, the letter (inside) address, and salutation to those shown below.

3. Insert spaces to change from block to modified block, and add punctuation after the salutation and closing to get mixed punctuation.

2304 McRae Boulevard | Central Falls, RI 02863 | Today's date |
Mr. Milton Malley | 505 Burleigh Street | Northfield, NJ 08225 | Dear Mr. Malley:

Problem 3 Changing from Block Style to Modified Block Style

Directions: **1.** Retrieve **L59b1**.

2. Change to modified block style with mixed punctuation.

3. Leave the return address, but change the letter address to the following: Mrs. Halina Neumann / Mid-Atlantic Historical Society / 1841 Indian Trail Road / Milford, DE 19963 / Dear Mrs. Neumann: /

4. Change *northwestern* to *Mid-Atlantic*, *exploration* to *settlement*, *Utah* to *Delaware*, and delete *trappers and.*

28 minutes

25c • Formatting Problems: Centering

Problem 1

Directions: **1.** Review how to retrieve a file from your directory (Lesson 17).

2. Retrieve Lesson 24c, Problem 2 (**L24c2**).

3. Move the lines so that the sports are listed in alphabetical order. Maintain the DS. (Move the line and the blank line following it in one step to avoid losing the blank line.)

4. Change the problem identification to Lesson 25c, Problem 1.

5. Check for DS; save as **L25c1**.

6. Print and give to your teacher for grading.

INTRAMURAL SPORTS

Volleyball	Baseball
Floor Hockey	Softball
Indoor Soccer	Golf
Badminton	Wrestling
Basketball	Racquetball
Tennis	Cross Country

Vertical Centering Calculation Review
Lines available 66
Less lines required............__
Lines remaining ....__
Top margin.........................__
Begin on line ....__

Problem 2

Directions: **1.** Retrieve **L23c1**.

2. Place the cursor below the last line of the problem and import L24c1.

3. Delete the identification of L23c1 and the heading line of L24c1.

4. Recalculate to center this problem on a full sheet of paper.

5. Change identification to Lesson 25c, Problem 2.

6. Save as **L25c2** and print.

Problem 3

Directions: **1.** Retrieve **L25c2** if it is not on your monitor.

2. Move the lines so that they are now listed in alphabetical order according to the city name. When you select the line to move, also select the blank line below it to maintain the DS.

3. Check to see that the DS is used throughout the problem.

4. Change identification to Lesson 25c, Problem 3.

5. Save as **L25c3** and print.

IMPORT and **INTEGRATE** Import or integrate means to bring a saved file into the problem with which you are currently working. The original file remains unchanged as you will now use another file name for the problem.

58c, continued

Problem 2

Directions: **1.** Retrieve **L57d2**. Insert spaces to change from block style to modified block. Add punctuation to change from open punctuation to mixed punctuation. **2.** Change the mailing address and salutation to the following: Mrs. Linda Charles / Redmond Memorial School / 617 Thunderbird Road / Redmond, WA 98052 / Dear Mrs. Charles: **3.** Change *April* to *March*.

Problem 3 Modified Block Style, Mixed Punctuation

Directions: Use the same format as the model shown in L58c1, page 119.

1845 Rockside Road / Falls City, NE 68355 / Today's date / Mr. Thomas Karr / Wales Ferry School / 393 Brighton Avenue / McCook, NE 69001 / Dear Mr. Karr:

One part of our social studies class work is devoted to awareness of local and world-wide events as they happen. Each week the students use clues provided by the teacher to find articles about these events as reported in weekly news magazines. Students in each class are divided into teams and at the end of the week compete to provide correct answers to the questions posed by the teacher.

Would the students in your social studies classes be interested in competing against some of our students? We could arrange a series of three matches, to be held alternately in each school, to determine the winning team. Clues and questions would be written by teachers from both schools.

If your students are willing to pursue such competition, please let me know so our teacher, Mr. Main, can meet with you to make definite arrangements.

Yours truly,

(Your name)

Learning the Figure Keys (Lessons 26-30)

Learning Goals

1. Tap the figure keys by touch, using the correct fingers.
2. Increase basic skills by refining stroking and operating techniques and by keying a variety of drills and timed writings.

Word Processing Concept Introduced in Unit 4

removal of files from directory

General Directions

Use 1″ side margins for all lessons in this unit. SS sentences and drill lines. DS between repeated groups of lines. DS paragraph copy. Use the preset tab for paragraph indention.

LESSON 26

1" side margins

7 minutes

26a • Keyboard Review

Directions: Key each sentence two times SS. DS between 2-line groups.

quick down-and-in motion as you tap the space bar

alphabet
```
Place your new video camera in the giant size box.
I took quite a long time to find the eject button.
```
easy
```
He held both of his hands at just the right slant.
Lay all the keys there when she is done with them.
```
| 1 | 2 | 3 | 4 | 5 | 6 | 7 | 8 | 9 | 10 |

8 minutes

26b • Location of 1 and 7

Reach to 1

1. Find 1 on the chart.
2. Find it on your keyboard.
3. Place your fingers over the home keys.
4. Reach to 1 with the a finger.
5. Touch 1a lightly without moving other fingers from their home position.

Reach to 7

1. Find 7 on the chart.
2. Find it on your keyboard.
3. Place your fingers over the home keys.
4. Reach to 7 with the j finger.
5. Touch 7j lightly without moving other fingers from their home position.

```
a1a a1a a1a 1a 1a 1a a1a
```
Key twice on same line
```
j7j j7j j7j 7j 7j 7j j7j
```

30 minutes

58c • Formatting Personal-Business Letters

Modified Block Style Letter with Mixed Punctuation

Review format for personal notes in *modified block style* where the date and complimentary close lines began at the center of the line of writing (51 for 12-pitch and 42 for 10-pitch). A personal-business letter is formatted in the same manner, with the return address placed on the two lines above the date and the inside address placed above the salutation. The beginning lines of the paragraphs may be blocked or indented to the preset tab.

Mixed punctuation indicates that a colon will follow the salutation and a comma will follow the closing.

Problem 1 Model of Modified Block Letter; Mixed Punctuation

Directions: Format for side margins of 1 1/2". Begin return address on line 14. Set a tab at the center of the line of writing.

Return Address: 226 Harmony Road | College Place, WA 99324 | Today's date |

Letter Address: Miss Janet Pryce | 1764 Jules Avenue | Silver City, NM 88061

Dear Miss Pryce:

Your questions about how a letter in modified block style is different from a letter in block style are good ones.

All lines (the return address and the date lines, the inside address and salutation, all paragraphs, and the closing lines) begin at the left margin in a block letter.

A letter in modified block style moves the placement of two items--the lines for the return address and date begin at the center of the line of writing. The tab at center is also used to begin the closing and signature lines.

Although the block style is faster to produce, as there are no tabs, some writers prefer the appearance of the modified block style.

Thank you for your inquiry. If I can be of further assistance, please let me know.

Sincerely, | (Your name)

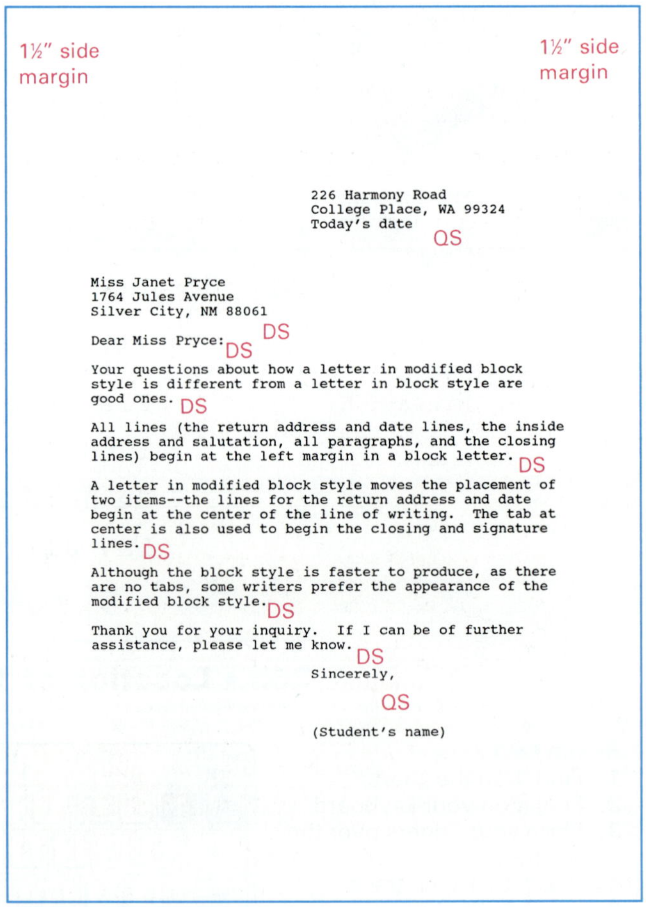
1½" side margin

1½" side margin

226 Harmony Road
College Place, WA 99324
Today's date
QS

Miss Janet Pryce
1764 Jules Avenue
Silver City, NM 88061
DS
Dear Miss Pryce:
DS
Your questions about how a letter in modified block style is different from a letter in block style are good ones.
DS
All lines (the return address and date lines, the inside address and salutation, all paragraphs, and the closing lines) begin at the left margin in a block letter.
DS
A letter in modified block style moves the placement of two items--the lines for the return address and date begin at the center of the line of writing. The tab at center is also used to begin the closing and signature lines.
DS
Although the block style is faster to produce, as there are no tabs, some writers prefer the appearance of the modified block style.
DS
Thank you for your inquiry. If I can be of further assistance, please let me know.
DS
Sincerely,
QS
(Student's name)

12 minutes

26c • Location Drills 1 and 7

Directions: Key each line two times SS. DS between 2-line groups.

Reach to 1

Reach to 7

1
```
ala ala ala la la la 11 aims, 11 aides, 11 and 111
Kay drove 111.1 miles.  Hire 11 boys and 11 girls.
```

7
```
j7j j7j j7j 7j 7j 7j 77 jobs, 777 jars, 77 and 777
I bought 77 books.  See page 777.  All 7,777 came.
```

number fluency
```
After 17 days at sea they docked on June 17, 1777.
Our firm sold 1,717 new cars and 1,177 new trucks.
```

| 1 | 2 | 3 | 4 | 5 | 6 | 7 | 8 | 9 | 10 |

26d • Technique Builder

6 minutes

Directions: Key each line two times SS. DS between 2-line groups.

key with flowing rhythm

1 and I|and go|and look|and grade|and limp|and right

2 to jump|to show|to start|to save|to have|to regard

3 the fee|the boy|the man|the date|the rest|the time

4 of their|of this|of that|of them|of facts|of great

5 did do|did go|did draw|did join|did extra|did link

12 minutes

26e • Continuity Practice

Directions: Key both ¶s DS. Proofread for errors. Repeat each ¶. Try to make no more than four errors per writing.

all letters used 1.1 si word wrap

keep your eyes on the copy

	gwam 1'	3'
Each time that you sit down to key, take a second or so to	12	4
decide just what it is you want to do. Your goal may be to	24	8
improve your stroking speed, or it may be to make fewer errors	37	12
than you made the last time.	43	14
One thing we know for sure is that you will do your best if	12	18
you work on only one skill at a time. It is quite hard to make	25	23
your fingers fly and still have all the words come out right.	38	27
When you zip along, you can expect to make a few mistakes.	50	31

gwam 1' | 1 | 2 | 3 | 4 | 5 | 6 | 7 | 8 | 9 | 10 | 11 | 12 | 13 |
3' | 1 | 2 | 3 | 4 |

30 minutes

57d • Formatting Personal-Business Letters

Problem 1

Directions: **1.** Retrieve **L50c3**. Add the following return address and sending address to change into a letter: 1710 Delmonico Avenue/Canoga Park, CA 91304/Mr. Paul Grissom/41 Ferguson Drive/Kenosha, WI 53142

2. Change format so that the margins are 1 1/2"; the return address begins on line 14.

Problem 2

Directions: Format for side margins of 1 1/2"; begin return address on line 14.

1010 Conklin Avenue | Sherwood, AR 72116 | Today's date | Mr. Cesar Butler | Maitland Memorial School | 432 Stillwater Avenue | Maitland, FL 32751 | Dear Mr. Butler |

Our school's music club is interested in participating in the Music Festival being held at Maitland Memorial School next April. We have been to festivals within our area, but we have not been away overnight.

What housing facilities are available near your school that we might use during the festival? We would need housing for about thirty students and three chaperons. Is there a choice of nearby restaurants for inexpensive meals? As we will charter a bus, it will be available for moving the group between the housing and the school for practices and performance; and we will not need public transportation.

What is available for relaxation and entertainment for our group during unscheduled time?

Answers to these questions will help us decide about attending the festival and whether we can make definite plans for our group's travel to Maitland.

Cordially yours | (Your name)

LESSON 58

1" side margins

5 minutes

58a • Keyboard Review

Directions: Key each sentence three times SS. DS between 3-line groups.

alphabet Val Gumis will quickly explain the fire hazards on this job.

fig/sym Megan keyed a 5-minute writing on page 76 with 98% accuracy.

easy The right angle to use in solving problems is the try angle.

| 1 | 2 | 3 | 4 | 5 | 6 | 7 | 8 | 9 | 10 | 11 | 12 |

10 minutes

58b • Paragraph Guided Writings

Directions: **1.** Take a 1' writing on the ¶ below. Note the last word you keyed; make this your goal word.

2. Take three 1' writings on the ¶. Try to reach your goal word as time is called. Key no faster or slower than it takes to reach your goal word.

3. Raise your goal by four words. Take three additional 1' writings. Try to reach your new goal as time is called.

all letters used 1.2 si — word wrap

One major use of the computer can be found in the world of art. With its help experts can now analyze all the layers of paint that a finished work might contain. It can give to them in an instant details that once would have required years to find.

LESSON 27

1" side margins

7 minutes

27a • Keyboard Review

Directions: Key each line two times SS. DS between 2-line groups.

keep arms and wrists quiet

alphabet You see best if you tilt the screen exactly right.
Pat vowed to make her quota for that zone by June.

1 ala ala la la la 11 and 111, add 11 and 11, age 11

7 j7j j7j 7j 7j 717 units, 77 jobs, 77 and 77 and 17

easy Make sure you sign your name on both of the forms.

| 1 | 2 | 3 | 4 | 5 | 6 | 7 | 8 | 9 | 10 |

8 minutes

27b • Location of 5 and 9

Reach to 5

1. Find 5 on the chart.
2. Find it on your keyboard.
3. Place your fingers over the home keys.
4. Reach to 5 with the f finger.
5. Touch 5f lightly without moving other fingers from their home position.

Reach to 9

1. Find 9 on the chart.
2. Find it on your keyboard.
3. Place your fingers over the home keys.
4. Reach to 9 with the l finger.
5. Touch 9l lightly without moving other fingers from their home position.

f5f f5f f5f 5f 5f 5f f5f   Key twice on same line   l9l l9l l9l 9l 9l 9l l9l

12 minutes

27c • Location Drills 5 and 9

Directions: Key each line two times SS. DS between 2-line groups.

Reach to 5

5 f5f f5f f5f 5f 5f 5f 551 feet, 55 firms, 55 and 55
Send 555 pens. We won 155 games. Build 515 sets.

9 l9l l9l l9l 9l 9l 9l 99 lines, 919 lots, 99 and 99
Use all 99. I fell 19 feet. He sold 919 in 1991.

Reach to 9

27d • Continuity Practice

6 minutes

Directions: Key the ¶ as many times as you can in the time allotted.

1.0 si   word wrap   words

The world of high tech has great news for those who do not 12
spell as well as they should. Software can now be used to help 25
them catch words they miss. 30

| 1 | 2 | 3 | 4 | 5 | 6 | 7 | 8 | 9 | 10 | 11 | 12 | 13 |

56e, continued

Personal-business letters are folded and inserted into large envelopes (No. 10 or 9 1/2" x 4 1/8" in size) for mailing.

FOLDING LETTERS FOR LARGE ENVELOPES

Step 1—Fold from bottom to top, making the fold slightly less than one third the length of the sheet.

Step 2—Fold the top down to within one half inch of the bottom fold.

Step 3—Insert the letter into the envelope with the last crease toward the bottom of the envelope and with the last fold up.

LESSON 57

1" side margins

57a • Keyboard Review

5 minutes

space quickly with down-and-in motion of thumb

Directions: Key each sentence three times SS. DS between 3-line groups.

alphabet Rex Fuji positively warned us smoking can be quite a hazard.

fig/sym Use their 800 number and order The Company We Keep ($12.95).

easy All of the big towns are right there at the end of the lake.

| 1 | 2 | 3 | 4 | 5 | 6 | 7 | 8 | 9 | 10 | 11 | 12 |

57b • Language Arts Skills: Keying from Dictation and Spelling Checkup

5 minutes

Directions: **1.** Your teacher will dictate the words in 56b, page 114. Key the words from dictation.

2. Check your work for correct spelling. Rekey any words in which you made an error.

57c • Continuity Practice from Rough Draft Copy

5 minutes

Directions: Key the ¶ at least two times DS. Make corrections as you work.

all letters used 1.2 si word wrap

words

While hightech has equiped us with tools to han dle many 12
tough jobs it has caused a few porblems too. For one one thing, 24
it gives us informatoin faster than wecan utilize it. machines 37
have done what the can do, we have been taxed to keep up wiht 50
them. 51

12 minutes

27e • Sentence Guided Writings

Directions: **1.** Take a 1' writing on each sentence with the call of the guide each 20". Try to complete each sentence as the guide is called. **2.** Take two 1' writings on the last sentence without the call of the guide.

		words in line	gwam 20"
1	Our roads can be safe for all.	6	18
2	*If you drive, learn the rules.*	6	18
3	Be sure your car is in good repair.	7	21
4	*Have your brakes and tires checked.*	7	21
5	Keep to your right and pass on the left.	8	24
6	*Slow down a bit when you drive at night.*	8	24
7	Wear a seatbelt when you are in a moving car.	9	27
8	*Never use your brakes when you are in a skid.*	9	27
9	Glance into the rearview mirror every ten seconds.	10	30
10	*Turn on the headlights so you can see and be seen.*	10	30
11	If you do not drive a car, pass these rules along.	10	30
12	*They can help others make our roads a safer place.*	10	30

LESSON 28

1" side margins

7 minutes

28a • Keyboard Review

Directions: Key each line two times SS. DS between 2-line groups.

keep eyes on copy

alphabet	Most all kids love to spend time down at the mall.
	Jacques bought pizza mix for that party last week.
1,7	Amy will be 17 on May 17. She lives at 7177 Pine.
easy	Turn right when you come to the end of that block.
	1 2 3 4 5 6 7 8 9 10

56d, continued

Return address: 162 Golf Links Road | Mount Rainier, MD 20712 | May 6, 19--

Recipient's address: Miss Shani Jenkins | 4317 Addison Avenue | Beacon, NY 12508

Dear Miss Jenkins

Our class is completing a unit on "Wildlife in the United States." We are disturbed to learn that several animals are on the list of endangered species and that, unless action is taken soon, they may become extinct.

We understand that you have been active in bringing this information to the public's attention.

Would you please send some suggestions that our class could use to inform the student body of this crisis. We are also interested in materials for posters that we could place in the school, but we would welcome any updated information that would add to what we have already learned.

Thank you for any assistance and information you can give us. All materials should be sent to me at the above address.

Sincerely | (Your name)

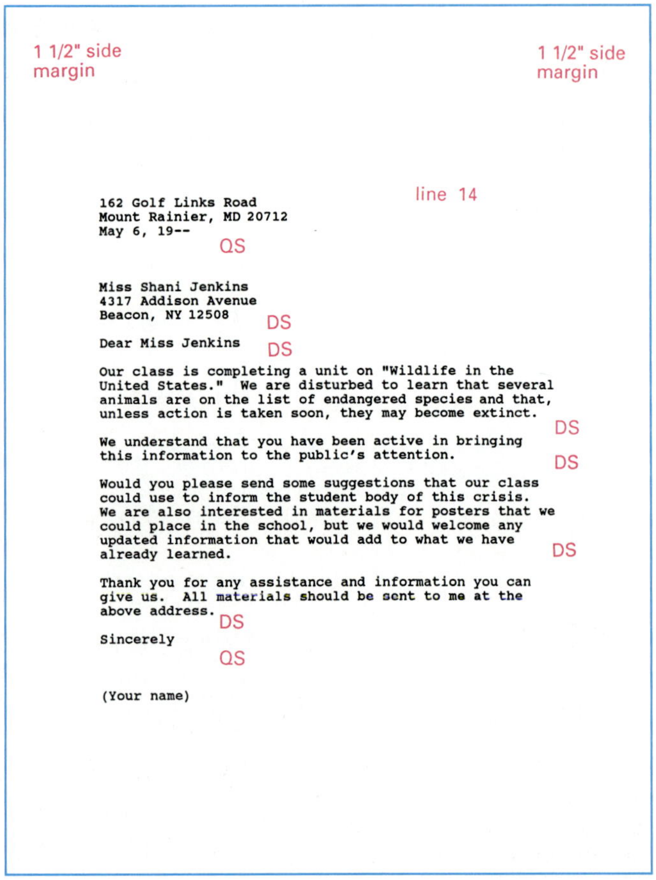

162 Golf Links Road
Mount Rainier, MD 20712
May 6, 19--

Miss Shani Jenkins
4317 Addison Avenue
Beacon, NY 12508

Dear Miss Jenkins

Our class is completing a unit on "Wildlife in the United States." We are disturbed to learn that several animals are on the list of endangered species and that, unless action is taken soon, they may become extinct.

We understand that you have been active in bringing this information to the public's attention.

Would you please send some suggestions that our class could use to inform the student body of this crisis. We are also interested in materials for posters that we could place in the school, but we would welcome any updated information that would add to what we have already learned.

Thank you for any assistance and information you can give us. All materials should be sent to me at the above address.

Sincerely

(Your name)

Problem 2

Directions: Retrieve **L46d1** and add the underlined portions to change a personal note into a letter. (Format on a full sheet with side margins of 1 1/2". Begin return address on line 14, and sign your name below the complimentary close.)

<u>8418 Cannon Road</u>
<u>Bettendorf, IA 52722</u>
October 1, 19--

<u>Miss Susan Parish</u>
<u>34 Greenleaf Terrace</u>
<u>Old Town, ME 04468</u>

5 minutes

56e • Folding Personal-Business Letters for Large Envelopes

Directions: Fold at least one letter keyed in L56d for insertion into a large envelope, following the steps in the diagram on page 117.

(continued on next page)

8 minutes

28b • Technique Builder

Directions: Key each line three times from dictation SS. DS between 3-line groups.

key smoothly; do not pause between phrases

```
1 of this|of this|of these|of these|of your|of their
2 to be|to be|to have|to have|to them|to them|to our
3 for the|for this|for that|for them|for your|for it
4 are in|are in|are for|are for|are on|are on|are at
5 in our|in our|in his|in his|in her|in her|in which
6 and it|and it|and it will|and it will|and it would
7 is not|is not|is not the|is not the|is not the one
```

8 minutes

28c • Location of 4, 8, and : (colon)

Reach to 4

1. Find **4** on the chart.
2. Find it on your keyboard.
3. Place your fingers over the home keys.
4. Reach to **4** with the **f** finger.
5. Touch **4f** lightly without moving other fingers from their home position.

Reach to 8

1. Find **8** on the chart.
2. Find it on your keyboard.
3. Place your fingers over the home keys.
4. Reach to **8** with the **k** finger.
5. Touch **8k** lightly without moving other fingers from their home position.

`f4f f4f f4f 4f 4f 4f f4f` Key twice on same line `k8k k8k k8k 8k 8k 8k k8k`

> The : is the shift of the ;. Touch ;:; three times. Space twice after : used as punctuation.

12 minutes

28d • Location Drills 4, 8, and : (colon)

Directions: Key each line two times SS. DS between 2-line groups.

Reach to 4

Reach to 8

```
4  f4f f4f f4f 4f 4f 4f 44 fans, 414 fins, 4,414 feet
   We saw 44 ships.  Divide by 414.  I sold 144 more.

8  k8k k8k k8k 8k 8k 8k 88 keys, 18 kites, 8,188 ties
   They ran 818 yards.  Ask for 88.  Leave on May 18.

:  ;:; ;:; :; :; Note:  To:  From:  Dear Mrs. Browne:
   She said:  I want these four:  Send the following:

number fluency
   It read as follows:  Ship all 418 to 159th Street.
   On June 18, 1989, we drew 45,179 fans to the game.
   | 1 | 2 | 3 | 4 | 5 | 6 | 7 | 8 | 9 | 10 |
```

10 minutes

56c • Timed Writings

Directions: 1. Take two 1' writings on each ¶; take the first for speed, the second for control.

2. Take a 3' writing on the ¶s below. Figure *gwam*. Compare the *gwam* and number of errors on the 1' writings with your 3' writing.

all letters used 1.2 si word wrap

	gwam 3'	
Inventors the world over are hard at work churning out all	4	45
kinds of gizmos they think will improve the way we live. Their	8	49
goal is to help us save time, effort, or money.	11	52
We have been told for years that we will soon be talking on	15	56
video phones and going to work by air. Robots will take care of	20	60
the housework, they say. Some products succeed, of course, while	24	65
quite a few do not.	25	66
Take the picture phone, for example. Think what that will do	29	70
to your telephone habits. You might not answer so quickly as you	34	75
used to. You may want to let it ring several times so you can	38	79
adjust your tie or fix your hair first.	41	82

gwam 3' | 1 | 2 | 3 | 4 |

20 minutes

56d • Formatting Personal-Business Letters

Block Style Letter with Open Punctuation

Review the format for a *block style* personal note with *open punctuation*, in which all lines begin at the left margin. The beginning lines of paragraphs are blocked. There are no marks of punctuation following the salutation and complimentary close.

Spaces Between State Abbreviations and ZIP Codes

Use the 2-letter state abbreviations that are preferred by the U.S. Postal Service, followed by one space and the ZIP Code. The 5-numeral ZIP Code divides the United States into geographic areas, the areas into sectional centers, and the centers into delivery zones. The recently added 4-numeral code divides the zone into sectors and the sectors into delivery routes. Individuals generally use the 5-digit ZIP, while companies with large mailings are encouraged to use the expanded 9-digit code.

Problem 1 Model of a Block Letter with Open Punctuation

Directions: Format for side margins of 1 1/2". Begin return address (sender's address) on line 14. Key the model letter shown on page 116.

10 minutes

28e • Paragraph Skill Builder

Directions: Key the ¶ once for practice; then take three 1' writings on it. Figure *gwam* on the best writing.

all letters used 1.1 si word wrap words

When you see a new word in print, try to guess what it means. 13
The way it is used in the sentence should give you a quick hint. 26
To find the exact meaning, though, you will need to look it up. 39
Then seize the chance to put your new word to work on the job 51
when you speak or write. 56

| 1 | 2 | 3 | 4 | 5 | 6 | 7 | 8 | 9 | 10 | 11 | 12 | 13 |

LESSON 29

1" side margins

7 minutes

29a • Keyboard Review

Directions: Key each sentence two times SS. DS between 2-line groups.

sit erect; keep your eyes on the copy

alphabet A fine text can equip you with good verbal skills.
Jud seized the chance to show me what he could do.

: colon Use the colon to show time: 7:15, 8:15, and 9:15.

easy The girls are just the right height for the chair.

| 1 | 2 | 3 | 4 | 5 | 6 | 7 | 8 | 9 | 10 |

5 minutes

29b • Location of 2 and 0 (zero)

Reach to 2
1. Find **2** on the chart.
2. Find it on your keyboard.
3. Place your fingers over the home keys.
4. Reach to **2** with the **s** finger.
5. Touch **2s** lightly without moving other fingers from their home position.

Reach to 0 (zero)
1. Find **0** on the chart.
2. Find it on your keyboard.
3. Place your fingers over the home keys.
4. Reach to **0** with the **;** finger.
5. Touch **0;** lightly without moving other fingers from their home position.

s2s s2s s2s 2s 2s 2s s2s Key twice on same line ;0; ;0; ;0; 0; 0; 0; ;0;

Formatting and Keying Personal-Business Letters (Lessons 56-60)

UNIT

Learning Goals

1. Further the development of basic keying techniques.
2. Further the development of basic keying skills.
3. Continue to improve language arts skills.
4. Continue to develop appropriate related understandings and skills.
5. Format and key personal-business letters in block and modified block style and with open and mixed punctuation.

Word Processing Concepts Introduced in Unit 10

changing a personal note into a personal-business letter
changing letter styles by using insert and delete

General Directions

Use 1" side margins for all lessons in this unit unless otherwise directed. SS sentences and drill lines. DS between repeated groups of lines. DS paragraph copy for timed writings.

LESSON 56

1" side margins

5 minutes

56a • Keyboard Review

Directions: Key each sentence three times SS. DS between 3-line groups.

keep wrists low and still

alphabet Jake Hooper was not fazed by required large volume tax cuts.

fig/sym Key distances in figures: We drove 695 miles in 1 3/4 days.

easy They said she should get a bid from more than one rock band.

| 1 | 2 | 3 | 4 | 5 | 6 | 7 | 8 | 9 | 10 | 11 | 12 |

5 minutes

56b • Language Arts Skills: Spelling and Proofreading Aid

Directions: Key each line three times SS. Carefully study the spelling of each word as you key it.

keep fingers deeply curved

1 remittance laboratory signature proposal eligible sufficient

2 via cooperate analysis definite capacity develop commitments

3 tremendous beautiful essential consequently survey recommend

Reach to 2

29c • Location Drills: 2 and 0 (zero) 7 minutes

Directions: Key each line two times SS. DS between 2-line groups.

```
   s2s s2s s2s 2s 2s 2s 22 sales, 212 sets, 122 steps
2  He is 22.  I am 21.  On May 22 we drove 212 miles.
   ;0; ;0; ;0; 0; 0; 0; 200 pets, 100 pens, 900 tons.
0  Each number ends with a zero: 10, 20, 40, and 50.
```

Reach to 0

29d • Technique Builder 5 minutes

Directions: Key each line three times from dictation SS. DS between 3-line groups. Do not pause between phrases.

```
1  and the sets|and the seats|and the ink|and the oil
2  if they were|if they look|if they bet|if they give
3  for the rest|for the inn|for the cats|for the pups
```

11 minutes

29e • Removing Unnecessary Files from the Directory

REMOVING UNNECESSARY FILES It is neither necessary nor wise to keep all the listed files in your directory. Too much space is used for data that you may no longer need and your directory becomes difficult to read. One important task for the operator is to remove files for which there is no longer a need. Be careful to remove only what you are really finished with, or you may find yourself rekeying the data.

Check the directions in the User's Manual for your software to learn how to remove files from your directory. Remove only the following files: **Les1** through **Les25**. **DO NOT** remove any problems (L21c1 through L25c4) as some of them will be retrieved and used later.

10 minutes

29f • Continuity Practice

Directions: Key both ¶s DS. Proofread for errors. Repeat the paragraphs. Try to make no more than four errors per writing.

keep elbows in; feet flat on floor

all letters used 1.2 si word wrap	*gwam* 1'	3'	
The ways in which quite a few men and women work have changed	12	4	29
in the past ten years. Hours are getting shorter. Use of	24	8	33
flextime has increased. Job sharing does not seem to occur	36	12	37
often.	37	12	37
More and more of our citizens are now working at home. In a	12	16	41
large number of cases, two persons from the same household do	24	20	45
this. With an office at home, they do not face the stress of	36	24	49
commuting.	38	25	50

gwam 1' | 1 | 2 | 3 | 4 | 5 | 6 | 7 | 8 | 9 | 10 | 11 | 12 | 13 |
3' | 1 | 2 | 3 | 4 |

55c, continued

Problem 2

Directions: Retrieve **L52c3**. Change the title as marked, then change the information in the second column. Finally, arrange the states in chronological order according to date of admission to the Union. Save as **L55c2**.

~~STATE NICKNAMES~~ DATES OF ADMISSION TO THE UNION

Louisiana	~~Pelican State~~ April 30, 1812
Pennsylvania	~~Keystone State~~ December 12, 1787
Idaho	~~Gem State~~ July 3, 1890
Utah	~~Beehive State~~ January 4, 1896
Montana	~~Treasure State~~ November 8, 1889

Problem 3

Directions: Retrieve **L55c2**. Add the following states and their dates of admission to the union. Arrange in chronological order when all information has been keyed.

Nevada	October 31, 1864
Delaware	December 7, 1787
California	September 9, 1850
Indiana	December 11, 1816
Alaska	January 3, 1959
Hawaii	August 21, 1959
Georgia	January 2, 1788
West Virginia	June 20, 1863
Wisconsin	May 29, 1848

Problem 4

Directions: Retrieve **L54d3** and add these states. Do not change spacing or tabs.

Maine	ME	Utah	UT
Maryland	MD	Vermont	VT
Massachusetts	MA	Virginia	VA
Michigan	MI	Washington	WA
Minnesota	MN	West Virginia	WV
Mississippi	MS	Wisconsin	WI
Missouri	MO	Wyoming	WY

LESSON 30

1" side margins

7 minutes

30a • Keyboard Review

Directions: Key each line two times SS. DS between 2-line groups.

alphabet She quizzed me on the value of certain junk bonds.
Be sure to put the wax on your skis before you go.

2 s2s s2s 2s 2s 22 sets, 221 slides, 22 or 222 suits

0 ;0; ;0; 0; 0; 10 pans, 101 plans, 10 or 100 plants

easy More than half of the men here paid their own way.

| 1 | 2 | 3 | 4 | 5 | 6 | 7 | 8 | 9 | 10 |

5 minutes

30b • Location of 3 and 6

Reach to 3

1. Find 3 on the chart.
2. Find it on your keyboard.
3. Place your fingers over the home keys.
4. Reach to 3 with the d finger.
5. Touch 3d lightly without moving other fingers from their home position.

Reach to 6

1. Find 6 on the chart.
2. Find it on your keyboard.
3. Place your fingers over the home keys.
4. Reach to 6 with the j finger.
5. Touch 6j lightly without moving other fingers from their home position.

d3d d3d d3d 3d 3d 3d d3d   Key twice on same line   j6j j6j j6j 6j 6j 6j j6j

9 minutes

30c • Location Drills: 3 and 6

Reach to 3

Reach to 6

Directions: Key each line two times SS. DS between 2-line groups.

3 d3d d3d d3d 3d 3d 3d 33 days, 333 hours, 33 and 33
Give us 333 feet. Take 3,333 gallons. I have 33.

6 j6j j6j j6j 6j 6j 6j 66 jolts, 66,666 jets, 6 or 6
I weigh 66 pounds. Send 666 now. Collect 66 now.

number fluency

We won our games 57 to 46, 48 to 39, and 31 to 20.
Flight 7658 landed at 12:49, just 30 minutes late.

In 1993 she sold 452 cans of pop and 396 hot dogs.
He called three new numbers: 823, 946, and 1,705.

| 1 | 2 | 3 | 4 | 5 | 6 | 7 | 8 | 9 | 10 |

LESSON 55

1" side margins

5 minutes

55a • Keyboard Review

Directions: Key each sentence three times SS. DS between 3-line groups.

use quick, sharp, tapping strokes

alphabet Have Fred explain why he objects to making up the last quiz.

fig/sym "Mike's address is 2874 North Alamar Avenue," replied Cindy.

easy Most of the tires on the bus are worn down and out of shape.

| 1 | 2 | 3 | 4 | 5 | 6 | 7 | 8 | 9 | 10 | 11 | 12 |

10 minutes

55b • Timed Writings

Directions: Key two 3' writings on 53b, page 108. Figure *gwam*. Submit the better of the two writings.

30 minutes

55c • Formatting Problems: Multiple-Column Tables

Problem 1

Directions: Four Current Events Matches have been held. Retrieve **L54d1** and record the scores for Week 4, calculating new totals. Arrange the teams according to scores, and indicate the winning team by enhancing the line in **bold** print.

BOLD TEXT The bold feature emphasizes text by printing characters darker than others. This bold effect is created when the printer strikes each designated character twice. Turn on the bold command by tapping the assigned key or keystroke combination (such as *the F6 or the Code and b keys*). Key the text to be printed in bold, which may appear highlighted on the screen. Turn off the bold command by tapping the same key or keystroke combination used to turn it on.

CURRENT EVENTS TEAM SCORES

	Old Score	Week ~~3~~ 4	New Score
Orange Team	~~400~~ 590	~~190~~ 100	
Purple Team	~~280~~ 420	~~140~~ 200	
Red Team	~~280~~ 490	~~210~~ 180	
Blue Team	~~270~~ 420	~~150~~ 210	
Green Team	~~270~~ 410	~~140~~ 190	

10 minutes

30d • Paragraph Skill Builder

Directions: Key the ¶ once for practice; then take three 1' writings on it. Figure *gwam* on the best writing.

all letters used 1.2 si word wrap

One of the big jobs that faces all of us as citizens is how to take good care of our present energy sources. There is a lot of air, sun, and water, for example, but their quality is now at risk. What we need to do is make better use of what we have.

14 minutes

30e • Sentence Guided Writings

Directions: Key each sentence for a 1' writing with the call of the guide each 20". Try to complete each sentence as the guide is called.

		words in line	*gwam* 20"
1	Alex will be 17 on October 17.	6	18
2	We had 17 copies of Volume 71.	6	18
3	See pages 59 to 95 for more advice.	7	21
4	Mark ran for only 59 yards, not 95.	7	21
5	Notice: do not confuse items 48 and 84.	8	24
6	Two groups of 48 add up to more than 84.	8	24
7	Their last trip took 20 hours and 20 minutes.	9	27
8	Jo put down .20 when it should have been .02.	9	27
9	Martha is just 36 years old, but her mother is 63.	10	30
10	If you have two sets of 33, your total will be 66.	10	30

27 minutes

54d • Formatting Problems: Multiple-Column Tables

Problem 1

Directions: Retrieve **L53c2** and make the changes marked. Calculate the New Scores by adding the Old Score to the points earned in Week 3. Save as **L54d1**.

CURRENT EVENTS TEAM SCORES

	Old Score	Week ~~2~~ 3	New Score
Orange Team	~~220~~ 400	~~180~~ 190	
Purple Team	~~160~~ 280	~~120~~ 140	
Red Team	~~120~~ 280	~~160~~ 210	
Blue Team	~~210~~ 270	~~60~~ 150	
Green Team	~~90~~ 270	~~180~~ 140	

Problem 2

Directions: Format on a full sheet DS. Leave 12 spaces between columns. Save as **L54d2**.

NATIONAL OBSERVATION DATES

Citizenship Day	September 17
United Nations Day	October 24
National Freedom Day	February 1
Loyalty Day	May 1
Wright Brothers Day	December 17
Forefathers' Day	December 21

Problem 3

Directions: Retrieve **L52c4** and add these states. Do not change spacing or tabs. Save as **L54d3**.

Illinois	IL	Pennsylvania	PA
Indiana	IN	Rhode Island	RI
Iowa	IA	South Carolina	SC
Kansas	KS	South Dakota	SD
Kentucky	KY	Tennessee	TN
Louisiana	LA	Texas	TX

Learning the Basic Symbol Keys (Lessons 31-35)

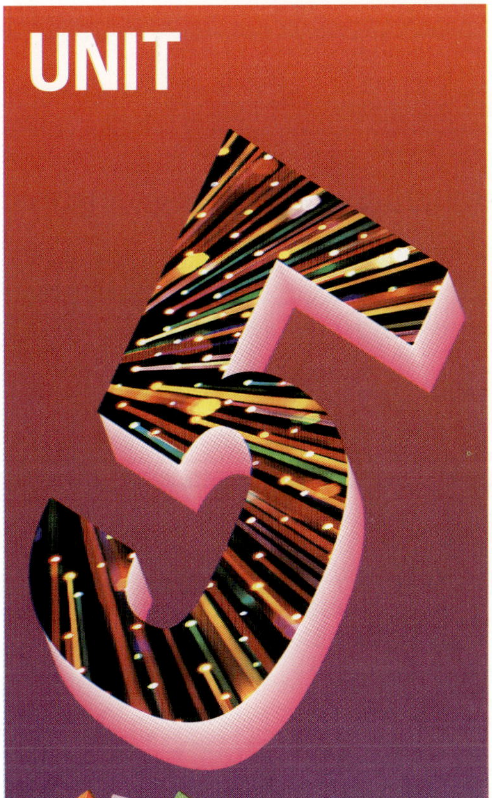

Learning Goals

1. Tap the symbol keys by touch, using correct fingering.
2. Space correctly after punctuation marks and symbols.
3. Learn to use the search and replace function of word processing.
4. Learn to correct rough draft material using two proofreader's marks.
5. Improve basic skills by further refinement of stroking and operating techniques and by continued practice of skill-building drills and timed writings.

Word Processing Concepts Introduced in Unit 5

automatic underline	insert
character string	proofreader's marks
delete	search and replace

General Directions

Use 1" side margins for all lessons in this unit. SS sentences and drill lines. DS between repeated groups of lines. DS paragraph copy if your software permits. Use the preset tab for paragraph indentions.

LESSON 31

1" side margins

5 minutes

31a • Keyboard Review

Directions: Key each sentence two times SS. DS between 2-line groups.

alphabet	Jenny loved to quote wild, crazy things from textbook pages.
figures	More than 350 kids from 14 schools competed here on June 26.
easy	I know that she told them to sit down in their usual chairs.
	I 1 I 2 I 3 I 4 I 5 I 6 I 7 I 8 I 9 I 10 I 11 I 12 I

5 minutes

31b • Location of $ (dollar), # (number or pounds), and / (diagonal)

Reach to $ (dollar sign)
1. Shift, then reach up to $ with the **f** finger.
2. Touch **$f** lightly without moving other fingers from their home position.

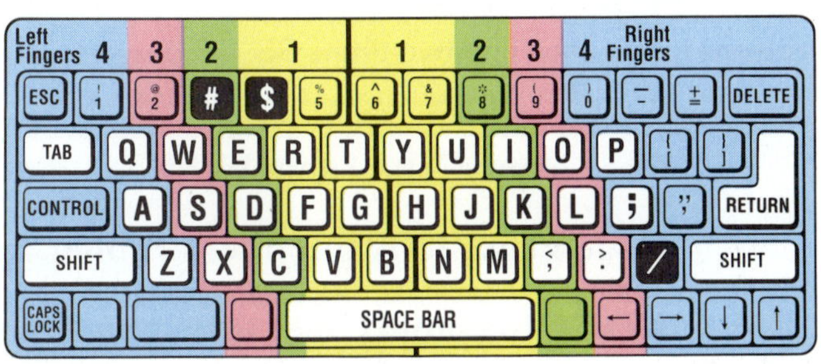

Reach to # (number sign)
1. Shift, then reach up to # with the **d** finger.
2. Touch **#d** lightly without moving other fingers from their home position.

f4f f$f f4f f$f $f $f $4

Key twice on same line

d3d d#d d3d d#d #d #d #3

LESSON 54

1" side margins

5 minutes

54a • Keyboard Review

Directions: Key each sentence three times SS. DS between 3-line groups.

alphabet Major taxes have clearly penalized quite a few bigger banks.

fig/sym Lot prices varied more than $765 during the years 1993-1994.

easy The profit you can make depends on both labor and materials.

8 minutes

54b • Speed Ladder Sentences

Directions: **1.** Take 1' writings on each sentence. Try to key each sentence four times within the minute.
2. Your instructor will call the return each 15 seconds to guide you.
3. The rate increases four words a minute with each succeeding sentence.

keep your eyes on the copy

		gwam 15"	words
1	Sit up as you key these words.	24	6
2	Your goal is to complete this line.	28	7
3	Keep your eyes on the copy in your book.	32	8
4	See if you can add some more words each time.	36	9
5	Tap the return key quickly as the guide is called.	40	10

5 minutes

54c • Technique Builder

Directions: Key each line two times SS. DS between 2-line groups.

1 three happy jetty room bill week inn message sleep mood well

2 issue guess look good less rubber apply proof speed too free

3 buzz allow apply feel fall soon funny offer muzzle add bluff

31b, continued

Reach to / (diagonal)
1. Reach down to / with the ; finger.
2. Touch /; lightly without moving other fingers from their home position.

;/; ;?; ;/; ;?; ;/ /; ;/

Reach to /

Reach to $

Reach to #

31c • Location Drills $, #, and / 10 minutes

Directions: Key each line two times SS. DS between 2-line groups.

Note: Do not space between $, #, or / and a figure.

$ Their four lunches cost them $4.25, $4.55, $4.75, and $4.95.
\# She wrote 33 pounds as 33#. Number 134 can be written #134.
/ Use the / to make fractions, as 1/3, 1/5, 1/8, 11/16, 15/16.

| 1 | 2 | 3 | 4 | 5 | 6 | 7 | 8 | 9 | 10 | 11 | 12 |

31d • Comparison Sentence Skill Builder 10 minutes

Directions: Key two 1' writings on each sentence SS. Compare rates on the three sentences.

easy Six of the eight girls signed both forms with the right pen.
fig/sym Our store priced Item #4685 at $37.50 beginning on 12/30/94.
shift Winners are Rod Monroe, Lana Wolf, Her Mee, and Wei Yen Lee.

| 1 | 2 | 3 | 4 | 5 | 6 | 7 | 8 | 9 | 10 | 11 | 12 |

31e • Speed Ladder Paragraphs

15 minutes

Directions: **1.** Take a 1' writing on ¶ 1 DS. **2.** When you complete ¶ 1 in 1', continue on to ¶ 2. Repeat this procedure as you try to complete all five ¶s in the given time. **3.** Take three 1' writings on any ¶ you cannot finish in 1'.

Your teacher may call half minute guides. You should be at or past the first • at 30" to finish the ¶ in 1'.

return and tab quickly at the end of each paragraph

all letters used 1.2 si word wrap

	gwam 1'	3'
One bit of advice you should heed is to keep your sense of	12	4
humor, even when things look their worst.	20	7
In fact, being able to laugh at oneself may well be the	11	10
secret to a good life and real success. That is no joke either.	24	15
A good laugh can make living much easier. A joke cuts	11	18
problems down to size. It lowers tension if tempers start to	23	22
flare and things get out of hand.	30	25
Humor brings out the best in other folks too. It helps them	12	29
relax so they can enjoy being with you. They respond in kind	24	33
when facts are given to them in a clever, funny way.	35	36
The greatest thing about a sense of humor, however, is that	12	40
it is so good for your health. A quip can do as much for how a	25	45
person feels as jogging around the block.	33	48

gwam 1' | 1 | 2 | 3 | 4 | 5 | 6 | 7 | 8 | 9 | 10 | 11 | 12 | 13 |
3' | 1 | 2 | 3 | 4 |

25 minutes

53c • Formatting Problems: Multiple-Column Tables

Problem 1

Directions: Retrieve **L51d1** and make the necessary changes.

REVISED PRACTICE SCHEDULE

Field Hockey Team	~~Johnson~~ Thomas Field
Soccer Team	Meade Field
Cross Country Team	~~Lyons~~ Hanes Track
Girls Tennis Team	Wilson Court
Boys Tennis Team	~~Ashe~~ Cooke Court
Pep Squad	Courtyard

Problem 2

Directions: Retrieve **L52c2** and make the changes marked. Then arrange in order to show the standings at the end of Week 2. Save as **L53c2**.

CURRENT EVENTS TEAM SCORES

	Old Score	Week ~~1~~ 2	New Score
Orange Team	220	~~220~~ 180	~~220~~ 400
Blue Team	210	~~210~~ 60	~~210~~ 270
Purple Team	160	~~160~~ 120	~~160~~ 280
Red Team	120	~~120~~ 160	~~120~~ 280
Green Team	90	~~90~~ 180	~~90~~ 270

Problem 3

Directions: Format the problem below on a full sheet DS. Leave 14 spaces between columns. Save as **L53c3**.

ENDANGERED SPECIES IN NORTH AMERICA

Grizzly bear	Bald eagle
Ocelot	Whooping crane
Red wolf	American crocodile
Eastern cougar	Utah prairie dog
Gila trout	California condor

LESSON 32

1" side margins

5 minutes

32a • Keyboard Review

Directions: Key each sentence two times SS. DS between 2-line groups.

alphabet Karen just expected him to acquire a zest for living by now.

fig/sym Our order #439, for 2 7/8 lbs., is made out for just $15.60.

easy When she tried to go back to first base, she was thrown out.

| 1 | 2 | 3 | 4 | 5 | 6 | 7 | 8 | 9 | 10 | 11 | 12 |

7 minutes

32b • Location of % (percent), & (ampersand), and - (hyphen) or -- (dash)

Reach to % (percent)

1. Shift, then reach up to % with the f finger.

2. Touch %f lightly without moving other fingers from their home position.

Reach to & (ampersand)

1. Shift, then reach up to & with the j finger.

2. Touch &j lightly without moving other fingers from their home position.

f5f f%f f5f f%f %f %f %5 Key twice on same line j7j j&j j7j j&j &j &j &7

Reach to %

Do not space between a figure and %.

Reach to &

Space before and after the &, which may be used in place of the word *and.*

Reach to -

Do not space before or after - (hyphen) or -- (dash)

Reach to -

Reach to - (hyphen) or -- (dash)

1. Reach up to - with the ; finger.

2. Touch -; lightly without moving other fingers from their home position.

;-; ;-; -;- -;- -- -; ;-

32c • Location Drills %, &, and -

8 minutes

Directions: Key each line two times SS. DS between 2-line groups.

% Interest rates at four banks were 8%, 8.5%, 8.75%, and 9.2%.

& Haller & Ling ordered 77 pairs of shoes from Sanchez & Sons.

- In mid-April we received a 4-star rating--the best possible.

10 minutes

all letters used 1.2 si

32d • Script Skill Builder

Directions: Key the following ¶ two times DS. Take two 1' writings. Figure *gwam.*

gwam 1'

Noise is now such a vexing problem that at least one 11
town we know has hired two cops to cite those who get out of 23
line. To get their job done, they use a sound analyzer. So 35
far they have quieted a few saloons, a noisy parrot, and one 47
loudmouthed rooster. 51

LESSON 53

1" side margins

5 minutes

53a • Keyboard Review

Directions: Key each sentence three times SS. DS between 3-line groups.

keep feet flat on floor

alphabet Pamela gave Nick exquisite old jewelry for the bazaar today.

fig/sym A record 127 people cast votes for Ramona as vice-president!

easy He tried to learn to keep his eyes on the ball at all times.

| 1 | 2 | 3 | 4 | 5 | 6 | 7 | 8 | 9 | 10 | 11 | 12 |

15 minutes

53b • Paragraph Guided Writings

Directions: **1.** Take a 1' writing on ¶ 1. Figure *gwam*. Add four words to your gwam for a new goal.

2. Take two 1' writings on the same ¶. Try to reach your goal on each writing.

3. Take a 1' writing on the same ¶. Drop back two to four *gwam*. Your goal is to key without errors.

4. Repeat Steps 1, 2, and 3 for the second and third ¶s.

all letters used 1.2 si word wrap *gwam* 3'

Most of us are so pressed for time these days that those who 4 | 40
market goods and services have a hard time keeping up. In the 8 | 45
era of fax machines and microwaves, what once seemed fast is not 13 | 49
quite fast enough anymore. 14 | 51

We think pizza should be delivered to the house in half an 18 | 55
hour or less. We get upset if someone makes us wait more than a 23 | 59
minute or so for a burger and fries. 25 | 61

If we do save bits of time here and there, perhaps the real 29 | 65
challenge is to learn what to do with them. Extra time is worth 33 | 70
something when it is enjoyed and used wisely. 36 | 73

gwam 3' | 1 | 2 | 3 | 4 |

5 minutes

32e • Learning to Use the Search and Replace Function

Directions: **1.** Key several lines of your initials, spacing between each set of initials.
2. Position the cursor at the beginning of the first line.
3. Using the search and replace function of your software, replace your initials with your full name.

CHARACTER STRING A group of letters, numbers, symbols, or a combination of them will be regarded as a character string or code.

SEARCH AND REPLACE Search and replace is a feature that searches forward (or backward) through a document until it finds the designated character string or code and then replaces it with a new string that the user designates. Some programs also allow you to delete a string using the replace feature. A discretionary replace (sometimes called selective search or search with confirmation) allows you to replace character strings selectively. A global replace will automatically replace every occurrence of the designated character string. By entering the proper command, the program prompts you with special directions such as "Search For:" and "Replace With:." When the command is executed, the program locates each occurrence of the character string and replaces it with the new string.

10 minutes

32f • Timed Writings

Directions: Key two 3' writings on the ¶s below. Figure *gwam*. Submit the better of the two writings.

all letters used 1.2 si word wrap	*gwam* 1'	3'
Ever since the keyboard we now use was first designed, dozens	12	4
of people have tried to improve on it. A problem they want to	25	8
solve is that a few of our least frequently used keys can be	37	12
stroked with ease, but all the common ones cannot.	47	16
One expert has come up with a device that has but eight keys,	12	20
each with three positions. The fingers do not have to jump around	25	24
so much, and keys are moved back and forth rather than tapped.	38	28
Another new machine is split in the middle so that it looks like	51	33
an open book face down.	56	34
Still others are working on ways to lessen the load of those	12	38
who have to spend a lot of time at the computer each day. An	24	43
office products firm now sells a foam wedge that tips the	36	46
keyboard toward the user. Its purpose is to relieve strain on	49	51
the hands, neck, and eyes.	54	52

gwam 1' | 1 | 2 | 3 | 4 | 5 | 6 | 7 | 8 | 9 | 10 | 11 | 12 | 13 |
3' | 1 | 2 | 3 | 4 |

52c, continued

Problem 2

Directions: Retrieve **L52c1** and arrange the teams in order, according to the highest score at the end of the first week's match. Save as **L52c2**. When you are finished, your table should look like this:

CURRENT EVENTS TEAM SCORES

	Old Score	Week 1	New Score
Orange Team		220	220
Blue Team		210	210
Purple Team		160	160
Red Team		120	120
Green Team		90	90

Problem 3

Directions: Format this problem on a full sheet DS. Leave 10 spaces between columns. Save as **L52c3**.

STATE NICKNAMES

Louisiana	Pelican State
Pennsylvania	Keystone State
Idaho	Gem State
Utah	Beehive State
Montana	Treasure State

Problem 4

Directions: Retrieve **L51d3** and add these states. Do not change spacing or tabs. Save as **L52c4**.

Connecticut	CT	New York	NY
Delaware	DE	North Carolina	NC
Florida	FL	North Dakota	ND
Georgia	GA	Ohio	OH
Hawaii	HI	Oklahoma	OK
Idaho	ID	Oregon	OR

LESSON 33

1" side margins

33a • Keyboard Review

5 minutes

Directions: Key each sentence two times SS. DS between 2-line groups.

alphabet Rick Wells put five dozen quarts of jam in the box for Gary.

fig/sym Only 60% can do the 25 push-ups required by the H & F tests.

easy Fix the handle so tight that he will not be able to turn it.

| 1 | 2 | 3 | 4 | 5 | 6 | 7 | 8 | 9 | 10 | 11 | 12 |

33b • Location of (and) (parentheses)

5 minutes

Reach to ((parenthesis)
1. Shift, then reach up to (with the l finger.
2. Touch (l lightly without moving other fingers from their home position.

Reach to) (parenthesis)
1. Shift, then reach up to) with the ; finger.
2. Touch); lightly without moving other fingers from their home position.

```
191 1(1 191 1(1 (1 (1 (9
```

Key twice on same line

```
;0; ;); ;0; ;); ); ); )0
```

Reach to (

Reach to)

33c • Location Drills (and) 10 minutes

Directions: Key each line two times SS. DS between 2-line groups.

Note: Do not space between ( ) and the words they enclose.

(Strike the 9, then shift to key (. Key the 9, then key (99.

) Strike the 0, then shift to key). Key the 0, then key 00).

Send your letters (keep them short, please) to me at Box 90.

( ) Do not hang sweaters (or clothes that stretch). (They sag.)

Beth Martin (Grade 8) had the top speed (42 words a minute).

Almost 900 kids attended the concerts in Babylon (New York).

LESSON 52

1" side margins

5 minutes

52a • Keyboard Review

Directions: Key each sentence three times SS. DS between 3-line groups.

keep arms and wrists quiet

alphabet Marvel Jackson was requested to pay a tax for the big prize.

fig/sym Thirty of the 120 students (25%) missed questions #79 & #80.

easy They paid for their eight chairs with the profits they made.

| 1 | 2 | 3 | 4 | 5 | 6 | 7 | 8 | 9 | 10 | 11 | 12 |

10 minutes

52b • Language Arts Skills: Spelling and Proofreading Aid

Directions: **1.** Key each line three times SS. DS between each 3-line group. **2.** Note the spelling of each word as you key this drill. **3.** Proofread carefully. Check any word about which you are uncertain against the original copy.

key without pauses between words

1 attempt coming fourth library prior finally until using paid

2 quantity excellent privilege particular substantial mortgage

3 efficient continuing guarantee superintendent accommodations

30 minutes

52c • Formatting Problems: Multiple-Column Tables

Problem 1

Directions: **1.** Key results of the first week's match as shown below on a full sheet DS. **2.** Leave eight spaces between columns. Since this is the first week, there is no Old Score to add to this week's total to get a New Score. **3.** Format the column as it will be used in later problems. **4.** Save as **L52c1**.

COLUMN HEADINGS Column headings are formatted to begin at the point of the tab and are underlined. A column heading may be the longest line in the column.

CURRENT EVENTS TEAM SCORES

	Old Score	Week 1	New Score
Blue Team		210	210
Green Team		90	90
Orange Team		220	220
Purple Team		160	160
Red Team		120	120

10 minutes

33d • Continuity Practice

Directions: **1.** Key the ¶ below one time DS. Proofread for errors.
2. Try to key correctly three times the words in which you made an error.
3. Try to key the entire ¶ without errors as many times as you can in the time remaining.

all letters used 1.2 si word wrap words

keep fingers deeply curved

	words
The job of carrying papers is not for the lazy person. You	12
have to get up early each day, and you have to work in all kinds	25
of weather. Once in a while you have to call on people who	37
forget to pay their bill. Those are some of the reasons that	49
explain why many boys and girls quit after only three to six	62
months.	63

| 1 | 2 | 3 | 4 | 5 | 6 | 7 | 8 | 9 | 10 | 11 | 12 | 13 |

15 minutes

33e • Timed Writings

Directions: **1.** Take one 3' writing. Figure *gwam*.
2. Take two 1' writings on each ¶.
3. Take one 3' writing. Figure *gwam*. Compare this rate with your first 3' writing.

all letters used 1.2 si word wrap

	gwam 1'	3'	
Studies show that most of us now have our car washed as	11	4	30
frequently as once a month. More often than not, we hire someone	24	8	34
else to do the job for us. At least that is what the carwash	37	12	39
people say.	39	13	40
Their research found out too, though, that a sizable number	12	17	43
of car owners expect to wash their cars right at home. They	24	21	47
still like to keep all the family wheels clean with a hose,	36	25	51
bucket, and sponge.	40	26	53

gwam 1' | 1 | 2 | 3 | 4 | 5 | 6 | 7 | 8 | 9 | 10 | 11 | 12 | 13 |
3' | 1 | 2 | 3 | 4 |

51d, continued

Problem 2

Word Processing Method of Setting Column Tabs

Step 1 Identify the longest item in each column and determine the number of spaces to be placed between columns.

Step 2 Use the automatic centering feature and key these items and spaces (Step 1) on the line.

Step 3 Move the cursor to the beginning of the first column; note (write down) the cursor position.

Directions: Using the method described above, key the table below DS on a full sheet of paper. Leave 12 spaces between columns.

Step 4 Repeat Step 3 for each remaining column.

Step 5 Clear all tabs in the ruler/format line.

Step 6 Set tabs in the ruler/format line at the positions noted in Steps 3 and 4.

Step 7 Delete the line keyed in Step 2.

Step 8 Key the table.

Note: Numerals presented in a table are aligned on the right side; therefore, it may be necessary to space after the tab to achieve the desired arrangement.

DISTANCES BETWEEN MAJOR CITIES

Philadelphia to Houston	1,508 Miles
Chicago to Cincinnati	287 Miles
Salt Lake City to Miami	2,532 Miles
Detroit to Boston	695 Miles
Atlanta to New York	641 Miles

Problem 3

Directions: Key the table below DS. (You will be retrieving it for later problems.) Center the heading on line 7. Set the tabs for the columns, keying and centering the line below:

Massachusetts (6) MA (14) North Carolina (6) NC

After the tabs are set, remove the line (this line is the longest in the complete problem--see L52c4, L54d3 and L55c4). Save as **L51d3**.

POSTAL SERVICE STATE ABBREVIATIONS

Alabama	AL	Montana	MT
Alaska	AK	Nebraska	NE
Arizona	AZ	Nevada	NV
Arkansas	AR	New Hampshire	NH
California	CA	New Jersey	NJ
Colorado	CO	New Mexico	NM

LESSON 34

5 minutes

34a • Keyboard Review

1" side margins

Directions: Key each sentence two times SS. DS between 2-line groups.

keep arms and wrists quiet

alphabet Bob Jade was given extra maps quickly as he was in a frenzy.

fig/sym Exactly 465 runners (of all ages) competed on July 30, 1994.

easy He will throw the rocks out of sight at the end of the lane.

| 1 | 2 | 3 | 4 | 5 | 6 | 7 | 8 | 9 | 10 | 11 | 12 |

5 minutes

34b • Numbers and Symbols

Directions: Key the ¶ below once DS.

all letters used 1.5 si word wrap words

A recently published book paints a unique (and amazing) 11
picture of America. Here are some interesting excerpts from it: 24
Americans eat 24,657,534 hot dogs every day and purchase 100 36
million M & Ms; the president of the U.S. earns $547.95 each day, 50
while Michael Jackson makes $164,383.67; and women spend 59 62
minutes (of each 24-hour period) cleaning house--but men spend 74
only 26. 76

| 1 | 2 | 3 | 4 | 5 | 6 | 7 | 8 | 9 | 10 | 11 | 12 | 13 |

5 minutes

34c • Location of ' (apostrophe) and ! (exclamation point)

Reach to ' (apostrophe)

1. The ' is to the right of the ; and is controlled by the ; finger.

2. Touch '; lightly without moving other fingers from their home position.

Reach to ! (exclamation)

1. Shift, then reach up to ! with the a finger.

2. Touch !a lightly without moving other fingers from their home position.

;'; ;'; ;'; ;'; '; ;' '; Key twice on same line a!a a!a a!a a!a !a a! !a

10 minutes

51c • Steps in Arranging Tables: Horizontal Placement

Step 1 Format equal left and right margins (1" margins are suggested, unless the table will be very wide).

Step 2 Clear all preset tabs. Set a tab at the center point of the paper you will use when you print (remember 12-pitch center is 51; 10-pitch center is 42).

Step 3 Determine the spacing between the columns (if a specific number of spaces is not given). **Hint:** Use an even number; six is always good.

Step 4 Find the longest item in each column.

Step 5 From the tab at center, backspace once for each two letters, figures, spaces, or punctuation marks in each column. If you have an extra character in any column, add that character to the first character in the next column. If one space is left over after backspacing for all the columns, disregard it.

Step 6 Backspace once for every two spaces to be left between columns. Since you will use an even number, there will not be any spaces left over.

Step 7 The first tab will be at the point at which you stopped backspacing. This is where the first column will start.

Step 8 Space forward once for each letter, figure, space, or punctuation mark in the longest entry in the first column and once for each space left between Columns 1 and 2. Set a tab for the second column. Continue in this way until stops have been set for each column. Space across the last column to determine the right margin.

Note: Once you are familiar with the backspace-from-center method of determining margins and tabs, you will learn a more automatic method of formatting a table.

Vertical Placement of a Table (Review)

Step 1 Count the lines in the copy to be centered. If your copy is to be double-spaced, remember to count the spaces between the lines. There is only one line space following each line of copy when material is double-spaced.

Step 2 Subtract the total lines to be used from the lines available on the paper you are using. (There are 66 lines on an 11" sheet.)

Step 3 Divide the number of lines that remain by two for the top margin. If the result contains a fraction, disregard it.

25 minutes

51d • Formatting Problems: Multiple-Column Tables

Problem 1 Tabulation Problem

Directions: Following the steps above, key the table below on a full sheet of paper DS. Leave 10 spaces between columns. Save as **L51d1**.

Vertical Centering Calculation Review

Lines available	66
Less lines required	13
Lines remaining	53
Top margin	26
Begin on line	27

line 27 PRACTICE SCHEDULE

Field Hockey Team	Johnson Field
Soccer Team	Meade Field
Cross Country Team	Lyons Track
Girls Tennis Team	Wilson Court
Boys Tennis Team	Ashe Court
Pep Squad	Courtyard

| 18 | 10 | 13 |

Reach to '

Reach to !

34d • Location Drills: ' and ! 8 minutes

Directions: Key each line two times SS. DS between 2-line groups.

Space twice after ! at the end of a sentence, which may be a single exclamatory word.

' Mr. and Mrs. O'Grady can't pay the bill for Karen's tuition.
Jack O'Bannion says he won't ever eat at Mandy's Cafe again.

! Get ready! Begin! Run faster! Try harder! Hurry! Great!
He won first place! Priscilla was elected! I hate spinach!

'! Keep your eye on them! Don't give up! Get off Kelly's car!
Danger! Stop! I can't see the bridge to O'Donnell's house!

34e • Continuity Practice 7 minutes

Directions: **1.** Key the ¶ below one time DS. Proofread for errors.
2. Try to key correctly three times the words in which you made an error.
3. Try to key the entire ¶ without errors as many times as you can in the time remaining.

all letters used 1.2 si | word wrap | words

If you go for things like bruised shins, flying straight up 12
high walls, and turning over once or twice in the ozone, 23
skateboarding is the sport for you. Of course you should be 35
sure to wear a helmet, wrist guards, and kneepads to ward off the 48
injuries. Get set to crash quite often, and do not expect any 61
net or pool of water to cushion your falls. 70

| 1 | 2 | 3 | 4 | 5 | 6 | 7 | 8 | 9 | 10 | 11 | 12 | 13 |

34f • Learning to Correct Rough Draft Copy 15 minutes

EDITING (Review) Editing is a process of changing a document.

INSERT Insert is an editing feature that allows you to add characters without rekeying the entire document. New text is inserted and existing text is pushed to the right or down to make room for the addition.

DELETE Delete is an editing feature that removes (erases) any character or characters, including blank spaces, identified (highlighted) by the cursor. Existing text to the right moves over and text below moves up to close the space. Use the backspace/erase key for one or two characters and the delete function for longer deletions.

Formatting and Keying Tables (Lessons 51-55)

Learning Goals

1. Format tables (with and without column headings) that present information clearly and attractively.
2. Use critical thinking skills to complete problems.
3. Continue development of language arts skills—including spelling, proofreading, and punctuation.
4. Continue refinement of stroking and operating techniques through meaningful practice.
5. Review the process of selecting files listed in the directory for later use and removing those that will not be needed.
6. Use word processing software to create a database and use a spreadsheet.

Word Processing Concepts Introduced in Unit 9

easy column formatting
enhancing copy (bold)
database
spreadsheet

General Directions

Use 1" side margins, unless otherwise directed, for all lessons in this unit. SS sentences and drill lines. DS between repeated groups of lines and paragraph copy (if your software permits). Proofread and correct errors when keying problems.

LESSON 51

1" side margins

51a • Keyboard Review

5 minutes

Directions: Key each sentence three times SS. DS between 3-line groups.

use quick sharp, tapping strokes

alphabet Juan Vasquez knows of body building exercise plans for them.

fig/sym He read 24 books in 1994--including The Russians and Poland.

easy Those who were in good shape ran down the field at halftime.

| 1 | 2 | 3 | 4 | 5 | 6 | 7 | 8 | 9 | 10 | 11 | 12 |

51b • Remove Unneeded Files from Directory

5 minutes

Remove files that are no longer needed from your directory.

LEAVE THESE FILES:

L21c1	L36c1	L38c1	L40b1	L44d2
	L36c2	L38c2	L40b2	L46d1
L24c3	L37c1	L39c1	L40b3	L50c3
	L37c2	L39c2	L43c	
	L37c3	L39c3	L43d	

34f, continued

PROOFREADER'S MARKS Copy that has been keyed or printed may be corrected by the use of symbols which indicate specific changes that are to be made in the final copy. Study these symbols, called proofreader's marks, then follow the directions below for keying the paragraphs.

^ for insert # for space

Directions: **1.** Format 1" side and top margins.
2. Key the following paragraphs DS once, making the corrections indicated by the proofreader's marks.
3. When you have finished keying the paragraphs, delete the following words:

Paragraph 1: *all*

Paragraph 2: *and more*

Paragraph 3: *just* and *new*

Paragraph 4: *very, some,* and *old*

Paragraph 5: *some*

Friends fill a vital role in life. They provide comfort as they let you know you are not all alone.

With every friend you explore a new path in life. You will learn more the wider your circle of friends becomes.

You might hit it off with someone right away, or it may take month before you so. Recognize that each new friendship moves at its speed.

Then you have some chances to get acquainted withthose outside your circle of friends.

While we know howimportant our friends are to us, this discussion willnotbe complete without some caution. The advice may be trite, but its true. To have a friend, you must be one.

One of the very best times to meet new people is when the school year begins.

LESSON 50

1" side margins

5 minutes

50a • Keyboard Review

Directions: Key each sentence three times SS. DS between 3-line groups.

alphabet Jerry Diamond packed the fine quartz in twelve larger boxes.

fig/sym Pam's cellular car phone cost $487 while mine was only $369.

easy Their first goal is to make enough to own their own bicycle.

| 1 | 2 | 3 | 4 | 5 | 6 | 7 | 8 | 9 | 10 | 11 | 12 |

10 minutes

50b • Timed Writings

Directions: **1.** Take two 3' writings on 49b, page 100. Proofread for errors. **2.** Figure *gwam*; submit the better writing.

30 minutes

50c • Personal Notes

Problem 1 Personal Note in Modified Block Style, Open Punctuation

Directions: **1.** Format the following problem on a full sheet of paper in modified block style with open punctuation and indented paragraphs. **2.** Format side margins at 2" and begin the date at the center of line 20.

January 18, 19--

Dear Mike

The theme for our school observation of National Freedom Day has been selected. It is

FREEDOM FOR EVERYONE

and will be observed on Friday, February 1.

The publicity committee has made posters, contacted the school newspaper, and planned an assembly for the student body. Our photographer will take pictures for the newspaper.

Sincerely

(Your name)

Problem 2 Changing From One Style to Another

Directions: **1.** Retrieve **L48c3** and delete spaces to change from modified block style to block style. **2.** Save as **L50c2**, print, sign your name above the keyed name, and give to your teacher.

Problem 3 Changing From One Style to Another

Directions: **1.** Retrieve **L48c1** and delete spaces to change from modified block style to block style. **2.** Save as **L50c3**, print, sign your name above the keyed name, and give to your teacher.

LESSON 35

1" side margins

5 minutes

35a • Keyboard Review

Directions: Key each sentence two times SS. DS between 2-line groups.

alphabet Bud Roper may take this quiz next week if Jack will give it.

fig/sym It's unbelievable that Jan's team won 106 to 98 in overtime!

easy Most of us show what we are by what we do with what we have.

| 1 | 2 | 3 | 4 | 5 | 6 | 7 | 8 | 9 | 10 | 11 | 12 |

7 minutes

35b • Location of " (quotation marks), * (asterisk), and _ (underline)

Reach to " (quotation)

1. The " is the shift of the ' and is controlled by the ; finger.

2. Touch "; lightly without moving other fingers from their home position.

Reach to _ (underline)

1. Shift, then reach up to _ with the ; finger.

2. Touch _ lightly without moving other fingers from their home position.

;'; ;"; ;'; ;"; "; ;" ";

Key each drill twice

;-; ;_; ;-; ;_; _; ;_ _;

Reach to * (asterisk)

1. Shift, then reach up to * with the k finger.

2. Touch *k lightly without moving other fingers from their home position.

k8k k*k k8k k*k *k k* *k

23 minutes

49c • Personal Notes in Modified Block Style, Open Punctuation

Problem 1

Directions: **1.** Format the following problem on a full sheet of paper in modified block style with open punctuation. Indent the paragraphs by using the preset tab.

2. Format side margins at 2" and begin the date at the center of line 20.

3. Key your name a QS below the complimentary close.

4. Proofread for errors. Save, print, sign your name above the keyed name, and give to your teacher.

February 4, 19--

Dear Paul

Can you believe that our winter break is almost here? Just three more days of school before we'll be heading for the slopes.

My plane leaves at 7:10 p.m., so I should be seeing you by 9:30. I'll be ready to ski whenever you are.

Maybe there are a few good points about your dad's transfer.

See you soon

(Your name)

Problem 2

Directions: **1.** Use the same format as Problem 1.

2. Send the following note to each of the people in **L47d1** and **L47d2** (there were four altogether).

November 2, 19 - -

Dear

The costume party for kindergarteners at Acton Elementary School was a huge success.

The judging was not easy, but you helped select really clever costumes. The food was delicious, and the children enjoyed the games.

Thanks for your part in planning and giving the party.

Sincerely

(Your name)

8 minutes

35c • Location Drills: ", *, and _

Directions: Key each line two times SS. DS between 2-line groups.

" Don't confuse "to" and "too" or "principal" and "principle."

Read three articles: "Show Time," "Smile," and "Vacations."

* Use * for a reference below. My quote was from Frank Bush.*

_ Indent _ spaces. Use your _ thumb. Please come _.

"_ This report is called "At Risk." The book title was Shogun.

_ They were assigned The Covenant and All the President's Men.

USING _ TO KEY A LINE TO FILL IN Use the _ to key a line for a fill-in form.

UNDERLINE TEXT AS YOU KEY (AUTOMATIC) Turn on automatic (continuous) underlining by tapping a keystroke combination (such as *Code and u*), or tap the assigned function key (such as *F6*). As you key, the text will be underlined. When you're finished, turn automatic underlining off by tapping the same key or key combination.

UNDERLINE EXISTING TEXT Position the cursor at the beginning of the existing text. One method is to hold down the left shift key and tap the hyphen key. Another method is to identify the block of text by entering a specific command (such as the *Alternate and F4 keys*) and then enter the underline command (such as the *F8 key*).

See the User's Manual for instructions on underlining with your software.

---

7 minutes

35d • Technique Builder

Directions: Key each line three times SS. DS between 3-line groups.

key with a steady rhythm

1 if they | they were | if they were | if she | she saves | if she saves

2 and he | and he | reads | reads | and he reads | and she | and she reads

3 they did | they did | they did only | she may | she may | she may only

4 to the | to the | race | race | to the race | for their | for their race

LESSON 49

1" side margins

7 minutes

49a • Keyboard Review

Directions: Key each sentence three times SS. DS between 3-line groups.

alphabet I'm amazed Dave Kowing expects to qualify in the broad jump.

fig/sym Hilary's check will be $246 when rates go from 7.8% to 9.1%.

adjacent keys Sandra said a few more people were going there after dinner.

hyphen Fifty-two east-west streets are two-way and six are one-way.

easy It will pay them to take some time to plan for their visits.

1 2 3 4 5 6 7 8 9 10 11 12

15 minutes

49b • Paragraph Guided Writings

Directions: **1.** Take a 1' writing on ¶ 1. Figure *gwam*. Add four words to your *gwam* for a new goal.

2. Take two 1' writings. Try to reach your goal on each writing.

3. Take a 1' writing on the same ¶. Drop back two to four *gwam*. Your goal is to key the ¶ without errors.

4. Repeat Steps 1, 2, and 3 for the second and third ¶s.

all letters used 1.2 si word wrap *gwam* 3'

There can be no doubt that an information age is now here in 4 45
full force. In fact, it seems to expand so quickly that most of 8 49
us do not have time to adjust to any product before a new one 13 54
comes along. 13 54

No more than a few short years ago, the small computer first 17 58
appeared on desks across the land. Within three years millions 22 63
were in use, and now nearly half of our work force is in some way 26 67
involved with them. 27 68

In many cases, though, this new age has not brought order to 31 72
business nor has it lowered our work loads. We have come to a 36 77
point where people are so crazy they call to tell you that your 40 81
fax line is busy. 41 82

gwam 3' 1 2 3 4

10 minutes

35e • Timed Writings

Directions: Key two 3' writings on the ¶s below. Figure *gwam*. Submit the better writing.

all letters used 1.2 si word wrap

	gwam 1'	3'	
Now that scientists have found out how to launch the parts of	12	4	56
satellites and then assemble them in space, one of their major	25	8	60
dreams will at last come true. This technique makes it possible	38	13	65
for them to build a new home in the sky.	46	15	67
These space stations, as they float way high above the	11	19	71
clouds, will get the energy they need from sunlight that is	23	23	75
collected on large panels. The men and women who live and work	36	27	79
in this new space home will be taxied back and forth from the	48	31	83
earth in a shuttle.	52	33	85
The thought of space stations is not new. They have been	12	37	89
seen both in print and in the movies for a long time. In fact,	24	41	93
the first story of a manned space station appeared in a magazine	37	45	97
well over a hundred years ago. It was a hollow brick sphere that	51	50	102
could be shot into space by a cannon.	58	52	104

gwam 1' | 1 | 2 | 3 | 4 | 5 | 6 | 7 | 8 | 9 | 10 | 11 | 12 | 13 |

3' | 1 | 2 | 3 | 4 |

8 minutes

35f • Spacing After Punctuation Marks: Review

Directions: Key each line one time SS.

Punctuation Guide

1. Space twice after end-of-sentence punctuation.
2. Do not space after a period within an abbreviation. Space once after an abbreviation; twice if that period ends a sentence.
3. Space once after a comma.
4. Space twice after a colon. Do *not* space before or after a colon when stating time.
5. Key the dash with two hyphens; do not space before or after.
6. Do not space before or after the hyphen in a hyphenated word.

1 Sit in the bleachers. The game starts soon. I hope we win.
2 Where is it? Will he go? Can they see? Who ate the fries?
3 Don't run! Be quiet! Turn down the volume! We'll be late!
4 Mr. and Mrs. White left at 10 a.m. We met the 1 p.m. plane.
5 Heather, Kaitlin, and Amy spent the summer in Paris, France.
6 Jot down these numbers: 35, 42, and 50. I arrived at 4:10.
7 Drop us a line--about 100 words or less--before September 5.
8 Our teacher said Mandy Jones-Carr turned in a 15-page paper.

| 1 | 2 | 3 | 4 | 5 | 6 | 7 | 8 | 9 | 10 | 11 | 12 |

48c, continued

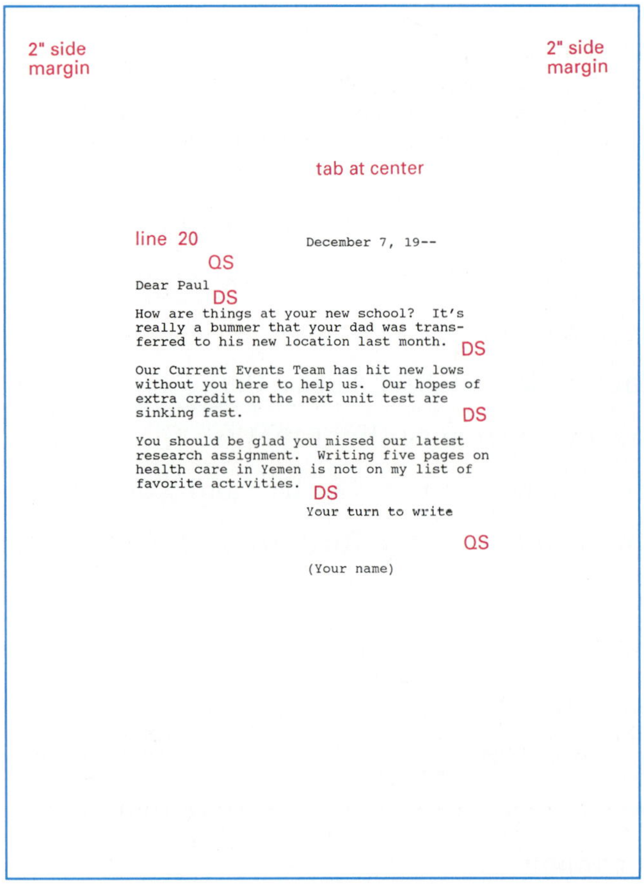

2" side margin

2" side margin

tab at center

line 20 December 7, 19--

QS

Dear Paul

DS

How are things at your new school? It's really a bummer that your dad was transferred to his new location last month.

DS

Our Current Events Team has hit new lows without you here to help us. Our hopes of extra credit on the next unit test are sinking fast.

DS

You should be glad you missed our latest research assignment. Writing five pages on health care in Yemen is not on my list of favorite activities.

DS

Your turn to write

QS

(Your name)

December 7, 19 - -

Dear Paul

How are things at your new school? It's really a bummer that your dad was transferred to his new location last month.

Our Current Events Team has hit new lows without you here to help us. Our hopes of extra credit on the next unit test are sinking fast.

You should be glad you missed our latest research assignment. Writing five pages on health care in Yemen is not on my list of favorite activities.

Your turn to write

(Your name)

Problem 2 Personal Note Changed to Modified Block Style

Directions: Retrieve **L46d2** and insert spaces to move the date and closing lines to change the style to modified block.

Problem 3 Personal Note in Modified Block Style

Directions: **1.** Use the same format as Problem 1. **2.** Save, print, sign your name above the keyed name, and give to your teacher.

January 12, 19 - -

Dear Chae

You are right. I do have some ideas for National Freedom Day. Even though it is an occasion that is overlooked by many people, we should plan events to call attention to February 1.

Each amendment to the constitution is important, but the Thirteenth Amendment has special meaning to a large segment of the U.S. population.

I will attend your meeting on Wednesday to share my thoughts with your committee.

Your friend

(Your name)

Formatting and Keying Short Reports (Lessons 36-40)

Learning Goals

1. Format a short report in correct form.
2. Key correctly words that are commonly misspelled.
3. Apply capitalization guides in keying sentences.
4. Key from rough draft containing common proofreader's marks.
5. Key from script with greater ease.
6. Increase keying skill by further refining basic techniques.

Word Processing Concepts Introduced in Unit 6

hard hyphen	soft hyphen
hard return/enter	soft return/enter
hard space	spell check
hyphen character	

General Directions

Use 1″ side margins, unless otherwise directed, for all lessons in this unit. SS sentences and drill lines; DS between repeated groups of lines. DS paragraph copy. Proofread and correct all errors in problems.

LESSON 36

1" side margins

5 minutes

36a • Keyboard Review

Directions: Key each sentence three times SS. DS between 3-line groups.

keep fingers deeply curved

alphabet I quite expected June was a lazy time for living back there.

fig/sym She said that 80.6% of her 34 car trips were under 15 miles.

easy He may sign his name on both of the forms if he has a proxy.

| 1 | 2 | 3 | 4 | 5 | 6 | 7 | 8 | 9 | 10 | 11 | 12 |

5 minutes

36b • Language Arts Skills: Spelling and Proofreading Aid

Directions: Key each line three times SS. DS between 3-line groups.

1 decision parcel ordinary maintenance canceled serious choose

2 belief familiar across wholly experience responsible visible

3 absence eighth congratulate immediate committee incidentally

LESSON 48

1" side margins

5 minutes

48a • Keyboard Review

Directions: Key each sentence three times SS. DS between 3-line groups.

tap each key with quick, sharp strokes

alphabet They flew D. G. Chavez home quickly by jet at their expense.

fig/sym Total fees amounted to $7,435--an 80% increase in 12 months!

easy At least eight of their members work there in the same firm.

| 1 | 2 | 3 | 4 | 5 | 6 | 7 | 8 | 9 | 10 | 11 | 12 |

10 minutes

48b • Sentence Skill Builder from Script

Directions: Take two 1' writings on each sentence. On the first writing, push for speed. On the second writing, drop back in speed and work for control.

	words
If you do not know which career you want, you are not alone.	12
Even most college students are unsure of their career goals.	12
To find a career you like, you need to look inside yourself.	12
You should try to find out what activities satisfy you most.	12

30 minutes

48c • Personal Notes in Modified Block Style with Open Punctuation

MODIFIED BLOCK STYLE In the modified block style, the date and complimentary close are keyed at the center of the line of writing (51 for 12-pitch printers and 42 for 10-pitch printers). The beginning lines of the paragraphs may be blocked or indented (preset tab).

OPEN PUNCTUATION (Review) Open punctuation means that there are no marks of punctuation following the salutation or complimentary close. Punctuation within the message follows regular punctuation rules.

Problem 1 Model Personal Note in Modified Block Style with Open Punctuation

Directions: **1.** Format the problem on page 99 on a full sheet of paper in modified block style with open punctuation and blocked paragraphs.
2. Format side margins at 2" and begin the date at the center of line 20.
3. Key your name a QS below the complimentary close.
4. Proofread for errors. Save, print, sign your name above the keyed name, and give to your teacher.

35 minutes

36c • Formatting Problems: One-Page Reports

SOFT RETURN/ENTER The soft return/enter is automatically entered by the program at the end of a line of copy when text is being "wrapped around" to the next line. When you adjust the margins, or insert and/or delete copy, the program automatically changes the position of the soft return. An example of the soft return occurs when you key a paragraph for a timed writing and do not tap the return/enter key until the end of the paragraph.

HARD RETURN/ENTER The hard return/enter is entered by tapping the return/enter key. Hard returns can be removed only by deleting them with a backspace erase or the delete feature. You have used the hard return/enter feature during practice exercises when you tap the return/enter key at the end of each line and twice between 2-line groups.

HYPHEN CHARACTER The hyphen character, as you have already learned, is a feature used for keying dates or minus signs in formulas.

HARD (REQUIRED) HYPHEN The hard, or required, hyphen is entered when the user taps the hyphen key. Regardless of where the hyphen appears within the paragraph, the program prints it. Hard hyphens are used in telephone numbers, a numeric range, certain phrases that should not be broken (jack-o-lantern), and compound words (self-confident). To prevent the minus or dash from being separated from related characters when it occurs at the end of a line, the user may have to tap a specific key (such as the *home* key) before tapping the hyphen key. A hard hyphen can be deleted by the user. Consult the User's Manual for your software to learn how to use the hard hyphen.

SOFT (GHOST OR NONREQUIRED) HYPHEN The soft, ghost, or nonrequired hyphen is an electronic feature that allows the user to decide whether a word should be hyphenated to avoid a very ragged right margin. When the hyphenation feature is "on," the cursor stops when a word will not fit on the line. Some programs automatically insert a soft hyphen; others allow the user to make the decision. Should the location of the hyphenated word change during reformatting, the soft hyphen is deleted automatically. Consult the User's Manual for your software for directions on using the soft hyphen feature.

HARD (REQUIRED) SPACE The hard, or required, space is a feature that guards against breaking a line of printed text between title and surname (Mr. Magoo), initials (B. L. Smith), and parts of a formula (a + b + c), etc. Inserting hard spaces between items of text causes the printer to regard the phrase as one word. The printer will print the text containing the hard space on one line. Consult the User's Manual for your software to learn how to use the hard space feature.

QUADRUPLE SPACE (QS) To leave a quadruple space, tap the return/enter key four times at the end of the last line before the quadruple space. This leaves three blank lines; you key on the fourth line.

(continued on next page)

25 minutes

47d • Personal Notes in Block Style with Open Punctuation

Problem 1

Directions: **1.** Format the following problem on a full sheet of paper in block style with open punctuation.

2. Format side margins at 2" and begin the date on line 20.

3. Key your name a QS below the complimentary close. Key the official title on the next line.

4. Proofread for errors. Save, print, sign your name in the space allowed, and give to your teacher.

October 14, 19--

Dear Aimee

The Student Council will be sponsoring a costume party for the kindergarten classes at Acton Elementary School.

Would you serve as a member of the planning committee for the party? We need to plan for refreshments, contests, and prizes.

Please think about serving on this committee, and let me know by Friday if you can help us. The committee will be meeting after school next Tuesday. I hope to see you there!

Sincerely

(Your name)
Activity Committee Chairman

Problem 2

Directions: **1.** Retrieve **L47d1**.

2. Prepare copies of the same note to the names below. Be sure to change the salutation for each one.

3. Save so that you have a file for each note. You might use **L47d2a**, **L47d2b**, **L47d2c** or **L47d2dBen**, **L47d2Dar**, **L47d2Chr** to distinguish one from another.

Ben Darice Chris

36c, continued

SPELL CHECK The spell check is a feature of word processing software that gives you a means of verifying the correct spelling of words in a document. The spell check does *not* eliminate the need to proofread a document, as it only verifies spelling, not the use of a word. (A correctly spelled, but incorrectly used word will not be brought to your attention.) During the spell check, the user has the opportunity to select the desired word from a list of possible spellings, to add the word to the dictionary, to edit and recheck the word in question, or to ignore the indication that the spelling may not be correct. Proper names and technical words are generally not included in the dictionary.

Practice

Practice using the spell check feature, first keying both sentences below. Position the cursor at the beginning of the first sentence and give the command to use the spell check. Ask for a list of spellings for the error in the first sentence. Observe that the two errors in the second sentence are not picked up by the spell check. Cursor to the errors and correct them.

The two students met with the principal aftre lunch yesterday.

The too students met with the principle after lunch yesterday.

Problem 1 Model of a Short Report

Directions: **1.** Key the report on page 72 using 1" margins DS.

2. Center the heading in all caps on line 13. DS and key your name, then QS to begin the report.

3. Proofread for errors, referring to the User's Manual for directions on using the spell check in your software.

4. Save as **L36c1**, print, and give to your teacher.

Problem 2 Short Report with Proofreader's Marks; Search and Replace

Directions: **1.** Key the report on page 73 using the same format as Problem 1.

2. Use the search and replace feature of your software, referring to the User's Manual to review directions. Rather than key the word *disk* each time it appears, key a *d*. When you have finished, move the cursor to home position, search for *d* and replace with *disk*.

3. Proofread for errors, using the spell check in your software.

4. Save as **L36c2**, print, and give to your teacher.

(continued on next page)

LESSON 47

1" side margins

47a • Keyboard Review

5 minutes

Directions: Key each sentence three times SS. DS between 3-line groups.

sit erect; keep feet flat on floor

alphabet Quint saw five black taxis jump the curbs and go zooming by.

fig/sym The Women's Club can meet at Olson's on April 30 and May 24.

easy Make sure he laid both world maps on the chair in row eight.

| 1 | 2 | 3 | 4 | 5 | 6 | 7 | 8 | 9 | 10 | 11 | 12 |

47b • Language Arts Skills: Keying from Dictation and Spelling Checkup

5 minutes

Directions: **1.** Your teacher will dictate words in 46c, page 94. Key the words from dictation.

2. Check your work for correct spelling. Rekey any words in which you made an error.

47c • Timed Writings

10 minutes

Directions: **1.** Take a 1' writing on ¶ 1. Figure *gwam*. Add four words to your *gwam* for a new goal.

2. Take two 1' writings. Try to reach your goal on each writing.

3. Take a 1' writing on the same ¶. Drop back two to four *gwam*. Your goal is to key the ¶ without errors.

4. Repeat Steps 1, 2, and 3 for the second and third ¶s.

keep wrists low and arms quiet

all letters used 1.2 si word wrap

	gwam 3'	
Before you start to look for your first job, you will be wise	4	43
to consider some techniques of job seeking that have been helpful	9	47
to others. They can also pay off for you.	11	50
For example, show that you are not lazy by listing the kinds	15	54
of work you have done. You might have delivered papers or taken	20	58
care of children. Be sure to include work for which you did not	24	63
get paid.	25	63
The strong points of your school record should be noted, of	29	67
course. It will help if you can say you missed only two days of	33	72
school in three years or that your keyboarding rate was one of the	37	76
best in the class.	39	77

gwam 3' | 1 | 2 | 3 | 4 |

1" left margin

1" right margin

MICROPROCESSOR HARDWARE line 13

DS

By (Student's name)

QS

This report is an attempt to identify some basic terms associated with microcomputers and word processors. A brief summary of some of the expressions common to all word processing programs follows.

DS body of report

A microcomputer is a small-sized computer with a keyboard, a monitor, a disk drive, and a printer, collectively referred to as hardware.

The main keyboard is similar to what you find on a typewriter. In addition to the alphabetic, numeric, and symbol keys on the main keyboard, other areas will contain function keys for the microprocessor, cursor direction keys, and a numeric keypad.

The monitor is an electronic screen that displays information that has been entered by loading in a program or by tapping the keys of the keyboard.

The disk drive reads and writes data that is stored on a disk. The disk (also known as a diskette or a floppy) may contain a pre-written program or data that the operator has entered.

The printer produces a hard copy (on paper) of the information that is shown on the screen.

One-page report

46d, continued

Problem 2 Personal Note in Block Style, Open Punctuation

Directions: Same as for Problem 1.

September 3, 19 - -

Dear Greg

Finally, after all this time, the date for tryouts for the soccer team has been announced.

The sign on the gym door calls for a meeting at Meade Field on Saturday at 11:00 a.m.

After scoring all those goals last season, you should have no problem making the team this year. I hope the hours of practice I've put in will pay off for me. Not being a part of the team is something I don't even want to think about!

See you Saturday

46e • Folding Personal Notes for Small Envelopes

5 minutes

Personal notes are usually folded and inserted into small envelopes (6 1/2" x 3 5/8") for mailing.

Directions: Fold at least one of the notes keyed in L46d for insertion into a small envelope, following the steps in the diagram below.

FOLDING LETTERS FOR SMALL ENVELOPES

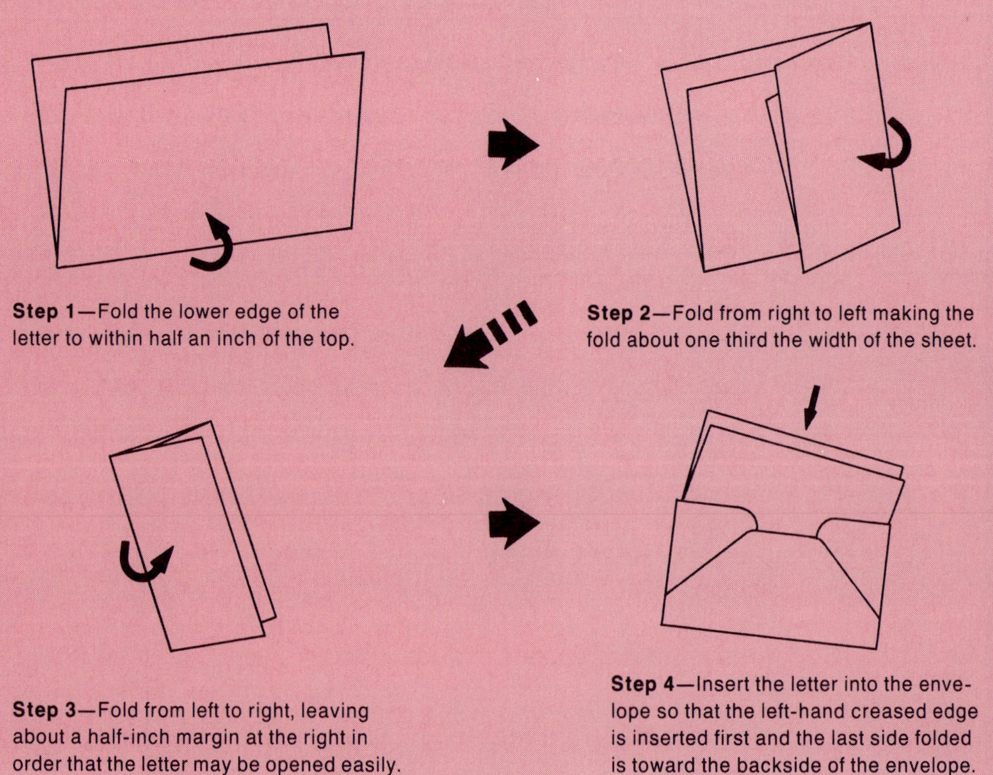

36c, continued

Review of Proofreader's Marks:

^ for insert # for space

New Proofreader's Marks:

lc or / for lowercase tr or ∽ for transpose

MICROPROCESSOR SOFTWARE

By (Student's name)

Software refers to the Programmed Instructions that tell the computer or word processor what to do. The instructions may be stored on a floppy disk that is coated magnetically. Data from a program disk entered may be into the system and shown on the screen.

Disks are made of very thin plastic. A disk that measures 5 1/4 inches is protected by a cover cushioned which has openings through which data is read or written. This floppy disk is stored in a Protective Jacket. A disk that measures 31/2 inches is protected by a Hard Plastic case. Although the hard case makes the disk more durable than the larger disk, the same gentle care must be proveded at all times.

The disk should be held only by the uppercorner and the exposed areas never should be touched as dust and oil from the surface of your fingers can ruin the disk. Disks should be protected from sunlight direct and kept away from extreme heat or cold. Bending or folding the disk may prohibit the readingand writing of the data stored on it. ¶ Disks should be stored in an upright position away from magnetic fields (telephones, dictation equipment, magnets, monitors, etc.).

LESSON 37

1" side margins

37a • Keyboard Review

5 minutes

Directions: Key each sentence three times SS. DS between 3-line groups.

keep wrists and elbows quiet

alphabet Bob was asked to quote from every zany jingle except theirs.

fig/sym Use a diagonal for "made" fractions such as 2 7/8 or 15 3/4.

easy They will spend half of their profit to pay for this emblem.

| 1 | 2 | 3 | 4 | 5 | 6 | 7 | 8 | 9 | 10 | 11 | 12 |

5 minutes

46c • Language Arts Skills: Spelling and Proofreading Aid

Directions: Key each line three times SS. DS between 3-line groups.

key each word letter by letter

1 toward similar practice valuable salary acknowledge hesitate

2 dollar financial procedure situation separate volume session

3 convenient responsibility circular calendar specific license

25 minutes

46d • Formatting Problems: Personal Notes in Block Style, Open Punctuation

BLOCK STYLE In the block style personal note, the date and complimentary close are keyed at the left margin. The beginning lines of the paragraphs are blocked.

OPEN PUNCTUATION Open punctuation means that there are no marks of punctuation following the salutation or complimentary close. Punctuation within the message follows regular punctuation rules.

Problem 1 Model Note in Block Style with Open Punctuation

Directions: **1.** Format the following problem on a full sheet of paper in block style with open punctuation.
2. Format side margins at 2" and begin the date on line 20.
3. Key your name a QS below the complimentary close.
4. Proofread for errors. Save, print, sign your name above the keyed name, and give to your teacher.

2" side margin 2" side margin

October 1, 19-- line 20

QS

Dear Susan DS

Spending the week at your cottage last month was great fun! The beach is a super place to spend time in the sun, and the waves were fun to ride. DS

It was great to be with you and your summer friends. We had a lot of fun. Perhaps some of your friends will be able to spend time here during a school break. DS

Thanks for inviting me and for the terrific time we had that week.

Your friend DS

QS

(Your name)

October 1, 19 - - line 20

QS

Dear Susan

DS

Spending the week at your cottage last month was great fun! The beach is a super place to spend time in the sun, and the waves were fun to ride.

DS

It was great to be with you and your summer friends. We had a lot of fun. Perhaps some of your friends will be able to spend time here during a school break.

DS

Thanks for inviting me and for the terrific time we had that week.

DS

Your friend

QS

(Your name)

5 minutes

37b • Language Arts Skills: Keying from Dictation; Spelling Checkup

Directions: Key the words in 36b, page 69, from your teacher's dictation. Check for correct spelling. Rekey any words in which you made an error.

35 minutes

37c • Formatting Problems: One-Page Reports

Review of Proofreader's Marks:

∧ for insert — # for space

lc or / for lowercase — tr or ∽ for transpose

New Proofreader's Marks:

cap or ≡ capitalize — ¶ begin new paragraph

Problem 1 Short Report with Proofreader's Marks

Directions: **1.** Review format for short reports.
2. Center the heading in all caps on line 13, DS and add your name, then QS.
3. Proofread for errors, using the spell check in your software.
4. Save as **L37c1**, print, and give to your teacher.

DISK DRIVES

By (Student's name)

Many microprocessors contain only one disk drive, but
∧ a microprocessor might contain two drives (A and B or 1 and 2) designed to be used by floppy disks for both the program disk and the data disk. other Microprocessors are equipped with a hard drive and a hard disk as well as a drive for a floppy disk. the hard disk is attached tothe Microcomputer (processor) and can be used to store programs as well as data. if desired, data could be written to the floppy disk. The harddisk stores more much information and is much faster to use than a floppy disk. ¶ The computer should be as little as possible moved but when itis necessary to move it, care should be give to avoid bumping it so that the Hard Disk is not disturbed. ¶ disk drives and all pieces of microprocessors shouldbe dusted regularly and used in an environment where the temperature and humidity are controlled.

Formatting and Keying Personal Notes (Lessons 46-50)

Learning Goals

1. Key personal notes in block and modified block style.
2. Use open punctuation in personal notes.
3. Key correctly words that are commonly misspelled.
4. Apply capitalization guides in keying sentences.
5. Increase keying skill by further refining basic techniques.

Word Processing Concept Introduced in Unit 8

changing letter styles by inserting/deleting spaces

General Directions

Use 1" side margins for all lessons in this unit unless otherwise directed. SS sentences and drill lines. DS between repeated groups of lines. DS paragraph copy. Proofread and correct all errors in problems.

LESSON 46

1" side margins

5 minutes

46a • Keyboard Review

Directions: Key each sentence three times SS. DS between 3-line groups.

keep feet on the floor

alphabet That back cover of my tax journal puzzled quite a few girls.

fig/sym Of their 296 bikes, 172 are 10-speeds and 124 are 3-speeds.

easy Their big bus made a right turn at the signal light in town.

| 1 | 2 | 3 | 4 | 5 | 6 | 7 | 8 | 9 | 10 | 11 | 12 |

5 minutes

46b • Technique Builder: Flowing Rhythm

Directions: Key each line three times SS. DS between 3-line groups.

stroke keys with a flowing rhythm

1 if the if the cases if the cases for the for the for the car

2 and the and the date and the date and the seat and the seats

3 she saw she saw only he did he did care they face they faced

4 if you if you ever if you trade and you and you and you were

37c, continued

Problem 2 Short Report with Proofreader's Marks

Directions: 1. Using the format for short reports, key the following problem. **Reminder:** Center your name DS under the heading, then QS.

2. Proofread for errors, using the spell check in your software.

3. Save as **L37c2**, print, and give to your teacher.

OPERATING THE CURSOR DIRECTION KEYS

Cursor direction keys let you move the cursor (that blinking light that shows where you are in the text) in any of four directions (left,right, up,and down) without erasing text.

If you want to move the cursor several lines at a time, you should use the page up or page down keys to save time. the cursor moves about twenty lines or so at a time, depending on how many lines you get on your screen. If you want to quickly move to the beginning line use the home key. In a like manner, the end key takes you to the end of line. To get to the beginning or end of the screen or the entire document, you will use the home and end keys repeatedly or with a function key.

Problem 3 Short Report with Proofreader's Marks

Directions: 1. Using the format for short reports, key the following problem. **Reminder:** Center your name DS under the heading, then QS.

2. Proofread for errors, using the spell check in your software.

3. Save as **L37c3**, print, and give to your teacher.

FUNCTION KEYS

The function keys of the keyboard allow you to work the with data you have entered into the microprocessor. as already indicated, the function keys used with the home or endkeys will move you quickly to the beginning orend of the document. by using one of the function keys, you can get a "help" menu will that tell you how to use the other function keys. You will find that you can delete (take out) data, move data from one part of the Document you are working with to another, check spelling of words in the document, center the text, duplicate paragraphs or sentences, or enhance portions of the text. enhancing lets you put the text in print bold, underline it, or return to regular printing.

SAVING OIL

By (Student's name)

Most of don't spend a lot of time discussing ways to save oil. Only when something drastic happens (~~like~~ the Iraqi invasion of Kuwait in 1990 ~~or a sudden large increase in the price of gasoline and home heating oil~~) do we realize that something beyond our immediate control may ~~cause a~~ change ~~in~~ the way we live.

What can we do to spend less of our hard-earned money and/or reduce our dependency on other countries for oil pro-ducts? One simple process ~~can~~ save as much as 1.3 million barrels of oil each day in the United States.

Many automobile owners prefer to change the oil in their cars ~~by~~ themselves rather than have it done at a com-mercial establishment. If these owners drain the old oil into a container ~~so it can be taken~~ to a collection site, the oil ~~can~~ be recycled. ~~At least one~~ major oil company now provides non-breakable containers for collecting used oil at stations with service bays. According to one state's Department of Environmental Protection, one gallon of used oil can produce the same amount of motor oil as 42 gallons of crude oil will yield. ~~And, the old oil requires only about one-third the energy needed to process crude oil into usable motor oil.~~

Recycling oil is just one way for the U.S. to become less dependent on other countries while cutting costs for the consumer.

ABC EXTRA

45d • Extra-Time Activities

Directions: If you have completed L45c and have time left, retrieve any incomplete problems in Unit 7 and finish them, carefully following directions for each problem.

LESSON 38

1" side margins

5 minutes

38a • Keyboard Review

Directions: Key each sentence three times SS. DS between 3-line groups.

tap the return/enter key quickly

alphabet Phil Singer wanted Liza to fly Jack to Quebec next November.

fig/sym Even sums like $580 or $476 don't require decimals or zeros.

easy He has to learn to handle those kinds of problems right now.

| 1 | 2 | 3 | 4 | 5 | 6 | 7 | 8 | 9 | 10 | 11 | 12 |

10 minutes

38b • Paragraph Guided Writings

Directions: **1.** Take a 1' writing to establish a goal rate.
2. Take two additional 1' writings, trying to reach your goal word just as time is called.
3. Add four words to your original goal. Take three 1' writings, trying to reach your new goal on each timing. Your teacher may call the quarter- or half-minutes.

all letters used 1.3 si word wrap

4 8
People don't just blow balloons up for parties any more.
12 16 20
They ride in them too. The riding ones, like their smaller
24 28 32 36
cousins, come in various sizes and colors. Some are as large as
40 44 48
jets. Liquid propane is used to make the air hot, and the excess
52 56
heat is let out through vents at the top.

30 minutes

38c • Formatting Problems: One-Page Reports

Problem 1 Short Report with Proofreader's Marks; Search and Replace

Directions: **1.** Using the format for short reports, key the following problem on page 77. **Reminder:** Center your name DS under the heading, then QS.
2. Key *fun* each time the word *function* appears. When you have finished the report, home your cursor and replace *fun* with *function.*
3. Proofread for errors, using the spell check in your software.
4. Save as **L38c1**, print, and give to your teacher.

(continued on next page)

44d, continued

Problem 2

Directions: **1.** Center the following problem DS on a full sheet of paper. **2.** Review proofreader's marks. **3.** Add your name and problem identification. **4.** Proofread and correct all errors. **5.** Save as **L44d2**, print, and give to your teacher.

```
        WORLDLEAGUE OF AMERICAN FOOTBALLSTADIUMS

                     1991 Season

                     Legion Field
                    Hughes Stadium

                     Alamo Stadium

                    Olympic Stadium

                    Giants Stadium
                  Florida Citrus Bowl
                Carter-Finley at NCState

                    Motjiuc Stadium
                     Waldstadion
                    WembleyStadium
```

LESSON 45

1" side margins

5 minutes

45a • Keyboard Review

Directions: Key each sentence three times SS. DS between 3-line groups.

alphabet Jack Walder bought five exquisite topaz pins in Mexico City.

fig/sym Mr. Kim's students raised $685.70 during the 1992-93 season.

easy He thinks he will be there to see them when the plane lands.

| 1 | 2 | 3 | 4 | 5 | 6 | 7 | 8 | 9 | 10 | 11 | 12 |

10 minutes

45b • Timed Writings

Directions: Take two 3' writings on 43b, page 88. Figure *gwam*. Submit the better writing.

30 minutes

45c • Review of Short Report Formatting

Directions: Review format for short reports on page 72, then key the following problem on page 92.

(continued on next page)

SPECIAL WORD PROCESSING FUNCTIONS

A favorite time-saving function is search and replace. Let's say that youare writing a paper on International Amnesty. if you writeout the term in full each time you use it, you will be using many keystrokes. use a letter or two as a short code instead of writing the full term. Stay away from single letters as a or i as they may be used as complete words within the paper. When you have finished the paper, return the cursor to the beginning of the text. tap the function key for Search and Replace, enter the code you used as the data to search for, and the full term you want to appear in the paper. In a very short time, the full term will be replaced with the codes, and you will have saved yourself a good number of keystrokes.

Moving text from one position in the document to another is a function that permits you to edit your copy with ease. The copy function is especially good for constructing forms or repeating statistics.

Problem 2 Short Report Shown in Script; Search and Replace

Directions: **1.** Using the format for short reports, key the following problem on page 78. **Reminder:** Center your name DS under the heading, then QS. **2.** Key *k* each time the word *key* appears, and *d* each time *document* is shown. Replace each code with the appropriate word when you have completed the report. **3.** Proofread for errors, using the spell check in your software. **4.** Save as **L38c2**, print, and give to your teacher.

(continued on next page)

LESSON 44

1" side margins

5 minutes

44a • Keyboard Review

Directions: Key each sentence three times SS. DS between 3-line groups.

key without pauses

alphabet Kim required only five major exercises with the big trapeze.

symbol She delivered my papers (<u>Los Angeles Times</u>) in half an hour.

easy See if they can do most of their work on these new machines.

| 1 | 2 | 3 | 4 | 5 | 6 | 7 | 8 | 9 | 10 | 11 | 12 |

5 minutes

44b • Language Arts Skills: Dictation and Spelling Checkup

Directions: **1.** Your teacher will dictate the words in 42b, page 87. Key the words from dictation.

2. Check your work for correct spelling. Rekey any words in which you made an error.

5 minutes

44c • Skill Comparison

keep your fingers deeply curved

Directions: **1.** Take a 1' writing on the easy sentence. Figure *gwam*.

2. Take a 1' writing on each of the other sentences.

3. Try to match or exceed your goal sentence *gwam* on each of the other sentences.

easy Their firms did not wish to take such a big risk right then.

direct reach Bryan brought a number of my many friends to hear the music.

script *Eight of the girls might visit both the towns and the lakes.*

rough draft ~~They~~ Those who pu ll on teh oars ~~do not~~ don't have time to rock the # boat.

30 minutes

44d • Centering Review

Problem 1

Directions: **1.** Center the following problem DS in a single column on a full sheet of paper.

2. Add your name and problem identification.

3. Proofread and correct all errors.

4. Save, print, and give to your teacher.

Vertical Centering Calculation Review

Lines available 66
Less lines required............___
Lines remaining ....___
Top margin.........................___
Begin on line ....___

TRACK AND FIELD EVENTS

Mile Run	Pole Vault
Marathon	Shot Put
Steeplechase	Discus Throw
Hurdles	Javelin Throw
Relay Races	Hammer Throw
High Jump	Decathlon
Long Jump	Walking
Triple Jump	

38c, continued

THE INSERT AND DELETE KEYS

Two other keys that make word processing easy to use are the "insert" and "delete" keys. With the insert key, you can add data anywhere in the document without losing material that you have already put in. The insert key will allow you to add as little as one space or character or as much as a sentence, a paragraph, or even pages of data.

The delete key is used to remove a limited amount of data from the document. If a large section of the document is to be removed, use the function key that lets you select that text and then remove it with a single keystroke.

If you accidentally delete more than you plan, the restore function will allow you to recover the deleted material -- and thus prevents panic caused by losing text you need.

LESSON 39

1" side margins

39a • Keyboard Review

5 minutes

Directions: Key each sentence three times SS. DS between 3-line groups.

alphabet	We might require five dozen packing boxes for our July crop.
symbol	Place added information (such as a date) within parentheses.
easy	We bought some more land down the lane from their big house.

| 1 | 2 | 3 | 4 | 5 | 6 | 7 | 8 | 9 | 10 | 11 | 12 |

39b • Technique Builder: Stroking

5 minutes

Directions: Key each sentence three times SS. DS between 3-line groups.

keep your eyes on the copy

one-hand	Barbara was served extra water. John swears Jill beat Lynn.
weak fingers	After passing the quiz, we happily asked for pizzas and pop.
double letters	Fourteen Mississippi schools offered bookkeeping /accounting.

| 1 | 2 | 3 | 4 | 5 | 6 | 7 | 8 | 9 | 10 | 11 | 12 |

15 minutes

43c • Formatting a Cross Reference Sheet for File Names

Directions: **1.** Following the directions in the User's Manual for your software, clear all preset tabs.

2. Format for 1" side margins.

3. Set new tabs 15 spaces inside the left margin and 10 spaces inside the right margin (go to the right margin, backspace 10 spaces, set tab).

4. Center the heading on line 13, DS. DS the listing.

5. List the short reports keyed for Unit 6, including file name, description of the contents of the file, and the date completed.

6. Save, print, and give to your teacher.

```
              CROSS REFERENCE SHEET FOR FILE NAMES

File Name    Description of Contents           Date

L36c1        Microprocessor hardware           (10/15)
L36c2        Microprocessor software
L37c1        Disk drives
L37c2        Cursor direction keys
L37c3        Function keys
L38c1        Special word processing functions
L38c2        Insert & delete keys
L39c1        File names
L39c2        Menus & directories
L39c3        Headers & footers
L40b1        Document formatting
L40b2        Proofreading the document
L40b3        Printing the document
```

15 minutes

43d • Review of Short Report Formatting

Directions: **1.** Review format for short reports, then key the following problem. **2.** Save as **L43d**, print, and give to your teacher.

TAKING BETTER CLASS NOTES

By (Student's name)

Do you have trouble taking notes in class? Do you take too many notes? What is important enough to write down? Here are a few suggestions that will help you write the facts your teacher believes are important.

Listen for words like *also*, *in addition*, *likewise*, *moreover*, and *furthermore*. These words alert you to further information or causes for the situation. When you hear these words, be ready to list more facts.

Be ready to shift your thinking when you hear such phrases as *different from*, *even though*, *still*, *the opposite*, and *yet*. The discussion before these phrases tells you one thing; these phrases let you know that there are exceptions to what you have just heard.

Comments like *for one thing*, *before*, *since*, and *in the first place* indicate that there is an order to the facts and that you should get ready to list them.

When you hear things like *most of all*, *pay particular attention to*, *a central issue*, and *the basic concept*, you need to concentrate more than ever. These phrases mean that the next information is really important--and will probably be on the test at the end of the unit.

35 minutes

39c • Formatting Problems: One-Page Reports

Review of Proofreader's Marks:

∧	for insert	#	for space
lc or /	for lowercase	tr or ∽	for transpose
cap or ≡	capitalize	¶	begin new paragraph

New Proofreader's Marks:

⁀	close up	ℓ	delete

Problem 1 Short Report with Proofreader's Marks

Directions: **1.** Using the format for short reports, key the following problem. **Reminder:** Center your name DS under the heading, then QS.
2. Proofread for errors, using the spell check in your software.
3. Save as **L39c1**, print, and give to your teacher.

FILE NAMES

What you decide to call your document is the File Name. The name should give some clue as to the con tents of the document. Be con cise in naming the document, as most filenames are limited to eight characters. if you happen to use the same file name for more than one document, only the last filed document will remain in the directory and be accessible to you. ¶ A cross reference sheet should be kept as a source of complete identification of the file names.

Problem 2 Short Report with Proofreader's Marks; Search and Replace

Directions: **1.** Using the format for short reports, key the following problem on page 80. **Reminder:** Center your name DS under the heading, then QS.
2. Key *d* each time the word *document* appears, then replace each *d* with *document* when you have finished the report.
3. Proofread for errors, using the spell check in your software.
4. Save as **L39c2**, print, and give to your teacher.

(continued on next page)

LESSON 43

1" side margins

5 minutes

43a • Keyboard Review

Directions: Key each sentence three times SS. DS between 3-line groups.

alphabet Hal G. Kumpf also said it was just six above zero in Quincy.

symbol The guard screamed out, "Don't you dare park in that space!"

easy I know for sure when items are for sale on the market shelf.

| 1 | 2 | 3 | 4 | 5 | 6 | 7 | 8 | 9 | 10 | 11 | 12 |

10 minutes

43b • Paragraph Guided Writings

Directions: **1.** Take three 1' writings on each ¶ below. Try to make no more than three errors on the first writing; one error on the second; no errors on the third.
2. Compare *gwam* on the three writings of each ¶.
3. As you try to reduce your errors, concentrate on each word as you key it. When you are aware of making an error, do not dwell on that error, as more errors will follow quickly.

keep your eyes on the copy

all letters used 1.3 si word wrap *gwam* 3'

The subject of life span is one that the experts know quite a 4 | 40
bit about. Not only do they know that women the world over live 8 | 44
longer than men do, but they realize that this fact is not unique 13 | 49
to human beings. The same thing is true for almost every other 17 | 53
species of mammal. 18 | 54

Just why females are the stronger sex is not so clear. Some 22 | 58
people say long life is due to genetic causes. Others think that 27 | 63
women tend to take better care of themselves. There may be some 31 | 67
truth in all the theories, whether they are based on biology or 35 | 71
behavior. 36 | 72

gwam 3' | 1 | 2 | 3 | 4 |

MENUS AND DIRECTORIES

You havebeen using word processing for quite some time. you have seen the menu that appears when you load in the Soft ware that you are using. Selecting from the directory listing has allowed you to get a Previous document, print from screen copy, clear your screen, or save the work you have completed. if you need to get a document filed previously, and you can not remember the exact file name, ask the microprocessor for a listing of the directory. From the listing you can select the document you need and retrieve it from the listing. You have had some experience in retrieving problems from your directory that you completed earlier to change or merge them with other problems.

The directory is a list complete of all documents you have saved. while it is convenient to use the Directory, you will find it necessary to remove un needed files to avoid clutter in the list.

Problem 3 Short Report with Proofreader's Marks

Directions: **1.** Using the format for short reports, key the following problem. **Reminder:** Center your name DS under the heading, then QS.

2. Proofread for errors, using the spell check in your software.

3. Save as **L39c3**, print, and give to your teacher.

HEADERS AND FOOTERS

If your final document will consist of more than one page, You should number each page after the first one. this can be done with either a header (at the top of the page) or a footer (at the bottom of the page), with the header being preferred by most authorities. Inaddition to the page number, the header or footer may also contain the title of the doc ument or other pertinent information. follow the directions in your software package to complete the header or footer.

5 minutes

42b • Language Arts Skills: Spelling and Proofreading Aid

Directions: Key each sentence three times SS. DS between 3-line groups.

1 statue preparation foreign already quality listen economical

2 occupy receive piece dining judgment grateful emphasis loose

3 freight surprise competent weather language succeed campaign

5 minutes

42c • Skill Comparison

keep wrists and elbows still

Directions: **1.** Take a 1' writing on the goal sentence. Figure *gwam.*
2. Take a 1' writing on each of the other sentences.
3. Try to match or exceed your goal sentence *gwam* on each of the other sentences.

goal sentence Everyone needs very good sight to see his or her own faults.

one-hand Get him a few cases of free milk. Jim gave up a great seat.

script *Some think that a bird in the hand is worth two in the bush.*

rough draft try not to talk if when you r mouth is full or you r head is emtpy.

30 minutes

42d • Technique Builder

Directions: **1.** Format the recipe shown below with 1 1/2" side margins.
2. Center the heading on line 13; leave one blank line after heading.
3. SS on a full sheet of paper; DS before direction lines (Mix in saucepan and bring to a boil, etc.).
4. Add your name and problem identification.
5. Proofread and correct all errors.
6. Save, print, and give to your teacher.

FAVORITE BROWNIES

Preheat oven to 400 degrees. Grease and flour a pan measuring 15 1/2" x 10 1/2" x 1". Set aside.

Mix in saucepan and bring to a boil:
1 stick margarine
4 tablespoons cocoa
1/2 cup shortening

Remove from heat, add, and stir:
1 cup water

Blend in:
2 cups sugar
2 cups flour

Add and stir:
2 eggs
1/2 teaspoon soda
1 teaspoon vanilla
1/2 cup buttermilk

Pour into greased, floured pan.
Bake for 20 minutes.
Remove from oven and frost immediately.

Frosting:

Bring to a boil in saucepan:
1 stick margarine
1/2 cup milk
4 tablespoons cocoa

Beat in and spread over warm brownies:
1 box confectioners sugar
1 teaspoon vanilla
1/2 cup chopped nuts

LESSON 40

1" side margins

5 minutes

40a • Keyboard Review

Directions: Key each sentence three times SS. DS between 3-line groups.

alphabet Max delivered the wrong size pack to Jeff quite by accident.

symbol You may wish to use "c/o" for the abbreviation "in care of."

easy Both of them asked to take their autos to the new body shop.

| 1 | 2 | 3 | 4 | 5 | 6 | 7 | 8 | 9 | 10 | 11 | 12 |

40 minutes

40b • Formatting Problems: One-Page Reports

Problem 1 Short Report Shown in Script

Directions: **1.** Using the format for short reports, key the following problem. **Reminder:** Center your name DS under the heading, then QS.
2. Replace each *d* with *document* when you have finished keying the report.
3. Proofread for errors, using the spell check in your software.
4. Save as **L40b1**, print, and give to your teacher.

DOCUMENT FORMATTING

The format for the d you are producing can be selected at any time, but most people find it easier to complete before the d is keyed into the microprocessor.

Default margins may be used, but the margins can be changed to meet specific d needs. Default margins are usually one inch on all sides so that there is a white frame around the printed d. If the margin formats are changed after the d is keyed in, the tabs that were originally set will move and may, therefore, have to be corrected.

Some documents are printed with single spacing, while others require double spacing. If you will print with single spacing, leave a blank line between paragraphs as you key in the work. If you will print with double spacing, do not leave a blank line between the paragraphs.

Your software may allow you to choose the spacing before you key in the data, or may require that you decide the spacing at the time you send the d to the printer.

15 minutes

41d • Centering Review

Directions: **1.** Center each of the following problems DS in a single column on a full sheet of paper. (See Lesson 21 if you need to review the procedure.) **2.** Add your name and problem identification to each problem. **3.** Proofread for errors, save, and print the problems.

Problem 1

Vertical Centering Calculation Review

Lines available....................66
Less lines required............. __
Lines remaining .... __
Top margin.......................... __
Begin on line .... __

```
         ABBREVIATIONS AND THEIR DEFINITIONS

          SS (single-space; single spacing)
          DS (double-space; double spacing)
    CS (columnar spacing; space between columns)
                LS (line spacing)
             CH (center horizontally)
              CV (center vertically)
                LM (left margin)
                RM (right margin)
                 TM (top margin)
               BM (bottom margin)
                SM (side margin)
          GWAM (gross words a minute)
            NWAM (net words a minute)
```

Problem 2

Simple Math Terms

Equation
Decimal
Quotient
Integer
Inequality
Percentage

Multiplication
Subtraction
Addition
Division
Parallel

Perpendicular
Rational Numbers
Volume
Simplest Form
Proportion

LESSON 42

1" side margins

5 minutes

42a • Keyboard Review

Directions: Key each sentence three times SS. DS between 3-line groups.

alphabet The quiz kept Jim and Dick Law busy for six very long hours.

fig/sym Sandra's score was 76%, Sean's was 85%, and Cindy's was 91%.

easy He knows you can locate all eight of the islands on the map.

1 2 3 4 5 6 7 8 9 10 11 12

40b, continued

Problem 2 Short Report with Proofreader's Marks; Search and Replace

Directions: **1.** Using the format for short reports, key the following problem. **Reminder:** Center your name DS under the heading, then QS.
2. When you are finished, replace each *d* with *document*.
3. Proofread for errors, using the spell check in your software.
4. Save as **L40b2**, print, and give to your teacher.

PROOFREADING THE DOCUMENT

When all the data has been entered into the d, you will want to use the spell check in the software to verify the accuracy of your spelling and keying. to avoid the possible loss ofyour d, it is advisable for you to file the d before using the spell check. ¶ using the spell check doesnot free you from reading through the d for completeness. The spell check can only determine if the words you used are in the dictionary and are spelled correctly. If you haveused a correctly spelled but incorrectly used word, the spell check can not make the distinction. ¶ whether you read through the d for completeness before or ~~and~~ after you print it, you must read it to see what it says, not for what you think you put in. If you make any corrections, you must, of course, resave the data.

10 minutes

41b • Paragraph Guided Writings

Directions: **1.** Take a 1' writing to establish a goal rate.
2. Take two additional 1' writings. Try to reach your goal word as time is called.
3. Add four words to your original goal. Take three 1' writings, trying to reach your new goal on each timing. Your teacher may call the quarter- or half-minute guides.

all letters used 1.3 si word wrap

Whether you drop out of school or not has little to do with the size of your brain. Yet we do know that one out of every five or six eighth graders is at serious risk of not getting through high school. Major causes include being home alone quite a bit and having limited language skills.

15 minutes

41c • Timed Writings

Directions: **1.** Take two 1' writings on each ¶. Figure *gwam*.
2. Take 2' and 3' writings on both ¶s combined. If you complete a writing before time is called, repeat until you are told to stop.
3. Figure *gwam*. Compare your 2' rate to the longer writing.

all letters used 1.3 si word wrap

	gwam 2'	3'
Getting some exercise didn't used to be a very big deal. You	6	4
could walk around the block or dig in the yard. At most, all you	12	8
really had to have was a pair of jogging shoes plus a healthy	18	12
supply of willpower.	21	14
Staying in shape is not the same now. The new exercise	27	18
devices are well equipped with lights, buzzers, screens, and	33	22
readouts. They measure your heart rate, tell you to speed up or	39	26
slow down, and furnish electronic cheers when you're done.	45	30

gwam 2' | 1 | 2 | 3 | 4 | 5 | 6 |
3' | 1 | 2 | 3 | 4 |

40b, continued

Problem 3 Short Report with Proofreader's Marks; Search and Replace

Directions: 1. Using the format for short reports, key the following problem. **Reminder:** Center your name DS under the heading, then QS.
2. For these paragraphs, use *pr* each time the word *printer* appears. When you are finished, replace each *pr* with *printer.*
3. Proofread for errors, using the spell check in your software.
4. Save as **L40b3**, print, and give to your teacher.

PRINTING THE DOCUMENT

Once your document has been checked for thoroughness, you are ready to send it to the printer. verify that the printer is turned on, that the paper supply is ade quate, and that the paper is in position for printing. if this is where you choose the spacing for the document, do so, and then give the print command to the printer. ¶The quality of the printed copy will be determined by the type of printer you are using. a dot-matrix printer is satisfactory for draft copy or in-house documents. If you are producing correspondence or the final copy of a term paper, use a letter-quality printer. A laser printer will produce sharp, distinctive copy that is especially suited to producing masters for multiple copies.

Reviewing Your Formatting Skills (Lessons 41-45)

Learning Goals

1. Continue refining stroking skills and operating techniques.
2. Continue reinforcing the operation of the tab, shift/caps lock, and return/enter key.
3. Review proofreader's marks and their uses.
4. Learn to format and use a cross reference sheet for file names and the contents of the files.
5. Review the vertical and horizontal placement of centered material.
6. Review the formatting and keying of short reports.
7. Learn more about the features of word processing programs.

Word Processing Concepts Introduced in Unit 7

backup copy
cross reference sheet for file names
help screen

General Directions

Use 1" side margins, unless otherwise directed, for all lessons in this unit. SS sentences and drill lines. DS between repeated groups of lines. DS paragraph copy. Proofread and correct all problems in this unit.

LESSON 41

1" side margins

41a • Keyboard Review

5 minutes

Directions: Key each sentence three times SS. DS between 3-line groups.

alphabet These new drug czars firmly backed every major export quota.

fig/sym All 7 of the 4-door cars had 59.8 cubic feet of cargo space.

easy The students wanted to visit all the towns shown on the map.

| 1 | 2 | 3 | 4 | 5 | 6 | 7 | 8 | 9 | 10 | 11 | 12 |

HELP SCREEN One of the function keys, usually the *F1* key, will give you a "Help" screen that will list the capabilities of the other function keys. Check the help screen before you ask your teacher how to do a specific task. If the help screen doesn't provide the assistance you need, then turn to your teacher.

BACKUP COPY A backup copy is a copy of an original storage medium such as a disk. A backup copy should be made of important files so that they will not have to be rekeyed if the original copy is damaged or lost.

Vertical Centering

Centering material so that it will have uniform top and bottom margins is called *vertical centering.*

1. Count the lines in the copy to be centered. If your copy is to be double spaced, remember to count the spaces between the lines. There is one line space following each line of copy when material is double spaced.

2. Subtract the total lines to be used from the lines available on the paper you are using. (There are 66 lines on a full sheet.)

3. Divide the number of lines that remain by 2. The answer gives you the number of lines in the top and bottom margins. If the result contains a fraction, disregard the fraction.

Horizontal Centering

Centering material so there will be equal left and right margins is called *horizontal centering.*

1. Format equal left and right margins. (**Note:** The paper you will print on is 8 1/2" wide. A 12-pitch printer will print 12 characters per inch; therefore 8 1/2 times 12 equals 102 characters. Half of 102 (51) is the center. A 10-pitch printer will print 10 characters per inch; therefore 8 1/2 times 10 equals 85 characters, and the center is 42 with the fraction being disregarded.)

2. Clear all preset tabs. Set a tab at the center point.

3. Backspace from center point once for every 2 characters, punctuation, or spaces in the line to be centered. If there is one character left, do not backspace for it. Begin to key at the point where you complete the backspacing.

Automatic Horizontal Centering

Automatic centering is a word processing feature that eliminates the calculations in the backspace-from-center method above. To center automatically, position the cursor at the left margin. Hold down the designated key or combination (such as *Code* and *c*, or *Shift F6*); the cursor moves to the center of the line. As you key, the cursor backs up (but may not print). To print the centered copy, tap the return/enter key.

You may find that you must first key the copy to be centered, then give the center command. Check the User's Manual for the software you are using for complete directions.

Horizontal Placement of Tables

1. Format equal left and right margins.

2. Clear all preset tabs. Set a tab at the center point of the paper you will use when you print (51 for 12-pitch, 42 for 10-pitch).

3. Determine the spacing between columns (an even number, 6 is always good).

4. Find the longest item in each column.

5. From the tab at center, backspace once for each 2 letters, figures, spaces or punctuation marks in each column. If you have an extra character in any column, add that character to the first character in the next column. If one space is left over after backspacing for all the columns, disregard it.

6. Backspace once for every 2 spaces to be left between columns. Since you will use an even number, there will not be any spaces left over.

7. The first tab will be at the point at which you stopped backspacing. This is where the first column will start.

8. Space forward once for each letter, figure, space or punctuation mark in the longest entry in the first column and once for each space left between Columns 1 and 2. Set a tab for the second column. Continue in this way until tabs have been set for each column. Space across the last column to determine the right margin.

Word Processing Method of Setting Column Tabs

1. Identify the longest item in each column and determine the number of spaces to be placed between columns.

2. Use the automatic centering feature and key these items and spaces on the line.

3. Move the cursor to the beginning of the first column; note (write down) the cursor position.

4. Repeat No. 3 for each remaining column.

5. Clear all tabs in the ruler/format line.

6. Set tabs in the ruler/format line at the positions noted in Nos. 3 and 4.

7. Delete the line keyed in No. 2.

8. Key the table.

Note: Column headings begin at the tab and may be the longest line in the column.

Keying Leftbound Reports

1. Leave a 2" top margin and a 1" bottom margin on the first page, 1" top and 1" bottom margins on all following pages. Center the heading on line 13, followed by a QS. If there is no title page, DS after the heading and center your name, then QS.

2. Format a 1 1/2" left margin and a 1" right margin.

3. DS the body, using 5-space paragraph indentions. DS before and after side headings. Retain at least two lines of a paragraph at the bottom of a page and carry forward at least two lines of a paragraph to a new page if possible.

4. Indent long quotations of four lines or more five spaces from each margin and SS them.

5. Number the pages after page 1, placing the page numbers on line 7 and aligning them with the right margin. Continue body of report on line 9.

leave 2" top margin

CONSERVING WATER

By (Student's name)

1½"left margin | 1" right margin

Enough rain falls in most parts of the United States to keep our lawns green, our gardens growing, and our reservoirs full.

If you look at a picture taken from outer space, you will notice that water mass exceeds landmass. But the large amount of water mass leads to one of our worries, for less than one percent of that water is drinkable. More than two percent of the water on earth is frozen in glaciers and ice at the North and South Poles. The remaining 97 percent of the water is locked in salt water oceans and coastal seas (Stewart, 1990, 225). The fresh water actually available for human use in lakes, rivers, and accessible ground water amounts to less than half of one percent of the total water supply. The purest, most easily developed supplies of water have already been tapped, and a growing number of users are fighting for access to the shrinking reserves (Coffel, 1989, 13). We don't have enough water to waste.

The average consumer uses about 50 gallons of water a day, or 240 gallons for a family of four (Handbook, 1991, 3). Humans require two to three quarts of water per day just to maintain the crucial liquid balance within the body (Coffel,

approximately 1"

(line 7) 2

1989, 16). Some of that water comes from the food eaten, but much of it is taken in as fluids. Amazingly, water is probably the only drink which is free of calories, sweeteners, caffeine, and alcohol (Stewart, 1990, 225).

The use of large quantities of water is an inescapable part of American life today. How can we reduce the amount of water we use?

Three-quarters of the water is used in the bathroom. As you may have heard in televised commercials, older toilets use more than five gallons with each flush. New toilets may use up to 3.5 gallons--a savings of 25 percent. By inserting a toilet tank dam, an additional half gallon of water is saved. The savings would then be 40 percent!

1½"left margin | 1" right margin

Are you one who likes to take a long shower? Some shower heads use between five and seven gallons of water per minute. Low-flow shower heads that use only 2.5 gallons of water per minute are available. Switching to a new low-flow shower head results in a 35 to 50 percent savings. And, much as you might enjoy that long shower, five minutes of scrubbing will get you clean.

Other ways to save water include running the dishwasher and washing machine only when full (or adjusting the water level setting), using a vegetable brush to remove dirt from fresh fruit and vegetables, and fixing any leaking pipes or faucets. Simply turning off the water while brushing your teeth saves at least four gallons of water each day.

approximately 1"

1"left margin | Model Unbound Report | 1" right margin

MICROPROCESSOR HARDWARE

By (Student's name) DS

QS

This report is an attempt to identify some basic terms associated with microcomputers and word processors. A brief summary of some of the expressions common to all word processing programs follows.

Keying Unbound Reports

1. Leave a 2" top margin and a 1" bottom margin.
2. Format 1" side margins.
3. Center the heading on line 13, DS and center the writer's name, followed by a QS.
4. DS the body, using 5-space paragraph indentions. DS before and after side headings.

Keying Reference Citations

Use run-in references (internal citations) to indicate sources of information. Order for run-in references is: Name(s) of author(s), the year of publication, and the page number of the source (Jones, 1992, 275).

Keying a Bibliography

1. Use the same top and side margins used for the first page of your report. Center the heading on line 13.
2. Start the first line of each reference at the left margin. Indent other lines five spaces. SS the entries, DS between entries. Order for each item is: Author's last name, first name. Name of Source. City: Name of Publisher, Date.

BIBLIOGRAPHY ____ line 13

margin

QS

indent 5 spaces →

Coffel, Steve. But Not a Drop to Drink! New York: Rawson
     Associates, MacMillan Publishing Company, 1989.

DS

Connecticut Department of Health Services. Connecticut Water
     Conservation Handbook. Hartford: American Water Works
     Association, Connecticut Section, 1991.

DS

Stewart, John Cary. Drinking Water Hazards. Hiram, Ohio:
     Envirographics, 1990.

FUNDAMENTALS OF WORD PROCESSING line 16

8DS

Your name DS

Keyboarding Class

8DS

Date

leftbound title page

1½" left margin

1" right margin

TABLE OF CONTENTS line 13

QS

DS

Formatting and Keying Personal-Business Letters, Business Letters

All letters are arranged attractively on the sheet of paper. An average-size letter will have the date on (approximately) line 16 and will have 1 1/2" side margins. Shorter letters will have a lower date line and larger side margins. Longer letters will call for a higher date line and smaller side margins.

In *block style,* all lines begin at the left margin: The return address, the date, the salutation, the beginning of each paragraph, and the complimentary closing lines.

In *modified block style,* the return address and date lines as well as the complimentary closing lines begin at the center of the line of writing.

Open punctuation means that no marks of punctuation follow the salutation and complimentary close.

Mixed punctuation calls for a colon after the salutation and a comma after the complimentary close.

Vertical spacing within the letters remains the same: QS after the date, DS between the inside address and the salutation, between the salutation and the first paragraph, between paragraphs, and between the last paragraph and the complimentary close. The complimentary close is followed by a QS and the keyed name of the writer of the letter. If there is a business title, it is keyed on the line below the keyed name. For a business letter, DS after the name/title and key the reference initials of the word processor at the left margin in lowercase letters.

Folding Letters for Inserting into Small Envelopes

Letters are folded for inserting into small envelopes according to the steps in the diagram below.

FOLDING LETTERS FOR SMALL ENVELOPES

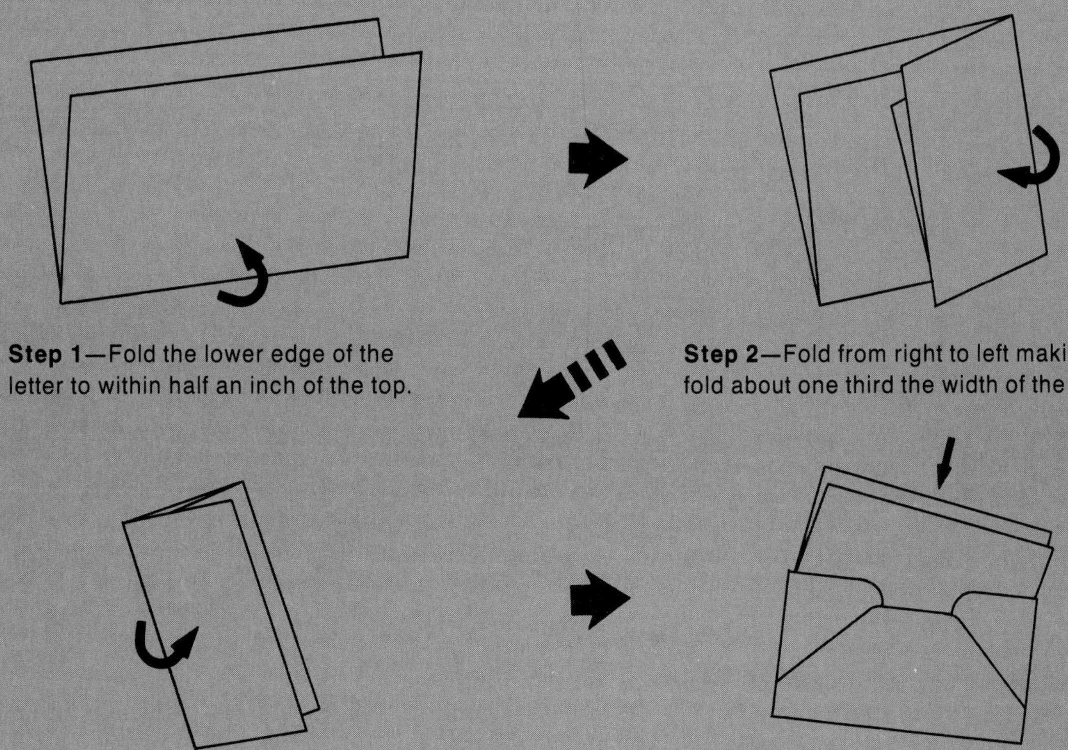

Step 1—Fold the lower edge of the letter to within half an inch of the top.

Step 2—Fold from right to left making the fold about one third the width of the sheet.

Step 3—Fold from left to right, leaving about a half-inch margin at the right in order that the letter may be opened easily.

Step 4—Insert the letter into the envelope so that the left-hand creased edge is inserted first and the last side folded is toward the backside of the envelope.

1½" side margin

1½" side margin

162 Golf Links Road
Mount Rainier, MD 20712
May 6, 19--

QS

Miss Shani Jenkins
4317 Addison Avenue
Beacon, NY 12508 DS

Dear Miss Jenkins DS

Our class is completing a unit on "Wildlife in the United States." We are disturbed to learn that several animals are on the list of endangered species, and that unless action is taken soon, they may become extinct. DS

We understand that you have been active in bringing this information to the public's attention. DS

Would you please send some suggestions that our class could use to inform the student body of this crisis. We are also interested in materials for posters that we could place in the school, but we would welcome any updated information that would add to what we have already learned. DS

Thank you for any assistance and information you can give us. All materials should be sent to me at the above address. DS

Sincerely

QS

(Your name)

Personal business letter
Block, open

1½" side margin

1½" side margin

226 Harmony Road
College Place, WA 99324
Today's date

QS

Miss Janet Pryce
1764 Jules Avenue
Silver City, NM 88061 DS

Dear Miss Pryce: DS

Your questions about how a letter in modified block style is different from a letter in block style are good ones. DS

All lines (the return address and date lines, the inside address and salutation, all paragraphs, and the closing lines) begin at the left margin in a block letter. DS

A letter in modified block style moves the placement of two items--the lines for the return address and date begin at the center of the line of writing. The tab at center is also used to begin the closing and signature lines. DS

Although the block style is faster to produce, as there are no tabs, some writers prefer the appearance of the modified block style. DS

Thank you for your inquiry. If I can be of further assistance, please let me know. DS

Sincerely,

QS

(Student's name)

Personal-business letter
Modified block, mixed

1½" side margin

1½" side margin

Today's date

QS

Parkview Business Machines
47 Olympic Boulevard
Fenton, MI 48430-1132 DS

Ladies and Gentlemen DS

As the new Director of the local Park and Recreation Commission, I am faced with a problem I hope you can help me solve. DS

The Commission has instructed me to obtain information about computer equipment that would best suit the needs of a small office. Providing correspondence between town officials, with local residents, and completing reports needed for commission and town meetings would be the primary uses of the equipment. DS

In addition, production of flyers to promote a variety of activities would be necessary. Also, statistical data about each activity must be available to the Commission at the conclusion of that activity. DS

Would you advise me on the specific hardware and available software that you would recommend for the requirements of this office. I can be reached at 555-7483 between 9 a.m. and 5:30 p.m. DS

Sincerely

QS

Erik Cullen
Director SS
DS
urs

Business letter
Block, open

1½" side margin

1½" side margin

Today's date

QS

Mr. Dale Pronga
Bob's Clothing Store
4325 Hickman Road
Napolean, OH 43545-3188 DS

Dear Mr. Pronga: DS

Thank you for giving me the opportunity to recommend (Student's name) for a position with your firm. DS

(Student's first name) worked with me for the past two years and I found (him/her) to be very reliable. (He/She) had a remarkable attendance record, and seldom called in to say (he/she) would be unable to report for work. Punctuality is crucial in my business, and I can report to you that (Student's first name) could be depended upon to be here on time and ready to put forth (his/her) best effort for my customers. DS

I am sorry to see (Student's first name) leave my store, but I can understand that (he/she) is anxious to put into practice some of the business aspects (he/she) has learned in school. DS

You can be assured that I recommend (Student's name) as an employee upon whom you can depend. DS

Yours truly,

QS

Paul Rozewski
Manager SS

urs DS

Business letter
Modified block, mixed

FOLDING LETTERS FOR LARGE ENVELOPES

Step 1—Fold from bottom to top, making the fold slightly less than one third the length of the sheet.

Step 2—Fold the top down to within one half inch of the bottom fold.

Step 3—Insert the letter into the envelope with the last crease toward the bottom of the envelope and with the last fold up.

Addressing Envelopes

1. Set a tab 10 spaces left of center for a small envelope, and five spaces left of center for a large envelope.

2. Space down 12 lines from top edge for a small envelope, and 14 spaces for a large envelope. Begin the address at the tab.

3. Use *block style*, *SS*. Use ALL CAPS; omit punctuation. Place city name, 2-letter state name abbreviation, and ZIP Code on last address line. One space precedes the ZIP Code.

4. For return address, use *block style*, *SS*, and ALL CAPS. Begin on line 2 from top of envelope, 3 spaces from left edge.

Two-Letter State Abbreviations

Alabama	AL	Indiana	IN	Nebraska	NE	South Carolina	SC
Alaska	AK	Iowa	IA	Nevada	NV	South Dakota	SD
Arizona	AZ	Kansas	KS	New Hampshire	NH	Tennessee	TN
Arkansas	AR	Kentucky	KY	New Jersey	NJ	Texas	TX
California	CA	Louisiana	LA	New Mexico	NM	Utah	UT
Colorado	CO	Maine	ME	New York	NY	Vermont	VT
Connecticut	CT	Maryland	MD	North Carolina	NC	Virginia	VA
Delaware	DE	Massachusetts	MA	North Dakota	ND	Washington	WA
Florida	FL	Michigan	MI	Ohio	OH	West Virginia	WV
Georgia	GA	Minnesota	MN	Oklahoma	OK	Wisconsin	WI
Hawaii	HI	Mississippi	MS	Oregon	OR	Wyoming	WY
Idaho	ID	Missouri	MO	Pennsylvania	PA		
Illinois	IL	Montana	MT	Rhode Island	RI		

Capitalization Guides (143, 156)

Capitalize:

1. The first word of a complete sentence.

2. The first word of a quoted sentence. (Do not capitalize fragments of a quotation resumed within a sentence.)

3. Languages and numbered school courses, but not the names of other school subjects.

4. The pronoun *I*, both alone and in contractions.

5. Titles of organizations, institutions, and buildings.

6. Days of the week, months of the year, and holidays, but not seasons.

7. Names of rivers, oceans, and mountains.

8. *North, South, etc.*, when they name particular parts of the country, but not when they refer to directions.

9. Names of religious groups, political parties, nations, nationalities, and races.

10. All proper names and adjectives made from them.

11. The names of stars, planets, and constellations, except the sun, moon and earth, unless these are used with other astronomical names.

12. A title when used with a person's name.

13. First words and all other words in titles of books, articles, periodicals, headings, and plays, except words which are articles, conjunctions, and prepositions.

14. The first and last words, all titles, and all proper names used in the salutation of a business letter.

15. Only the first word in the complimentary close.

16. All titles appearing in the address of a letter.

17. The title following the names of the dictator in the closing lines of a business letter.

Spacing Guides (68, 138)

1. Space twice after a period at the end of a sentence except when it comes at the end of the line. When it does, return/enter without spacing.

2. Space once after a semicolon or comma.

3. Space once after a question mark within a sentence; twice after a question mark at the end of a sentence.

4. Space twice after a colon except when stating time.

5. Space twice after an exclamation mark that ends a sentence.

6. Key the dash with two hyphens. Do not space before or after.

7. Space once after a period that ends an abbreviation.

8. Do not space between the $ and the number which follows it.

9. Do not space between a number and a following % sign.

10. Do not space between parentheses and the material they enclose.

11. Do not space before or after the apostrophe unless the apostrophe is at the end of a word.

12. Do not space between quotation marks and the material they enclose.

13. Do not space before or after a dash.

14. Do not space before or after a hyphen in a hyphenated word.

Number Expression Guides (138)

1. Key even sums of money without decimals or zeros.

2. Key distances in figures.

3. Use figures to key dates.

4. Spell a number beginning a sentence even though figures may be used later in the sentence.

5. Use figures with **a.m.** and **p.m.** Use words with **o'clock**.

6. Key amounts of money, either dollars or cents, in figures.

Punctuation Guides (68, 148, 152, 165)

1. Use a period after a sentence making a statement or giving a command.

2. Use a period after an initial.

3. Do not use a period after a nickname.

4. Use a period after most abbreviations.

5. Use a question mark after a direct question.

6. Use a period after requests and indirect questions.

7. Use an exclamation mark to express strong or sudden feeling.

8. Use a comma after each item in a series, except the last one.

9. Use a comma to separate consecutive adjectives when the *and* has been omitted.

10. Use a comma to separate a dependent clause that precedes the main clause.

11. Use a comma to separate two complete clauses separated by *and, but, for, or, so, yet*.

12. Use a comma to set off a day from year, city from state, and hundreds from thousands.

13. Use a comma to set off a short direct quotation from the rest of the sentence.

14. Use commas to set off interrupting words that are nonessential to the sentence.

15. Use a comma to set off interjections (yes, no, well) if there is a break in continuity.

16. Use commas to set off the name of the person addressed.

GLOSSARY

Alternate (ALT) Key Used with selected function keys to perform certain operations (might be called Option Key)

"Arrow" Keys Used to move cursor in the direction of the arrow (up, down, left, right)

Automatic Centering A formatting feature of automated equipment that places words or lines of copy at an equal distance from the right and left margin settings upon command (equal copy on either side of the center point)

Automatic Page Break A feature that allows the user to select the number of lines allowed on a page

Automatic Underlining A formatting feature that underlines a word or words separately or continuously upon command

Back Arrow See **Backspace**

Backspace To move the cursor to the left one space at a time by tapping the backspace (back arrow) key once for each character or space

Backspace Erase An editing tool that allows you to backspace and delete a previously keyed character or characters

Backup Copy A duplicate of an original file

Bidirectional Printing A feature that allows a printer to print in either direction (left to right or right to left)

Block Style A format for notes and letters in which all lines begin at the left margin

Bold A formatting feature that prints the designated text darker than the rest of the copy to add emphasis

Boot To start the computer DOS system

Caps Lock A key that causes all letters to be CAPITALIZED without having to depress a shift key for each stroke

CRT (Cathode Ray Tube) See **Monitor**

Centering See **Horizontal Centering**, **Vertical Centering**

Character A keystroke; a letter, number, symbol, or command

Character String A group of letters, numbers, symbols, or a combination of them

Clipboard Section or area of computer's RAM used to temporarily hold information when cutting and pasting (moving)

Cold Start or Boot Used when the computer hardware has not been powered on

Columns Vertical lines of information that are represented by alphabetic letters and/or numbers or symbols

Command A direction to the software by the user

Control The power to cause the hands and fingers to make correct motions; also the ability to hold keystroking speed down so that errors (mistakes) are kept to an expected or acceptable number

Controlled Page Break A special command inserted by the user to ensure that a page remains intact during automatic pagination

Copy Material that has been or is to be keyed; a word processing feature that allows the operator to define text at one location and duplicate it in another location

CPU (Central Processing Unit) The internal operating unit or "brains" of an electronic computer system

Cursor A lighted point on a display screen where the next character or space can be entered

Cut and Paste The process that allows you to move and copy highlighted information through the clipboard from one file to another file

Database Information that is organized and set up in an electronic file that can later be edited and/or sorted for different purposes

Data Disk Contains the files you create with a software program

Default Standards Preset specifications in word processing software that control line length, tabs, etc.

Delete A word processing feature that allows the operator to remove a defined block of text (such as a character, a word, a line, a sentence, etc.)

Delete Key Used to remove characters from the screen one by one

Dictionary See **Spell Check**

Directory A listing of documents filed on computer software

Disk A magnetic, Mylar-coated, record-like disc encased in a protective cover used for reading and writing by a central processing unit (common sizes are 5 1/4" and 3 1/2")

Disk Drive A device or unit into which a disk is inserted so information can be either retrieved or recorded on by the CPU

Disk Use Light Lights up when the built-in drive is reading data from a diskette or writing data on a disk

Diskette See **Disk**

Document Keyed copy such as a letter, report, or table

DOS (Disk Operating System) A program recorded on a disk that causes a computer to operate or function

Dot Matrix Printer A printer that uses closely grouped dots to form letters

Double Spacing One blank line left between lines of text

Editing The process of changing a document

Electronic Files Storage on magnetic media or in memory

Enter Key See **Return/Enter Key**

Escape (ESC) Key Used to cancel a function or exit a program section

Exit/Quit Leave the word processing program before powering down

File See **Document**

File Name The name or code assigned a document; limited number of characters, no space within name

Floppy Disk See **Disk**

Footer Repetitive information, usually a page number, that appears on the bottom of each page of a document

Format The layout of a document; includes line length, spacing, margins

Format Line See **Ruler/Format Line**

Formatting a Disk (Initializing) The process of preparing a disk to receive information; must be done before you can add or save files to it

Formatting a Document The process of arranging a document in proper form

Function Keys Keys, usually labeled with F and a number, whose roles are defined by the software

Ghost Hyphen See **Soft Hyphen**

Graphics Package Word processing software that displays visual materials such as graphs, charts, etc.

Hard Copy A computer printout on paper of the screen display

Hard Disk A large disk, usually housed within a metal case, that has greater storage capacity than floppy disks; often used for more permanent storage

Hard Hyphen Entered by tapping the hyphen key; will be printed where it appears

Hard Page Break See **Controlled Page Break**

Hard Return Entered by tapping the return/enter key; can be removed only be deleting with backspace erase or the delete feature

Hard Space A feature that guards against breaking a line of printed text between title and surname, month and date, or formula parts

Hardware The physical equipment that makes up a computer or word processing system

Header Repetitive information, which usually includes a page number, that appears on the top of each page of a document

Help Screen Provides information about commands

Horizontal Centering The placing of text so that half the copy is on each side of the horizontal center point

Hyphen Character A feature used for keying dates or minus signs in formulas to prevent the minus from being separated from related characters when it occurs at the end of a line

Import Copy or move a file into another document

Initializing See **Formatting a Disk**

Input The text and data that enter an information system; the process of entering text and data

Insert Editing feature that allows you to add characters without rekeying the entire document (new text is inserted and existing text is pushed to the right or down to make room for the addition)

Integrate Copy or move a file or parts of files into another document

Justified Text A feature which causes the right, as well as left, margin to be even

Key To tap keys to record or display text and data; also enter, key in, keyboard, and input

Keyboard An arrangement of keys on a "board" that is attached to or apart from a machine such as a computer or word processor; also the act of keyboarding

Left Shift Key Used to key capital letters and symbols controlled by the right hand

Letter-quality Printer A printer that produces output of acceptable quality for office correspondence

Lines Per Inch A printer option that controls the number of lines printed in each vertical inch; normal default value is 6 lines per inch

Main Menu Base of operation for software, gives options for using software

Margins The blank space to the left and right sides and at the top and bottom of a page

Media (Plural of Medium) The material on which input is recorded and stored, such as floppy disks, hard disks, etc.

Memory The ability of a word processor to retain information for later retrieval

Menu A list of options from which a keyboard operator may (or must) choose when using a word processing machine

Microcomputer Also called a personal computer, makes document creating, formatting, and editing easy when word processing software is used

Microprocessor A small computer that has word processing capabilities when software is added

Modified Block Style A format for notes and letters in which the return address (if used), date, and closing lines begin at the center of the line of writing; may have indented paragraphs

Monitor The piece of equipment used to display text, data, and graphic images on screen

Move Editing feature commonly called "cut and paste" that allows the user to remove (cut) a block of text from one location in a document and place (paste) it in a different location in the same document

Networked System Where communication devices are linked together

ON/OFF Control Used to "power up" or "power down" the system

Orphan The first line of a paragraph when in appears at the bottom of a page

Output Information that leaves an information system, usually presented to the user as a screen display or printout

Page Break The point (generally a given line count) at which a page ends; the printer automatically advances to the beginning of the next page

Page Numbering The automatic numbering or renumbering of the pages of a document

Pagination The automatic division of a document into pages, according to a preset number of lines per page

Peripheral Equipment that works with a word processing system but is not part of it, such as a printer or a scanner

Platen The cylinder (roller) in the printer around which the paper travels during the printing process

Platen Width A printer option that controls the distance the print head can travel from left to right on the printer; default value is often 8 inches

Power Down Leave the software and turn off all equipment

Power Light Comes on when the microcomputer's power is on

Power Up Start the computer

Print To produce, using a printer, a paper copy of information displayed on a screen or stored in word processing memory

Printer A unit attached to a computer or word processor that produces copy on paper

Printout The printed paper output of a word processor; the hard copy

Prompt A message displayed on the screen of a word processor telling the user that the machine is awaiting a specific command

Pull-Down Menus Alternative to using function keys to select commands and features

RAM (Random-Access Memory) Temporary memory that stores programs and data for your microcomputer

Retrieve To recover or get a saved document

Return/Enter Key Used to return cursor to left margin and down to the next line; also used to enter system commands

Right Shift Key Used to key capital letters and symbols controlled by the left hand

ROM (Read-Only Memory) Permanent memory in your microcomputer; includes instructions for microcomputer to operate, process, and store data for programs

Ruler/Format Line Line at the top or bottom of the screen (or accessible within a document) used to set the document format consisting of left and right margins, tab stops, text alignment and line-spacing

Run-in Reference Indicates source of information within the text of the document

Save To record data on a disk

Scroll To "roll" the text up and down or from side to side to show more characters on a display screen

Search A feature that allows the word processor to read through the document to locate a character string or code

Search and Replace A feature that searches through a document until it finds the designated character string or code and then replaces it with a designated new string

Shift Lock See **Caps Lock**

Soft Hyphen An electronic feature that allows the user to decide whether a word should be hyphenated to avoid a very ragged right margin; should the location of the hyphenated word change during reformatting, the soft hyphen is deleted automatically

Soft Return Automatically entered by the program at the end of a line of copy when text is being "wrapped around" to the next line

Software A set of instructions for the operation of a word processor, housed on a floppy disk

Source Document The original hard copy from which data are entered

Space Bar Used to move cursor to the right one space at a time or to add space between characters (will erase keyed text)

Spacing The space between lines of text

Spell Check A means to verify the correct spelling of words in a document

Stand-alone System A system in which one work station operates independently of all other systems and peripherals

Startup Disk The disk used to start up a software program

Strikeover/Replacement Mode Editing feature that allows you to position the cursor and key over (strikeover) characters; existing text is automatically erased and replaced by new text

String A group of characters, numerals, and/or symbols

Tab Key Used to move cursor to tab stops

Tabs Stops set in the ruler/format line that allow you to indent paragraphs and lists and to align columns in tables

Tabulate To line up text in neat columns or indent for preset paragraph indentions

Technique A keyboard operator's form or keying style

Template Disk Special type of data disk that contains files which are already created

Temporary Margins Used for long quotes, indented an equal number of spaces from each margin (usually 5)

Text See **Document**

Underline An option for placing a line under a character during printing

Vertical Centering The placing of text so that half the copy is on each side of the vertical center point

VDT (Video Display Terminal) See **Monitor**

Warm Start or Boot Used when the hardware has already been powered on

Widow The last line of a paragraph when it appears at the top of a new page

Widow/Orphan A word processing feature that prevents the occurrence of widows and orphans during automatic paging

Word Processor Software that allows you to create, modify, and print documents

Word Processing The act of writing and storing letters, reports, and other documents on a computer, electronic typewriter, or word processor; may also include printing of the final document

Word Wrap A word processing feature that permits information to be keyed on successive lines without having to tap the return/enter key at the end of each line

Work Station The equipment and area of an individual word processing operator

Wraparound See **Word Wrap**

Special Index